To Cor

"KEEPING THE MEMORIES ALIVE"

Ray Clanton

AF817766

FIRE, FEAR AND GUTS
The B-29 and Her Gallant Crewmen

Written by Raymond W. Clanton, A-C 73rd Bomb Wing

© 2005 by Raymond W. Clanton

All rights reserved.
No part of this book may be used
or reproduced in any manner without
prior written permission from the publisher,
except in the case of brief quotations
embodied in critical reviews and articles.

Publisher - Ray/Jan Publisher

Covers designed by: Jan Clanton

ISBN 0-9625253-2-4

Contact:
Ray Clanton
PO Box 1800
Camp Verde, AZ 86322

Email: ww2clanton@hotmail.com

Website: www.b29flyer.com

Dedication

It is with a profoundly deep sense of humility and respect that I dedicate this book to all the service personnel, who during World War II, were based on or attached to the Marianas Islands – Saipan – Tinian – Guam, in the Pacific Theater of Operations.

Acknowledgements

It is with a deep sense of pride and gratitude that I express my ever lasting thanks to my wife Jan for her contributions and encouragement in the development of this book. The front and back covers are her creations.

My story and those of other combat airmen would have remained forever dormant had it not been for her unselfish dedication to this project. A huge amount of time, effort and expertise went into this labor of love.

I owe another special thanks to the lovely and gracious Peggy Clanton for her considerable contribution in the marketing of this book.

I direct mailed 3,000 promotional letters and requests for hair-raising accounts of B-29 airmen in combat. The response was overwhelming.

The accolades and expressions of encouragement I have received have given purpose to developing a book of historical value dealing with the preservation of the personal accounts of the heroic deeds of the B-29 airmen.

Further, many have pre-ordered “The book” on a faith and trust basis only. That expression of confidence in my honesty and integrity renders me speechless. No easy task.

I also want to express my special appreciation to those combat veterans that submitted their stories for consideration in this book. It has been a gratifying experience.

This wonderful group of dedicated Americans have earned my deepest respect for the support they have provided throughout this endeavor.

Please permit me to state with all the sincerity I can muster “THANK YOU ALL!”

Introduction

“The Book” includes not only my story but the spellbinding exploits of other B-29 combat airmen, two POWs stories, a non combatants saga, an account of an airman’s psyche when facing death and much, much more – including some appropriate humor.

Every World War II enthusiast, student of history, Air Force museum or gift shop visitor, vet and his grandchildren and many others will be filled with a sense of understandable pride when they realize the courage and valor the airmen displayed flying their B-29 Superfortress on these life-threatening missions.

“Fire, Fear and Guts” is a revealing composite of significant historical events as recorded by those who lived them. It covers the gamut of dramatic human emotions. The stories are compelling. They depict a graphic portrayal of the air war over the Empire of Japan and its chilling effect on the airmen who put their lives on the line.

This book is divided into two sections-Part I and Part II.

Table of Contents

Table of Contents
(continued)

20

Part I

This book is divided into two sections. Part I is my (Raymond W. Clanton) story. It deals with my military training, certain combat experiences and some personal reflections. I have presented this narrative on a one on one basis. This technique introduces the reader to thrilling and substantive word pictures. Thus, a subtle desire to read more is created.

MILITARY RECORD & COMMENTS & CERTAIN COMBAT REFLECTIONS INVOLVING THE B-29 SUPERFORTRESS OF RAYMOND W. CLANTON – 0-760571

Post Office Box 1800
Camp Verde, AZ 86322

1944 Looking to the future

2004 Still proud to be an American

ENLISTED: Army Air Corps – 7/22/42, age 20 years
ACTIVE DUTY: Santa Ana A.F.B., California – 2/4/43
COMMISSIONED: 12/5/43
SPECIALTY: Pilot, Army Air Corps.

COMMENCE OVERSEAS DUTY: Arrive Saipan 12/6/44, as pilot (co-pilot) on B-29 Superfortress with 881st Squadron, 500th Bomb Group, 73rd Bomb Wing, 20th Air Force, Army Air Corps. There were 5 bomb wings, which made up the 21st Bomber command of the 20th Air Force operating in the Marianas-Saipan, Tinian, Guam. The 73rd was the first to strike Japan from the Marianas. After take off the B-29's were immediately in hostile territory flying 1500 miles to Japan with no fighter cover and little or no air/sea rescue. The 73rd absorbed over 33% of the losses sustained by the 5 bomb wings involved.

END OVERSEAS DUTY: Depart Saipan 10/23/45, as Airplane Commander.
DISCHARGED: 11/30/45 - RANK: 1st Lt.
COMBAT: 27 missions as Pilot (co-Pilot); 6 missions (4 were P.O.W missions) as Airplane Commander

DECORATIONS: Asiatic-Pacific ribbons with two Bronze Stars, Air Medal with Three Oak Leaf Clusters, Distinguished Flying Cross with two Oak Leaf Clusters, Presidential Citation Ribbon.

*SPECIAL NOTES:

- Because the B-29 Superfortress was the state-of-the-art flying machine of it's day, the pilot (1st pilot) was designated airplane commander, and the co-pilot was designated pilot.

- One of few pilots in 500th Bomb Group to make Airplane Commander.

SPECIFICATIONS OF THE B-29 SUPERFORTRESS

Wing Span:	141 ft.
Length:	99 ft.
Vertical Stabilizer:	29 ft.
Engines:	4 (2200 h.p. ea.) Wright cyclone, 18 cylinder
Cruise speed:	200 to 220 mph, indicated air speed
Top Speed:	370 mph at 25,000 ft. - ground speed
Range:	Flying low and lightly loaded – 5,000 plus miles
Range:	Fully loaded-7 tons at 30,000 ft.- 3,000 plus miles
Cost:	$600,000. (B-17 and B-24, $200,000. ea.)
Innovations:	Central fire control system would sight the target and fire the guns remotely. Pressurized cabins front and rear with connecting crawl tunnel. Fly higher, faster with bigger payload with greater range.
Armament:	10 fifty caliber machine guns and 1 twenty mm cannon
Weight, loaded:	140,000 lbs
Fuel Capacity:	10,500 gallons

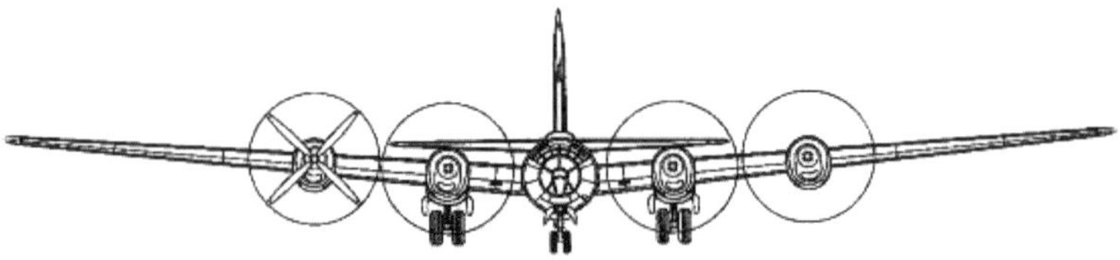

used with permission and under© of Squadron/Signal Publications, Inc.

Queen of the Skies

The B-29 has a special place in the evolution of flight lore. A place reserved for royalty. Her bloodline was pure.

Once airborne she became the unquestioned "Queen of the skies." Nothing even remotely approached her majestic beauty of design. She was a siren, a temptress. Veiled beneath her intrinsic beauty was a latent instrument of death and destruction.

B-29 Superfortress

A measure of her destructive prowess can best be illustrated by examining her credentials, some of which you are already aware. She could fly faster and higher and farther with a significantly larger payload than any other plane in the sky.

Her cabins in which the crewmen operated were pressurized and connected by a crawl tunnel. That was a real innovation in a combat aircraft. So, too, was the automatic gun-sight and firing mechanism combined and interlocked with a central fire control system. The gunners sighted (aimed) their guns by means of an instrument (device), which also fired them. Imagine that, the gunners never touched their guns.

Further, a flight engineer was an intricate and essential part of the crew. He monitored all systems of the aircraft through an array of instruments, dials, and gauges located on a vertical panel approximately 3 feet by 3 feet. He also recorded the planes fuel consumption and advised the pilots of the fuel flow in relation to the required flow line in order to sustain flight for the 3,000-mile missions.

Formation flying was a real challenge because of the constantly changing throttle settings. I'm sure you're aware of how you affect your own m.p.g. in driving your car when you're on and off the gas pedal. Inconsistent throttle settings affect an aircraft in the same manner.

Fuel consumption was arguably our worst enemy, particularly when the Japanese fighters and flak were neutralized or eliminated.

The radio and radar operators had the most sophisticated equipment in the world. Everything was state of the art. They could perform functions never done previously.

After this assessment of certain of her capabilities and assets it's a given extension to support her coronation as: "Queen of the skies."

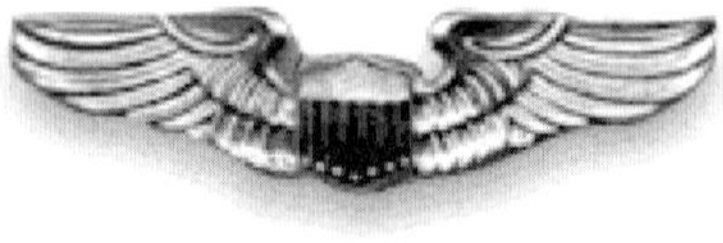

Preflight Training

I enlisted in the Army Air Corps in July of 1942 as an aviation cadet. I was called to active duty in February of 1943. My class was designated 43K. This indicated I would be graduating in December of 1943.

In the interim I attended a college (Board of Fire Underwriters) for insurance special agents. I also attended evening classes at L.A. Junior College majoring in mathematics and navigation. In those days we weren't called to active duty immediately because many training facilities had not been completed.

Preflight training was much like boot camp in the Army. Here we were issued our uniforms, assigned our barracks and bunks (beds), given our medical exams, taught to make a bed the Army's way and provided a footlocker. Further, we learned the intricacies of marching properly, standing inspections of all types, absorbing the insults of the upper classmen, attending ground school, mess hall (a place to eat), K.P. (washing dishes or preparing food), latrine duty (cleaning toilets), etc. Actually, I liked marching, military routine and discipline because I understood the reason it had it be that way.

Another item of significance did manifest itself very early on. It became eminently clear that an aviation cadet was so low on the chart of command you couldn't see him. We were required to address our enlisted men instructors as "sir." They literally had the power of life and death over us. Objecting to anything or disobedience of any kind meant only one thing – "you're washed out" (eliminated from aviation cadet training). I hasten to advise you, we learned the meaning of discipline in no uncertain terms. Also, orders were to be obeyed without question.

I must insert one of my overpowering concerns about being

unable to object to or appeal to anyone about an injustice or an objectionable situation. I trust you younger readers will recognize morality in the '40s was defined substantially different that it is now. A gay person during this period and later was defined as a happy individual. That definition was exemplified in song and verse for decades. Gradually a metamorphosis of sorts took place. The repugnant terms faggot, queer, and weird vanished and were supplemented with the word gay. And that's how it was.

I had a real personal anxiety problem all through pilot training. "What would I do if I were approached by a superior who was gay?" Would I be "washed out" if I refused his advances? Now that, for me, presented a real dilemma of staggering proportions. Thank God, I didn't have to deal with that issue. It is my opinion the military at that time should have cut all of us servicemen some slack, even we lowly aviation cadets. However, it was "cover-up" time and that's how the matter was handled and thus ignored.

Freedom of speech is a precious jewel in our form of government. It was never more profound for me than it was at that time.

In the classification process each aviation cadet was given an array of medical, physical, psychological, coordination and mental tests to determine his qualifications to become a pilot, navigator or bombardier. A part of this procedure included a test to determine one's depth perception. Such a determination was a vital factor in flying period and, flying tight formation in particular. My examination was unusual by any standard.

As we passed from one examining station to another, lines, of course, would form (so what's new?). Some extended from inside to outside. I make mention of this only because the element of light had such a significant effect on my depth perception test. The evaluation area consisted of a tunnel-like segment within a building. As I recall it was somewhere between 25 and 50 feet in length and about 3 feet square. Placed on one end was a stool to accommodate the examinee. The other end was designed to handle two black vertical rods approximately 8 inches in length and ¾ of an inch in diameter, each mounted on a separate track and brightly lighted. Two nylon cords about ¼ of an inch in diameter were connected to the vertical black rods. The nylon cords extended to the examinee's position.

When I walked into this room it appeared very dark because I had just been exposed to the bright sunlight. It was much the same as walking into a movie theater. I'm sure many of you have experienced the difficulty one has in locating a seat if your eyes are light sensitive. Mine are. You'd have to chuckle at my inability to locate the stool. The examiner actually took me by the arm and sat me down. He handed me the nylon cords and said, "Line up those rods at the end of the tunnel so each is the same distance from you." Then he switched on the very bright lights at the end of the tunnel. I said to myself, "I can't even see them."

Now, here's the kicker. You may call it, "Divine intervention" or "The Luck of the Irish." I knew I had to stall for time to permit my eyes to adjust to the darkness and brightness. The combination had literally rendered me blind. I fumbled with the cords, purposely dropped one and made some dumb comments about the weather and military life. After about 6 or 7 minutes of these tactics my eyes adjusted well enough to allow me to see the black rods. I must advise you I had no idea where they were in relation to one another and to me. So, I gambled. I moved the left rod up about an inch and the right one back about 2 inches. I said, "That's it." The examiner replied, " OK, now close your eyes while I reset the rods."

Next he said, "Open your eyes and do it again." I opened my eyes and by now I could see the black rods. I took long strokes with the cords in an attempt to get a sense of distance. It didn't happen, so I made a calculated estimate of how I thought the examiner had the rods set up. I moved the left rod toward me about 4 inches and the right one about 6 inches and dropped the cords. I said again, "That's it." He repeated the scenario. This time I could see and I set the rods as my vision perceived them. Again, I said, "That's it." The examiner's perplexing comment was "Are you sure that's the setting you want?" "Oh boy," I thought to myself, "The guessing game is on again." Obviously, I didn't know if he was trying to trap me or give a legitimate second chance. I elected to stay with my original choice. I replied, " Yes sir, that's the setting I want."

To this day I have absolutely no way of knowing if my three settings were within the acceptable tolerances. Perhaps one was very good and the other two were "close enough." The whole subject is open to all kinds of speculation. It's disconcerting not knowing which options I utilized worked and which did not. However, I passed and that, after all, is the bottom line.

I qualified for pilot training as my primary m.o. (classification). Also, for training as a navigator if I washed out as a pilot.

Assembling the B-29 Superfortress

Primary Training

I took my primary training at Thunderbird #1, Army Air Corps Base in Phoenix, Arizona. There was a real contrast between this base and Santa Ana from which I had just come. Thunderbird #1 was a civilian-type facility which the Air Corps had leased and the flight instructors were civilian pilots. When we first saw it many of us blinked twice and said, "What happened, can this be real?" It had all the trappings of a country club, but make no mistake, the military presence was there and in full control. Discipline and obedience were the orders of the day – every day.

Good fortune smiled on me when a gentleman by the name of Mr. Bannik was assigned my instructor. He was a great guy and a superb teacher. His methods would later (in basic training) save my military career as a combat pilot. He had a special air about him which generated respect and confidence in what he said. The instructors referred to us as "mister" so and so (last name) which for a while seemed somewhat uncomfortable. However, it beat the heck out of what the upperclassmen called us.

We qualified in P.T. Stearmans. The Stearman was a bi-wing airplane with excellent handling characteristics. Though it looked very much like the vintage aircraft of World War I, it made an ideal primary trainer. Takeoff and landing speeds were in the 55 to 70 mph range and it had two cockpits. I was the first to solo in my group. During this flight I felt a sense of joy and exhilaration I had never experienced previously. Flying alone produced a stimulating and invigorating emotion far beyond my ability to express. Nothing I had done previously even remotely approached that completely uninhibited sensation of being aloft in that little Stearman soaring through a cloudless blue sky that only Arizona can produce. "Only Heaven can be better than this," I said to myself.

In primary training we learned a number of basic maneuvers. Examples were: Lazy 8's, chandelles, power off stalls, power on stalls, stall recoveries, spins, spin recoveries, forced landings, slow rolls, snap rolls, inverted flight and power landings to mention a few. We were admonished not to attempt outside snaps or a split S because the stress placed on the wings of the aircraft exceeded the design limits. However, I had a compelling urge to see if I could execute an outside snap. So I made the attempt and I'm here to say the wings stayed on. Now when I look at what the consequences could have been, I must admit it was a real dumb trick. Incidentally, this writing is the first admission I've ever made of this unauthorized tactic.

Flying an airplane was an answer to all my dreams and prayers and also my grandfather's dream for me. He requested my parents name me after the Wright brothers by making my middle name Wright. It was an appropriate fit.

This period in my life was the most gratifying and enjoyable part of my entire military career.

P.T.-17 Stearman

Basic Training

I then went to Minter Field, Bakersfield, California, for my basic training. The instructors were 1st. and 2nd. Lieutenants. Here the romance almost ended. Each instructor was assigned to six cadets. I had the misfortune to be assigned to one who was p.o.ed by his position in life. He had embarked upon a plan to wash out an inordinate number of his cadets which I am sure he felt would cause him to be reassigned to combat duty.

On a formation instruction flight he tried to intimidate me to a point where I would challenge him in anger. He grabbed the stick and wrapped it forward and back, driving my head against the canopy. It hurt like hell. He expected me to fire back, giving him an excuse to wash me out on the spot. It didn't work. He gave the stick back to me and I had the almost uncontrollable urge to put that B.T. 13A in a dive and scare the pants off him, but we pulled out of formation and headed for base. When we landed he said, "Clanton, you're taking your washout ride with the Major tomorrow."

The next morning the Major met me on the flight line and said, "This is your washout ride." "Yes Sir!!!" I replied. When we reached the proper altitude, he instructed me to do a lazy 8 maneuver. I did it the way my instructor taught me, and the Major asked me, "Why did you do it that way?" Since we were not permitted to criticize our instructors or to make any lame brain excuses, I asked the Major, "How do you want me to do it?" I did it his way, which was the way I had learned in primary training. I did it and several other maneuvers as I had learned them in primary training, and passed my washout ride. Thank God the efforts of the instructor to make me his fifth victim failed.

AN UNCOMMON INCIDENT

During basic training an incident occurred which shook the

very fabric of the entire base. Hopefully, I can create a word picture surreal enough to make you feel a part of it.

As was the custom an aviation cadet of excellent stature and outstanding character was selected our "Captain of Cadets" by the officers in charge. Their choice was popular because he was a great guy and a credit to the uniform. No one ever spoke of him in any way other than in admiration and respect.

One evening about halfway through basic training some of my fellow aviation cadets and I were sitting in our barracks having a bull session. Suddenly out of nowhere a B.T.13A came roaring in on us. He was at rooftop level, with the throttle wide open giving us a buzzing such as none of us had ever experienced. It was a shock of unbelievable proportions. Jim, one of my fellow cadets said, "What the heck was that?" As he was speaking all six of us jumped up and ran outside to see what was happening. I said, "Look at that guy, he must have 'flipped his biscuit'."

After he passed over us he buzzed the officers quarters, administrative buildings, hangars, and rows and rows of B. T.13A's. Then he climbed to approximately 2,000 feet, did a dangerous vertical bank (a stall was a real possibility) and headed for the deck with a thunderous roar. Just skimming the rooftops he passed over us again. I said to Jim," We need to get out of here, this is bad stuff." He replied, "Yeah, you're right, but there's no place to go." So we all stood outside wondering what was happening and watching this drama unfold. His flying pattern was erratic. It was a cross between a sloppy lazy 8 and an imperfect elliptical circle. I wondered if this guy were an aviation cadet who had gone berserk, or one who had been provoked over the edge by the action of some instructor or superior officer. I could empathize with the "provoked over the edge" part.

He repeated the buzzing routine about five times. He was

creating a panic situation all over the base. Suddenly for some inexplicable reason the pilots voice was on the public address system. Everyone could hear him. We recognized the voice as that of the Captain of Cadets. Jim said, "I can't believe it's______." But it was. His voice was hysterical and his ramblings were illogical. He kept repeating, "I'm gonna get that s.o.b Captain_____. I'm going to kill him. I'm going to get even. He deserves to die. I can't take anymore." Remarks of that nature were continuous.

After 15 or 20 minutes had elapsed a voice from the control tower, which we identified as that of the Commanding Officer, attempted to start a dialogue with the C.O.C. His first words were, "Cadet________ please land your plane, you don't want to hurt your fellow cadets." The C.O.C. screamed back, "Don't give me that bull, I know you're going to court marshal me if you get the chance." The C.O. came back with, " Just land your plane. I give you my word you'll be treated fairly." The C.O.C. shouted into the mike, "The hell with you. I'm gonna get that bastard Captain _______. Trot him out so I can see him." To that the C.O. gave a curt, "Can't Do."

In this crisis situation we were much more than a little uncomfortable. We knew he wasn't going to pull out of one of his dives. It was evident someone was going to die before this episode ended. The banter between the C.O. and the C. O.C. continued with the stress level reaching new heights. The menacing tension was becoming unbearable. You see, a horizontal crash would have wiped out several buildings and barracks, and the resulting fires would have amplified that. God only knows how many officers, men and cadets would have died.

Next, the C.O.C. in a voice bordering on hysteria shrieked into the mike, " I'll show you I can fly this thing – watch!" With that he pulled the plane up to an altitude of 7,000 to 8,000 feet, did a roll over and dived for the deck under full throttle, and the prop set at high pitch. In that mode the plane created an ear-piercing noise much like that of a screaming banshee, the harbinger of death. He leveled off just over the officer's quarters less than 75 feet above the ground. Then he headed for the cadet's barracks, passed barely above the rooftops and turned toward the control tower. Just before slamming into the control tower (I'll warrant the guys in that tower thought they were dead) he veered off to the left, still under full power, pulled back on the stick and headed for the stars. He held that position till the plane stalled out, rolled over, and started to spin in.

The throttle was still wide open and the engine was now wound so tightly it could explode at any time. The prop noise was deafening as he crashed near the end of the east runway amid a ball of fire. It was over but what a waste. He would have made a wonderful, inspirational leader. He was the kind of man you would want your son to emulate.

Less than one hour after the crash the C.O. issued an urgent order. It said, "Get the cadets in the air." He properly and accurately interpreted the emotional impact the flipping of our C.O.C. had on all of us. He wanted us in the air in an attempt to circumvent any adverse psychological reaction this uncommon incident may have caused. His foresight created the desired effect. It was a very disturbing experience because of the manner in which it occurred and the admired individual involved. We all suffered a great loss that night and we knew it.

Ray in a B.T.13A

ADVANCED TRAINING

I had my advanced training at Stockton Field, Stockton, California. Almost every aviation cadet wanted to be a fighter pilot because of the adulation connected with it. We wanted to become "aces – Heroes," if you please. However, I believe the motivation goes much deeper than those superficial terms. I feel the compelling desire to fly a fighter, when defending ones homeland and/or way of life, is deeply embedded within our psyche. It is a natural extension of our basic instincts.

Remember, all through time, dating back to the first caveman, men first fought only with their hands and feet and connecting body parts. When our ancestors invented the club, they initiated the evolution toward the sophisticated tools of war we now employ. A combat fighter plane is one such tool. It provides the means by which the pilot who has honed his skills can use most of his body parts in the defeat of his enemy. Kinda like the caveman did, isn't it? I trust this is not too much of a stretch for you. Anyway, it is food for thought.

Back from the philosophical to the practical (real world). The fighter pilot has the entire "wild blue yonder" as his battleground while the bomber pilot can carve out only a small, precise segment of the sky for his. Further, the fighter pilot has the thrill and exhilarating excitement of hand-to-hand combat to stimulate his competitive juices while the bomber pilot has only the mundane mission assignment as his. There is not an abundance of self-gratification in dropping a load of bombs.

When the Air Corps changed from a defensive struggle to an aggressive mode the impetus for training bomber pilots began in earnest. To my great disappointment, my entire class of 43k went to twin engine advanced training to become bomber pilots. During my junior and high school years I lived near Lockeed (now Burbank) airport in Southern California where the P-38 was built and tested. Naturally it was my passion to fly this beautifully designed fighter. It was not to be. I completed my advanced training with two citations for flying proficiency.

P-38 My Dream to Fly.

Graduation time had arrived. It was December 5, 1943. My mother and girlfriend had traveled from the San Fernando Valley (Southern California) to be a part of this momentous occasion in my life. It was a beautiful day in all respects. I had that sense of satisfaction and fulfillment one gets when he feels he has accomplished something special. I'll tell you I was ecstatic for having survived the rigors of aviation cadet training. That episode in basic training was a close call. However, all of the negatives were dimmed and rendered superfluous by the joy and elation of the moment. The "pomp and circumstance" was in full array. The ceremony was similar to what you've seen a hundred times. But, this one was special to us cadets because we were the honorees. After the commanding officer presented all of us with the gold bars of a 2nd Lieutenant and our cherished silver wings, the formal part of the ceremony was concluded.

The personal portion commenced immediately thereafter. My girlfriend pinned my gold 2nd Lieutenant bars on my epaulets and awarded me a memorable ceremonial kiss. My mother pinned my coveted silver wings on my blouse (bad name for the coat part of an officer's uniform) and gave me a big hug and kiss. We were both overcome with emotion. At that moment the sense of pride I felt was overpowering. I'm sure we both felt grand-dad was looking down on all that had transpired, nodding his approval. The "four" of us were on Cloud Nine.

Except for my distasteful experience with my basic training instructor, my journey had been satisfying and rewarding. The "bonds and chains" as an aviation cadet were gone, and suddenly we were human again. A part of our training had been an attempt to determine if we could "take it" emotionally. "Take it," meaning orders, discipline, insults, and sacrifice. Many aviation cadets had been "washed out," not because they lacked the physical coordination to fly but because they couldn't or wouldn't conform to these requirements. It was difficult to submit one's independence to military code. Yes, I was grateful and thankful for not having "blown my top" along the way. I'll never forget my unbridled happiness of that day.

Tom Sanders photo

Two of the several B-29s I flew in combat

TRANSITION TRAINING

I completed my flight training at Roswell A.F. base in Roswell, New Mexico. Here I learned to fly the B-17 Flying Fortress. What a superb airplane. Also, it was a real pleasure to be treated like a normal person. We were even permitted to call our instructors by their first names. My instructor was 2nd Lt. Gary Clark, a great guy and a gifted instructor. My cup runneth over. My joy and happiness could not be overstated. I had achieved a life long goal. I was a flying officer in the Army Air Corps. Lt. Clark, like my primary instructor, Mr. Bannik, made flying a totally gratifying experience. First Lt. Huber, my Advanced Training instructor, was great also. That *** 2nd Lt. Finefrock at basic training was the antithesis of them.

When I completed my transition training Lt. Clark told me I was in a very enviable position. He said I had qualified to go to war in the European theater flying a B-17 as a first pilot or, become a B-17 instructor as he had done or, go into the newly formed B-29 (I had only heard rumors of the secret super plane) program. I nearly jumped out of my skin when he described this fantastic opportunity to become a part of the newly formed 20th Air Force. The B-29 was the heir apparent to end the war with Japan. She was a paragon of "firsts." Numbered among her firsts were: she could fly farther, and higher and faster with a bigger payload by a large margin than anything else in the sky. She was the panacea General Hap Arnold, Air Force Commanding General, was seeking in his quest for a bona fide strategic bomber. Her development near her earliest conception became his baby.

This super plane was originally designed and slated for action in the air war over Germany. However, as the war unfolded the requirement for a strategic bomber, with which to attack Japan, became apparent. "Bingo," the B-29 was the solution.

The fit was ideal. Looking at a map it was obvious the prudent way to attack the empire was from the Marianas – Saipan, Tiniam and Guam. The flight covered 3,000 miles plus – 1,500 miles out and guess what, 1,500 miles back. After flying that far, delivering a payload of significant size was imperative. Releasing it from altitudes up to 33,000 feet would lessen the enemy fighters' effectiveness and flak accuracy. Sounded good to me. Naturally, I jumped, leaped, yelled, and screamed, "I'll take the B-29 offer." Little did I realize I'd be participating in the refinement of that plane.

A B-17 in combat.

HOLDING FOR B-29 TRAINING

I spent about 6 weeks at Clovis Air Force Base at Clovis, New Mexico. The living conditions were miserable. I shall not belabor that point but instead I'll describe the reasons for my statement.

Our barracks were in part constructed with a wainscoting of wood paneling four feet in height. The balance of the walls and ceiling were canvas. I'm positive most of you have at sometime during your life encountered the 100-degree plus heat of the western deserts. Maybe you have endured one or two of the dust-choking sandstorms and then experienced the bone-chilling nights – perhaps amplified by a freezing wind chill factor. Well, that's what we had. Day after day and night after night, it was the same. This base was the worst facility to which I was assigned during my entire military career.

The barracks were heated with coal-burning stoves. Each morning when you lifted your head from your pillow you would view a well-defined silhouette of your profile. It was an etching in coal dust. I only make mention of this coal-dust-saturated air because of the humor it brings to mind. Wouldn't the environmentalist of today have a hayday with the clean air syndrome?

The comments above equate only to stateside comparisons. They are in no way intended to parallel combat field conditions because there is not even a remote resemblance.

It was here two other pilots and I saw our first B-29 Superfortress. It was such a secret we had to sneak into the hangar to see it. We were astonished by its size and beauty of design. We wondered if anything that huge could really fly. The irony here is that at this point in time it really didn't fly too well.

An experience I had at this base is worth stating since it vividly reflects the animosity I held for Lt. Finefrock, my basic training instructor. While walking along a dusty walkway on a very cold and blustery night, I spotted a guy whom I thought was he. I immediately started directly toward him and grabbed him by the lapels of his heavy overcoat fully intending to choke the hell out of him or punch his lights out. Just before I went for his throat, I realized I had the wrong man. I, of course, said, “Hey buddy I made a mistake, you’re not the guy I wanted, I’m sorry.” He replied, “By God, I’m glad I’m not. That hate in your eyes could scare a person to death.” We laughed and said, “Goodbye, have a great war.” That was a dumb remark and never would have been uttered by anyone who had been in combat and faced death on an almost daily basis.

Glenn McClure photo

Walker Air Force Base – 1944-45

This view looks across the barracks, Administration buildings and on to the runways. Two B-29s are barely visible over the chimney in the background. When I returned to Walker in 2003 only two of these brick chimneys and two deteriorating hangars remained standing. All other evidence of this once bustling operation is gone.

B-29 TRAINING

Walker Air Force base in Victoria, Kansas is where I learned to fly the B-29 and met my-wife-to-be. Any story written about the B-29 states unconditionally that it was committed to combat without the normal shakedown and correction modification procedures. We had a graphic example of one of the design flaws during a gunnery training session. The target was being towed in a normal pattern and our gunners were practicing their first experience with a remotely controlled sighting and firing mechanism. There came a call from the right blister gunner. "Right gunner to pilot, over." I replied, "Pilot to right gunner, what's the problem bronc, over?" He said," The target is in such a position I have to fire through No. 4 prop." I said, " Go ahead and fire, this plane has fire interrupters." Guess what! – wrong.

The strange thing about this malfunction was that the engine didn't develop any unusual vibrations. It should have. Those propeller blades were lathe machined to extremely tight tolerances. They were held within a very few thousandths of an inch of perfect. It seems inconceivable the imbalance would not have caused big time problems. Perhaps the holes and nicks were so closely matched in wind resistance that there was no imbalance. Now, that's a stretch even for me. Please see the photograph of this potentially catastrophic event.

The press would really have had a field day with this story. Imagine a headline "B-29 shot down over Kansas or shot down by one of it's own gunners." I could absorb 10 pages writing about the repercussions and turmoil that would have caused. Generals, inspectors, investigators, and specialists of all types would have inundated Walker Air Force Base. That's enough conjecture. No real damage was done for which we were all grateful.

After landing a cursory inspection of the propeller only amplified the belief that it could not function properly in that condition. We had put over 100 holes in it. In some places it was almost severed as you can plainly see in the photograph.

Prior to combat, that particular design flaw was eliminated by inserting a fail-safe switch in the electrical circuitry.

Actually, we were debugging it while in training. Frequently, we were unable to complete our assigned training schedules because we had so few planes and they were far too often grounded for either repairs, maintenance, or modifications. Pilot efficiency, formation flying, landings and takeoffs, emergency procedures and so forth suffered greatly. The bombardiers had too few actual drops and the gunners had too few live ammo practice runs. So what were we doing in combat? That proverbial question kept repeating itself.

The impetus to put the heat on Japan for the impeding invasion was increasing. It appears the Generals at the top of the heap were willing to accept a B-29 loss ratio far above that which had been experienced with our current long-range bombers, the B-17 and the B-24. Their losses due to mechanical failure were minimal. However, least we forget, losses due to fighter attack and flak were abnormally high.

Looking at the complete picture objectively one could consider us sacrificial lambs. Many lives would have been saved had the assault on Japan commenced after Iwo Jima was secured. Iwo Jima provided a haven for combat damaged B-29's and a base of operations for the P-51's. They became our much needed fighter cover. As I make this statement it brings to mind a sobering realization. More lives would have been spared had the B-29 been given six months more to correct and refine it's deficiencies before being committed to combat. Further, the fact that crews would have been more thoroughly trained is not an insignificant consideration. The whole esprit de corps would have been elevated.

In retrospect, it seems General Hap Arnold's focus was to demonstrate the effectiveness of a strategic bomber. In pushing his agenda forward he was able to convince the powers that be that a separate air arm was essential in modern warfare. Some of us paid the ultimate price but the AIR FORCE does now exist.

Please note, this is not an indictment of General Hap Arnold. Roosevelt and Churchill were pushing hard too. Therefore, permit me to outline some of the other factors which influenced the decisions of those atop the totem pole.

Bases had to be cleared for incoming crews and space had to be made for the B-29's rolling off the assembly lines. Further, with the war in Europe winding down, onerous problems of gigantic proportions were emerging. The whole war production juggernaut was in full gear and spewing out war materiel of every type and nature at an ever-increasing pace. That impetus had to be sustained. Any reduction would have ruptured the whole system. Also, any evidence of uncertainty would have adversely affected civilian support of the war. A factor no one in authority wanted to see emerge. Therefore, because it represented a significant portion of the production capacity of the country, the B-29 became a part of the analysis and conclusion to commit it to combat prior to completion of all test criteria.

Later, as you would anticipate, with good ol' American ingenuity other B-29 facilities were established. Several were located in Nebraska and a few in Texas and other places around the U.S. The new facilities along with the originals enabled other bomb wings to be formed and subsequent planes and crews emerged properly prepared and ready to fight.
One thing was never corrected. It was the engine. The four engines were designed to lift 120,000 lbs. Frequently, our take off weight exceeded 140,000 lbs. Therefore, the Wright engine manufacturer had a legitimate reason for the engines failures. Yes, modifications were on going. Performance improved greatly, but only to a point. Engine failure remained a bone of contention throughout the war.

In analyzing this section it is readily recognizable that dynamic forces were in play on two fronts. The press to crush Japan without delay and the drive to keep the war materiel juggernaut functioning probably answers that proverbial question – so what are we doing in combat?

My crew with one man missing.

Love is a many splendored thing
Thank God! I returned to my bride.

Proud Pilot.

PERSONAL RELECTIONS

About one week after I arrived at Walker Air Force Base my right gunner and great friend Bronc came to me and said, "Lt., you have got to see this gal working as a secretary in the parachute department. She is a real sexy sweater girl." When I saw her I said to myself "holy cow, she makes Lana Turner (sweater girl of the '40s) look like (Popeye's) Olive Oil. After a while I summed up enough nerve to ask for a date. She said yes and I borrowed my navigator's car and we went to the officers club at the base for a big dance. That was the start of a great courtship. Her mother and sister and brother liked me. Her father hated the ground I walked on and probably the air I flew in. During our courtship I had to hitch rides to take Peggy on a date. We did a lot of walking and bus riding. After our dates I spent many nights sleeping on the mayor's front porch waiting for the bus. Also, I spent too many nights sleeping in the bus that was going to take me out to the base. When I recall my lack of sleep I wonder how I could have seen the flight instruments. Ahh, The wonder of youth.

When Peggy and I arrived at the Officer's Club on one of our dates for another evening of fun and frivolity, the music was in full "swing" and that special aroma of a piano bar lounge permeated the air. That triggered my impulse to dance. Shortly thereafter, I found myself dancing up a storm with a Major's adorable wife. The conceited showoff that I was, especially when on the dance floor, doing a "jitter bug" (dance of the '40s) routine with a pretty gal, drew the attention of all in the entire room. Remember now, the military is not a democratic society. As the number was ending, I inquired of the Major's wife, "How about the next dance?" Her enthusiastic reply was, "Sure, and how about the one after that?" I pulled her close and whispered, "You got it."

The next selections were in the "swing" beat with a little

"lindy" thrown in for good measure. You gotta believe we were really grooving. It was quite an exhibition. Near the finish of the last number I caught a glimpse of the Major's face. His disapproval was obvious. I got the message "loud and clear" and returned his wife to their table. My close friend, Craig, had taken over my escort duties of Peggy. After another drink or two to fortify my courage, I went back to the Major's table and said, "Is it ok if I dance with your wife again?" She was smiling sweetly and started to rise when the Major interceded with a curt, "Sorry, our dance." The tone of his voice and his facial expression telegraphed an uncompromising message – "bug off."

The rejection shocked me into the world of reality. I thought to myself, "Boy, how dumb can you be? This guy can really give you a hard way to go." I had made an ass of myself and probably embarrassed the Major. It is a well-known fact; you do not get favorable reports in your promotion file offending a superior officer especially by flirting with his wife. I fretted over this incident for many months. Several of my pals kept giving me the "needle with a twist." They would make remarks like "Your ass is grass," "You're in deep doo-doo," etc. As far as I knew, I never received an unfavorable rating.

This episode had all started so innocently during one of the "change partner" dances. Everyone was having a great time dancing, laughing and having a few brews. For some inexplicable reason I happen to end up with that Major's beautiful little wife who was a dancing doll. I think it's now time for me to take the fifth (amendment that is) and drop the subject.

Later I learned Peggy was considering dumping me because of my inattention and the spectacle I had made of myself showing off like a high school kid. Thank God, I got my act together before that happened.

Before I went overseas Peggy and I were married in a little church in Russel, Kansas, October 9th, 1944. We had 2 children, Sharon and Rich and 5 grandchildren and two great granddaughters. We still laugh and joke about our first few weeks of married life. Just let your imagination run wild when you picture two virgins – yes, virgins learning the art of lovemaking. I know that is hard to believe in this day and age but it was true. Beyond the fantastic physical experience was a deeply embedded emotional connection that lasts a lifetime. Everyone should be so lucky. Incidentally, her father and I became great friends and he became one of my key people in my concrete block manufacturing business in North Hollywood, California.

Recently I passed through the town of Victoria, Kansas, where as stated previously, I trained to fly the B-29 Superfortress. There I had the good fortune to meet the Town Engineer. When I told him I had been a B-29 pilot, he recalled the excitement and thrill he experienced as a 10 year-old boy watching us fly those huge planes in combat formation. He further said his parents and other townspeople were not all that thrilled by having the huge influx of military men into their little town. They didn't want their daughters dating the flyboys whose future was not all that secure. That statement sent my thought back to Peggy's father and his reaction to my dating his daughter. It was the norm of the day.

HELL ON THE HOME FRONT

When my brother went to enlist he learned he had scars on his lungs. Somehow the death of our little sister from diphtheria ten years earlier damaged his lungs. He then suffered the most humiliating, degrading shock of his life. He was classified 4F for military service. This term was so repugnant in those days that it would make any patriotic American want, in some way, to strike out in defiance and anger. To his everlasting credit he rejected the normal impulses which would accompany such a crushing blow to one's ego. Can you imagine the impact on his emotions?

He was to all outwardly appearances a happy, healthy young man, which made it all the worse for what he had to subsequently endure. All his friends had gone into service. He had been rejected and left alone. That loneliness had to be awful to absorb. You see, anyone who was able-bodied was expected to be in uniform. If you were not, you were subjected to the most humiliating ridicule, insults and criticism you can possibly imagine. It was common for him to be walking along a street and be heckled by some serviceman or civilian. They would shout such words as "Draft Dodger"-"Slacker"-"Coward"-"Bum"-"Sissy" and a litney of profanity just to make the whole insult complete.

Absorbing those kinds of hits could very easily have caused a lesser man to jump in the "bottle" in a fit of self-pity. But not my brother. A defeatist he was not and is not. He rose above all the negatives to become a key man in the steel yard at Lockeed Aircraft during the war.

After the war Dad, "Hoc," and I built one of the most successful concrete block manufacturing businesses in the United States. We created more innovative concepts in the manufacturing process and obtained more patents along the way than anyone else in the game.

My next publication will feature the pioneers of that industry, how it developed and some very revealing surprises about the people involved. We sold the business to Kaiser Steel Corp. in 1960. "Hoc" went to U.C.L.A. where he graduated with honors. He made the Dean's List. Yes, I'm very proud of my younger (2.5 years my junior) brother. Please do not think I am so naïve as not to realize certain people deserved the scorn and rejection they received. There were those who took a variety of avenues to be classified 4F. Some became conscientious objectors, others pleaded infirmities, while others hit the education trail. A few left the country etc, etc.

In summation, I wish to state I felt then and do now the deepest empathy for my brother. It was and is easy enough to place myself in his shoes and imagine how I would have reacted to such an assault on my ego. I'm not at all convinced I would have handled the situation as well as he did and has. You see, this stigma lasted many, many years after the war. He could not participate in conversations about his experiences in combat nor could he be part of the many honors afforded us veterans. What a bummer.

Finally, I salute my brother for his unmitigated guts and the manner in which he conducted himself during all those years of unwarranted, emotional abuse. Understand, he is a guy who would have been a bona fide hero under certain combat conditions. Also, those of you who may have encountered a similar type of prejudice, please know there are many of us who acknowledge and honor the contributions you all made to the war effort. Those of you who worked in defense plants or other essential industries were far more important to the fighting men than those individuals who were in uniform performing necessary but not indispensable tasks. That is why you have our respect and ongoing thanks.

My brother and I riding our bikes to church.

General Henry (Hap) H. Arnold
Commanding General
Army and 20th Air Force

During WWII General Arnold faced innumerable challenges and responsibilities. It is well documented, he handled them with courage and dispatch. The arena in which he functioned was pressure packed and demanding. It appears he has two primary passions.

Number one was the development and establishment of the Air Force as a viable and separate arm of the military services.

Number two was the development of the Boeing B-29 Superfortress Strategic Bomber. Her deployment and subsequent domination of the air war over Japan is now legendary.

Oddly enough both were inalterably entwined.

Though there were moments of anxiety along the way each dream became a reality. We now have an Air Force which is equal and autonomous with the Army, Navy and Marines. And the B-29, in her hay-day, as you know was hailed "Queen of the Skies."

A Few War Time/Combat Memories

The first mission flown by the 73rd bomb wing from Saipan to Japan occurred 11/24/44. One hundred and eleven planes took off but only 24 reached the target. When I heard that ratio, I said to Port, our flight engineer, "What kind of percentage is that? How could so few bomb the primary target?" Port was the intellectual on our crew but he shrugged off my query with "Your guess is as good as mine. You know one thing's for sure; we can't accept statistics such as those for long."

However, of the 24 B-29's that reached the primary target only 2 were lost and 11 were damaged. That is an acceptable loss ratio as long as you're not among those missing for breakfast. It was puzzling because it was so comparatively low. The Japanese quickly corrected whatever defect was exposed by this mission and the loss ratio abruptly changed to intolerably high.

Mission #1

My first combat mission was flown on 12/11/44. It was a photo recon mission to target No. 357 (Musashino Aircraft Engine Plant) in Tokyo, Japan. We encountered only light flak, no hits and blinding searchlights. The brightness shocked everyone into a new world. Though briefing had alerted us to the white, silvery brightness there was no way they could convey the intensity of those beams. I shouted to the airplane commander seated next to me, "I can't see, for God's sake, don't you get hit or we're in deep trouble." He counseled, "Close your eyes for a couple of minutes, then open them slowly and look down when you do it." Yep, he was right. Other than the light intensity surprise the mission was a long 12 hours and uneventful.

Mission #2

The second mission was much the same. Of course, we were prepared for those blinding searchlights and they were no big deal. These first two missions are of the type appropriately designated as "milk runs." Too bad our crew was not selected for more of those. Naturally every crew had the same secret wish.

Mission #3

The third journey to the empire was a typical combat mission. We encountered very heavy flak and formations of very aggressive fighters. All had the same mind set, "Knock those damned B-29's and their despicable, capitalistic crews out of the sky." Let me assure you if those were not their exact thoughts their actions proved them "close enough."

Rather than repeatedly describe in detail a typical combat mission, permit me to refer you to the section titled "The Bomb Run." Each mission carried the same exposure, the same hazards. The degree of severity was materially lessened with the advent of the P-51's for fighter cover and Iwo Jima as a haven for battle stricken B-29's . The fire raids presented an entirely different type of vulnerability which I'll cover later.

The radio operator lost his right hand, which ended his military service. The bombardier and left and right gunners sustained minor hits by flak or fighter lead. They were not removed from the combat roster.

An interesting tactic employed by the Japanese pilots was to pull up from below the B-29 formations and to rock on the rudders while firing their guns. This literally created a "wall of lead" through which the B-29's had to fly. Several superforts were lost on this mission to Nagoia, Japan. Four

Purple Hearts were awarded the injured men.

Nagoia always remained the most undesirable target in my book. The flak was concentrated and disturbingly accurate. I flat hated that stuff. You'll see that evaluation repeated more than once as the commentary unfolds.

I recall the severe winds aloft in the form of a 160 to 300 mph plus jet stream. This was a phenomenon of staggering proportions. It completely disrupted the strategy formulated to cripple the capacity of the Japanese to produce war materiel.

When first discovered it produced a mind-boggling dilemma. Our instruments would be indicating an air speed of 200 mph but when the jet stream reached the higher velocities we would actually be backing up in relation to the ground. What a bewildering experience.

Ok, so now try a downwind bomb run. No, it's not "bingo" time. If anything the problem was only amplified. Combing an indicated air speed of 200 mph with a tail wind in the average range of 200 mph produced a groundspeed that exceeded the design limits of the Norton bomb sight. Is it any wonder bombing accuracy was lousy? Before reaching the target the B-29's had absorbed numerous, tenacious fighter attacks, passed through a jungle of flak, experienced turbulent weather conditions and now this "devil be damned" jet stream. Makes one want to seek another vocation, doesn't it?

As stated above, the bomb sighting mechanism was the Norton bomb sight. Though it was of superior design and concept, it had its limitations. No way could it compensate for winds of such magnitude. I'm certain that jet stream rattled cages all the way up to Gen. Hap Arnold. Bomb runs, because of the sitting duck syndrome, just got worse. Therefore, that jet stream almost single handedly compelled the strategy of the airwar to be modified.

This condition did manifest itself in a most personal way. Incidentally, I'm still relating our involvement with Mission #3. The airplane commander gave me plane control as we headed into the target zone, a decision which shocked me. I've never been able to comprehend why. If he were looking to put a "quick study" on a green horn pilot, he succeeded.

We were flying the right-hand side of the element. The lead plane made his right turn to align with the bomb run heading. As he continued his turn he found it necessary to increase the steepness in an attempt to compensate for the speed of the jet stream. Unfortunately, I had to place our plane in a position to cause it to almost stall since the radius of our turn was much less than that of the lead plane. When I felt the plane starting to shudder I shouted to the airplane commander, "She's stalling, I've got to dump her." I did this by pushing the stick (control column) hard forward. It is at this point, if you had the option to go, you would say, "Let me out of here" – yeah, sure at 30,000 feet you couldn't exactly step out and walk away.

Now here is the tension-packed picture. We were under heavy fighter attack as we began sliding under the formation less than 50 feet away from the open bomb bays with those 500-pound bombs swinging ominously in their latches. That haunting vision made such an indelible impression in my memory banks that my recollection today provides me with a picture as clear as though it were yesterday. Had we hit a bump or turbulence in the air, any number of factors could have triggered the release of those bombs.

Remember those fighters were still boring in spouting their hot breath of lead. A mechanical or electrical malfunction could have been initiated by any of forgoing. The tension was of such a magnitude as to cause one to literally stop breathing. It was in fact a situation which would cause anyone to "clip washers" (expression of emphasis) without apologies.

We were unable to get back into formation due to the extra fuel we needed and didn't have to power up. We sustained heavy fighter attack as we headed for home. After deplaning on Saipan, we discovered just how proficient those Japanese pilots were. Further, we took some flak hits which had they been made a few inches from that point either way would have had a disastrous impact on us. Making only a cursory examination we counted more than 300 holes in our plane.

Many sobering questions arose with no plausible answers. We crewmen keep asking one another, "How could we absorb that kind of damage without someone being killed or having a control cable or fuel line or some other vital organ severed?" In retrospect, it's amazing we survived this one and others like it. I know everyone on board was grateful for having survived our first, true combat mission. Yes, we're back to "divine intervention," etc. I won't bore you with another repetition of those phrases.

Mission #5

Two more Purple Hearts were awarded to two injured crewmen on my 5th mission while flying pilot on an alternate crew. The navigator's chest was ripped open by flak. This man handled his injury with admirable dispatch. His demeanor and courage has remained with me all these years. He was not a particularly rugged individual. Certainly, not in the mode of a 230-pound line backer. Yet, there he was, no complaining or hysteria or vocalizing about his fear of dying. The pain had to be excruciating. The wound was ugly and deep. I did not observe the gunner's injury, which is the reason for the absence of comment. Please permit me to make another editorial insertion. It is about the fact that the navigator wasn't sent state side. That lack of compassion (a word not commonly found in military dictum) bothered me then and does now. It was grossly unfair to require him to complete his missions after having escaped death by the narrowest of margins. However, the powers that be saw it otherwise. He was patched up and sent to Hawaii for approximately six weeks. After a little R&R he was returned to Saipan and completed his combat missions. We can all be proud of this type of man and the courage he displayed. Oh yes, the gunner lived and he too completed his quota of combat missions.

Mission #9

The ninth mission was a "sweat" combat mission. The usual concerns and apprehension accompanied takeoff. The 1,500 miles to Japan were long and boring. This sortie provided the normal chills and thrills I've previously described.

However, the trip home nearly qualified us for a very unceremonious journey to Valhalla. This mission ended with the plane landing with both inboard engines (#2 & #3) out and props feathered. The #1 engine quit just after touchdown, and #4 was sputtering during the roll out. The plane had to be towed from the runway to its hard stand. It was completely out of fuel.

The shortage of fuel was discovered approximately 200 miles from Saipan. The pilots decided to have the engineer transfer fuel from the inboard to the outboard engines' tanks. The rationale for this decision was to hopefully keep the outboard engines running during the critical phase of landing at Isley Field. Isley Field is elevated and, therefore, presents a cliff, which in itself is a foreboding hazard to aircraft on final approach. Landing short is death. What a dilemma.

This, of course, influenced the pilot's decision. It would be touch and go. Other considerations for the "go for it" decision was the knowledge that B-29's with combat damage don't float too well or long after ditching. Also, B-29's at this point in the war were in very short supply and precious to preserve.

The pressure kept mounting as the engineer continually advised the pilots of the dwindling fuel supply. Also, the navigator reported miles and times to touchdown. And that cliff at Isley Field kept looming higher and higher, as well as that ocean water colder and deeper. Yes, this was truly the epitome of a "sweat mission."

Bud Child and Ray Clanton
2 pilots and a B-29
Best friends through high school and in combat '45 and through life

The Greatest Mission

It seems fitting, at this point to insert an observation of how such a dramatic switch in tactical use of a strategic bomber developed. In 1944-45 the British had conducted incendiary raids over Europe with considerable but not sensational success. Our Dr. Raymond H. Ewell of the National Defense Research Committee had done impeccable research and feasibility studies utilizing the formidable M-69 incendiary bomb. Ewell made his findings known to Gen. Arnold and his staff. Ewell was a major player in the whole scheme of things.

Gen. Haywood S. Hansel who commanded the XXI Bomber Command prior to Gen. Curtis LeMay replacing him in January 1945 had scheduled missions which would evaluate the practicality of mass raids utilizing the new M-69 incendiary bomb. Because of bad weather and that abominable jet stream the results were inconclusive. Gen. Rosie O'Donnel, commanding general of the 73rd bomb wing pushed for area bombing months prior (during U.S. training flights) But Gen. Hansel rebuked his recommendations.

Gen. Hansel was a committed exponent of daylight, high level, precision bombing. This, too, was the designated plan established at the top. However, the agonizing reality of a failed concept, after the first five or six missions should have been acknowledged by those in command to these at the top. It had to be tough to accept. Few of us celebrate failure. But the plan as conceived under such a myriad of uncompromising conditions (that bad weather, and dastardly jet stream, etc.) was impossible to implement.

The question that puzzles me most is, why was so much time required to employ the incendiary raids? Lives could have been saved. However, please know, I recognize that factor is not high on the list of priorities when formulating a battle plan. It can't be, it's the nature of war, and a rocket scientist is not required to confirm that.

When I write the bombing results up to March 9, 1945 were poor, it's the misstatement of the century. Lousy doesn't even cover it. The amount of money, yes, money, expended was awesome. Throw in men, equipment and materiel and you have a loser of staggering proportions. That's right; Uncle Sam wasn't getting a realistic bang for his bucks. Do you envision the winds of change?

Gen. Hansel had been unceremoniously replaced (for reasons not all of his making) by Gen. LeMay who was considered the panacea for the faltering B-29 program. Though results improved modestly, they were in no way acceptable. You can bet your bottom bippie Gen. LeMay could see his destiny written all over the walls Gen. Hansel had vacated two and one half months earlier.

Gen. LeMay was looking at another imposing enemy, metaphorically speaking of course, lurking at home were the other services, ready to pounce on his bones, should the B-29 program be deemed impotent. Yes, there has always been an ongoing intense rivalry between the military services. Had the gamble to develop a strategy for low level, high density incendiary attack consummated in failure, his dreams and aspirations and those of many others would have perished in the confligation they created. However, the gamble paid off, big time. The scope and influence was awesome. This one dynamic mission changed the entire concept of the air war over Japan. I doubt if ever in the history of warfare so few men (334) so dramatically changed the manifesto of war. In the most modest of terms this fire raid was devastating in all aspects.

When the initial reports of the spectacular results were received at Guam Headquarters the exuberance and jubilation soared through the Marinas and throughout the 20th Air Force and must have latched onto a segment of that jet stream to carry the historic news, to the good ol' U.S.A. Gen. LeMay and the proponents of area incendiary bombing had been vindicated and made whole. Strike photos received a few days later only added to the crescendo. General Lemay had to be the most relieved guy on the planet. The albatross was hanging on no longer. His elation and euphoria must have soared to the heavens on a plume of his famous cigar smoke. It was a period of unprecedented satisfaction and jubilation.

By any unit of measure this was the most all-consuming raid ever inflicted on an enemy. It was without challenge the greatest mission ever flown. No other event had such an indelible impact on history. In the aftermath of this configration there rose from the smoldering cauldron of Dante's Inferno the majestic B-29. She was now eminently qualified to reestablish her regal status as "Queen of the Skies." No other plane in the world could have matched her accomplishments.

A few months later she would further solidify her position of eminence by delivering the atomic bombs on Hiroshima and Nagasaki. No other plane in the world could have fulfilled those missions. Further she had by deed and purpose properly admonished those who had vilified her. They could now in "Lock Step" march into oblivion.

This mission as described in the forgoing had to be by a huge margin the most significant one in which I participated. The following is my recollection of that event. As of 3/9-10/45 B-29 losses were above acceptable limits and the effectiveness of our precision bombing was not all that great.

In this atmosphere, the commanding general of the 21st Bomber Command, Curtis LeMay, issued an order tantamount to suicide, or so many believed. Remember, the B-29s were bombing from 25,000 to 30,000 feet. His epic order called for each B-29 to fly individually (no formal formation) at an assigned altitude between 4,500 and 7,000 feet. These would be night missions with no fighter cover (obviously). Each B-29 would drop an average of 7 tons of incendiaries randomly on a specified target.

Many airmen felt this plan was a sure invitation to death. The words "revolt, ground me, mutiny, no go, stuff it, stupid," etc. were part of the scuttlebutt among the flying crewmen. However, orders are orders, and only a select two or three refused to fly. History now reflects how successful this concept was.

The first fire raid called for a "maximum effort" of 300 B-29s, each with an average bomb load of 7 tons of incendiaries committed to burning Tokyo to the ground. Members of the 500th Bomb Group were the last scheduled over the target. As they approached landfall, a huge red glow filled the horizon. Tokyo was ablaze, with the largest and most horrific firestorm ever created by man. It was a look into hell (cover depicts a haunting realism). The enormous heat from the burning city generated tremendous up and down drafts. As the last planes passed through the dense smoke clouds, unbelievable turbulence occurred.

Our plane encountered a down draft so severe that all whose seat belts were not tightened were thrown from their positions, and everything that was loose flew over the cockpit and throughout the plane. Even our mikes and helmets were torn from our heads. The plane lost 1,000 feet of altitude before we knew it. Fortunately, I had my seat belt tightened and was able to hold the plane stable. Had I not, this occurrence could have been a disaster. For laughs, I became a hero in my own mind. If ever the phrase "war is hell" was appropriate, these fire raids made it.

The Japanese suffered terribly in the aftermath of the horrible firestorms created by 300 B-29s dropping 2,100 tons of incendiaries on a given populated target. The damage inflicted on the enemy in the zone affected was tantamount to near extinction. One million people were rendered homeless, 83,000 perished (Japan's own count set the number at over 200,000) and many thousands more were horribly injured. Production of war materiel in the affected area was brought to an abrupt halt.

General Curtis LeMay
Commanding General
21st Bomber Command

After a distinguished career in executing certain phases of the air war over Germany and a short stint with the 58th Bomb Wing in India. General LeMay took over B-29 operations in the Marianas in January of 1945. He was a no nonsense guy as we Junior officers perceived him. I have always equated his demeanor to that of General Patton. He was to the Army Air Corps as General Patton was to the Army. A phrase depicting General Patton's philosophy of war is contained within the words "old blood and guts." His soldiers modified the words to - "our blood your guts." Somehow I have no difficulty identifying General LeMay with in those parameters.

General LeMay's greatest claim to fame came about through the development and execution of the devastating fire raids. Through this concept virtually all cities in Japan with a population exceeding 50,000 where annihilated. As the war was ending cities in the 30,000-population range were next on the agenda.

Shake – Rattle – Roll

Actually, there was something very unique about a takeoff in a fully loaded B-29. It was a real adventure. Though the mind set of a combat pilot is almost 180 degrees opposed to that of a non-combatant, the B-29 brought into play circumstances which modified that conclusion. The over powering concern which affected everyone on board was the total lack of confidence we had in the performance of those unreliable engines. Each takeoff, stated in the crudest of terms, was a real "crapshoot." "Lady Luck" was the third pilot in the cockpit. Peering down the 8,500 feet of runway there was a degree of uncertainty and apprehension each time I (we) started our "take off roll."

I'm sure, from time to time, you have seen pictures of the B-17's in England pulling out of their "hardstands" (parking areas) into the taxiways and forming endless, foreboding lines waiting their turns to move into position for takeoff. The B-29's modus operandi was the same until we pulled into takeoff position. Getting that 140,000 plus pounds off the ground required additional procedures and considerations.

When our turn came, if I were in the left seat I gave her the gun and pulled into position for takeoff, stopped and laid on the brake pedals. Next the starter waved his right arm in a circular motion indicating, "Rev up your engines." Wing flaps were set at 25 or 12 ½ degrees by the pilot (co-pilot). The Flight Engineer increased the fuel to air mix ratio to auto-rich and placed the engine's cowl flaps at trail. Both pilots had their hands on the throttles as we moved them forward. As the rpm's and manifold pressures were reaching "military power" the plane began to vibrate and shake. The noise level was deafening – probably off the decibel scale. I was watching the starter and the control tower. The pilot monitored the rpm's and manifold pressures ever conscious of the red lines on the instruments and the cylinder head temperatures. Then, when it seemed the plane was about to disintegrate the starter gave the forward wave and the tower flashed the green light. It was "SHAKE, RATTLE AND ROLL" time. A fitting phrase from an old song.

I released the brakes and she started her laborious roll. She rumbled down the runway with the pilot calling out the air speed which was S.O.P. in a B-29. I was ever mindful of the towers position and the torque of the engines. A pilot must lead the torque by gently feeding in enough left rudder to keep the plane rolling in a straight line.

When the speed reached about 135 mph I had to make a conscious effort to hold her on the ground to develop more speed before we became airborne. I had seen the tower flash by in my peripheral vision a moment before and I therefore knew, we were committed to a "go." Subconsciously, I loved the roar of those engines and I said to myself, "Please, Lord, keep those 'fans' turning." When the pilot called out 145 I eased back on the control column (stick) and hauled her into the air with the command "gear up" (wheels). As soon as our flight was stable I gave the pilot the thumbs up sign, which told him "flaps up." I eased back on the throttles as I established our 500 feet per minute rate of climb. The flight engineer closed the cowl flaps as the cylinder head (engines) temperatures dropped. We were on our way to Japan, 1,500 miles distant. I can laugh now when I think we went through all that, and I only hit the hot spots, just to get airborne.

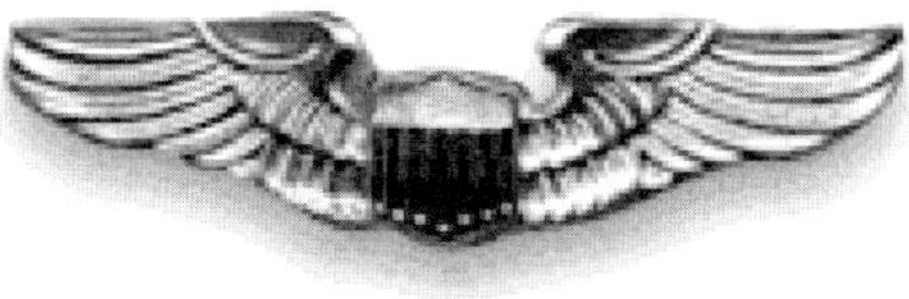

Colonel John E. Dougherty
500th Bomb Group Commander

Colonel Dougherty was an outstanding leader who led by example, a trait I greatly respected and admired. He projected an air of confidence that permeated the entire bomb group.

His tenacious determination to put the bombs on the assigned target earned him our countries second highest honor, the Silver Star. The commanding officer of the 73rd Bomb Wing, General Rosie O'Donnell found it necessary to issue an order requiring him not to exceed his quota of combat missions.

Certain of the missions in which he participated are catalogued within this book.

The Bomb Run

Here's what the bomber pilot (a/c) and his crew faces as they hit the coastline. Reaching landfall most always invited fighter attack. Depending on the direction from which they came, the first to spot one would shout over the intercom, "fighters at 5 o'clock high," or "5 o'clock low," or "2 o'clock level," or "2 o'clock low," etc, etc. You get the idea. The crewman who spotted them announced their location in relation to their position on the clock. Forget the conventional ethics of intercom procedure. No formality such as, "pilot to gunner, over," or "gunner to pilot, over" was in play. Rather it was, quite simply stated, uncontrollable pandemonium.

Guys were shouting, screaming, shrieking, yelling, hollering over the intercom. The voices came sometimes in unison or muddled or overlapping or disjointed or unintelligible. Through this jumble of confusion some words were discernible. "Here comes one at 12 o'clock high," "I got that s.o.b.," "He's on fire," "Boy that was close," "God, he's gonna ram us," "There goes a B-29 down," "Two Zeros at 4 o'clock low," "I got him," "Here comes another one," "Z square 00 has #2 on fire," "Help, I've been hit," and so on and on it went until the formation turned on to the bomb run.

Amid all this confusion the fighters kept boring in from all directions, pouring an avalanche of lead at the lumbering giants plodding along at about one-half their speed. In this maze of tension and pressure and death, the guns of the B-29 sounded a constant staccato giving some degree of hope and confidence to the beleaguered crewmen. They needed that lift.

On the bomb run they became the epitome of sitting ducks. It was necessary to establish the most stable platform possible in order to maximize the accuracy of the bomb drop. No variance in altitude, attitude or direction was permitted. Once on the bomb run heading, the pilots and bombardier could see black puffs of smoke fill the air in front of the formation. It was flak, like in "Bombs bursting in air" and it had a devastating effect on man and plane. I hasten to tell you, I hated that stuff.

Most often the formation had just encountered an aggressive, determined fighter attack in the form of a real "turkey shoot." I guess you know who the turkeys were. Now they faced an even more foreboding menace. This was about passing into that zone, (no, not twilight) commonly known as "Flak Alley." All aboard knew some plane or planes were going down. Most all would sustain some damage and have crewmen wounded.

It is here the airplane commander and his crewmen had to bring their "guts" into play. They "sucked it up," "Set their jaws," "Fixed their focus," "Applied their concentration," and plowed into that shrapnel jungle that was "Flak Alley." Terror, no. Scared, Hell Yes! But you did it anyway. No, you're not a hero. It's your job. It's not humility. It's fact.

Despite the impending clash with fate the formation continues on the bomb run. At the appropriate time the bombardier opens the bomb bay doors. He hits the toggle switch when he sees the bombs dropping from the formation leaders plane. The formation planes drop on the lead planes release. IT'S BOMBS AWAY! Close bomb bay doors and head for the Marinas (Saipan). Oops, there's more flak to clear and the formation braces itself for another encounter with the lurking fighter planes. They're primed for an unrelenting attack as soon as the formation clears "Flak Alley."

Most of the formation is still in tact. The fighters bore in, guns blazing and the scenario as described above repeats itself. Those that have survived the two fighter attacks and the caldron which was "Flak Alley" could appropriately repeat with credence "Enough is enough, already." Great, now all they have before them is 1,500 miles of enemy water to negotiate. Though some are severely crippled by enemy fire, and all carried the scars of battle, they will be home free – safe and sound – this time.

Perhaps you'd like to know how I handled myself in this arena of potential doom. Hopefully you won't find this self-serving dialogue. I hated and feared the flak jungle far more than fighter attacks. The overpowering factor seemed to be the inability to see it coming and knowing when you did it could be fatal. The thought of this brush with death created a stress level of overwhelming proportions.

Acknowledging fear was the key. That admission made it possible to develop the mind set to stay the course. So I admitted to myself, "I'm scared as hell, but give me those controls and I'll put those damned bombs on the target." That was my crutch whether I was flying as airplane commander or pilot. There you have it. I wonder how other guys handled their apprehension and fear.

Glenn McClure photo

B-29's Approaching Landfall

These planes are flying "loose" formation. They had rendezvoused off the coast of Japan several minutes earlier. As they approached their IP (Initial Point for the bomb run) the formation would tighten. The planes would be within a very few feet of one another to maximize their considerable firepower.

During the first several months of operation the B-29s had no fighter cover. Therefore, prudent use of their extensive firepower was essential. Further, the elements would "stack" themselves in such a manner as to concentrate a greater number of guns on a given target.

Variables In Psyche

Now, I'd like to address the over-worn word "hero." I vehemently oppose the reference to us as "heroes." A few people were and I salute them in solemn reverence and respect. However, 99.9 percent were not. That is true in all wars, present, past, and future. The word brave or bravery or valor are perhaps more accurate descriptive terms. Storming the beaches at Guadalcanal, Saipan, Iwo, Normandy and all the others required a special psyche, something unique and unusual within the man. Tank warfare, open combat, jungle encounters, search and destroy missions and all the rest did too. Flying combat or on bombing runs were in the same category.

Therefore, it is my conclusion, many service personnel did perform deeds of bravery even though they were scared and abhorred dying.

On the other hand one must differentiate between a man in combat who functions despite his fears and one who has no fear and cancels the desire to live with the bravado of a hand wave. I've previously admitted my fear. Therefore, I'm unable to respond to the alternative. However, I, as you must know by now, have an opinion.

The fearless individuals must possess a psyche similar to that of an Evel or Bobby Keneval or a NASCAR driver like Richard Petty or a Dale Earnhardt, or a test pilot who usually flies till he dies (General Chuck Yaeger, breaker of the sound barrier is a rare exception) and let's remember the astronauts, etc, etc. These people, who have a very special persona, regularly face serious injury and death without fear.

That differential will open a virtual Pandora's box of conjecture. Wouldn't this speculation be great fodder for an open forum? Since I have the privilege of the last word please permit me to conclude this section with this comment. I would attempt to do the dangerous vocations mentioned above, and do them undoubtedly poorly. I would do them not as an option but only, and I repeat only, under the veil of duty and I would know fear.

BONA FIDE HEROISM

I recall the Kamikaze attacks on the B-29's. Further, I remember seeing one of those jokers bent on suicide smashing through a superfortress in our formation. It was a sickening sight. It "shook" all of us badly, but, it had the enduring effect of furthering our resolve to heap as much hurt as possible on the enemy. Most Americans react in that manner.

Another reflection is that of Lt. Ebert (not on our crew) stepping into an open bomb bay with no parachute at 25,000 feet to release some armed bombs which had become jammed. At this altitude flesh freezes to metal. That only adds to the precarious nature of his life-threatening venture. He succeeded in discharging the bombs. He saved his plane and crew. This is the stuff from which heroes, true heroes are made.

Also, there was the spontaneous reaction of Staff Sgt. Henry Erwin, radio operator, to the preignition of a phosphorous flare or incendiary bomb on the deck of his B-29. He displayed impeccable courage with an absolute disregard for his own preservation and well-being. Knowing all too well he was facing horrible pain and disfigurement or even death he acted without hesitation. He grabbed that piece of metal burning at about 2,000 degrees and ejected it through the pilot's window. That burning member could have detonated the entire bomb load of incendiaries. All aboard would have been lost and the plane would have disintegrated in a huge, violent fireball.

I am filled with wonder by the unselfish action of Sgt. Erwin. His commitment to sacrifice life (he nearly died) and limb for his fellow crewmen places him in the unique category reserved for genuine heroes. There was only one Congressional Medal of Honor awarded to any member of the 20th Air Force. Sgt. Henry Erwin was that very special man. Further, I've included our own Raymond Porters heroic deed in Part II of this book. All three of these men willingly put their lives on the line and saved the lives of their crewmen. They belong to that special fraternity very few men can pledge.

A B-29 after Crash Landing

At this point in time I do not know how much of damage this B-29 sustained while flyable. Obviously, it absorbed a terrible trauma after touch down. Judging by condition of the fuselage I would conclude those who were alive on landing survived the crash.

11th Mission

After the eleventh mission, our crew was rotated stateside to Muroc Air Force Base in Southern California for lead crew training. It amounted to a very fortuitous gift in the form of our deployment to Muroc. Remember, the losses sustained by the B-29's during the first few months of combat were unacceptably heavy. It was not a good time. The computations made by many crewmen revealed a staggering statistic. The dauntless Superfortresses would have been wiped out before anyone completed 25 missions. A revelation such as that would grab anyone's undivided attention.

A RENDEZVOUS IN SAN FRANCISCO

As I approach this segment I am filled with an over abundance of ambivalence. It is difficult to acknowledge one's naivety or lack of sophistication, particularly in the field of sexual expertise. For better or worse that's where we're headed.

The experience which I am about to reveal occurred when our crew was rotated stateside for lead crew training. We had been in combat only five months, five very perilous months.

Because our third mission had taken out our radio operator we did not have a complete crew during the month of February 1945. Also, there were no replacement crewmen available. Therefore, we drew a pass on some very high loss ratio missions. It was very fortunate circumstance for us remaining crewmembers.

In March 1945 we flew all but one of the "Fire Blitz" raids which I've covered in detail previously.

April 4, 1945, we were assigned a new airplane commander. He was the greatest pilot with whom I've ever flown. Some of his exploits are detailed in Part II under "The Hugh McNamer Story." When "Mac" (McNamer) took over we participated in the violent April missions. I shall not describe each sortie we flew. All combat missions flown in conjunction with the high-level precision bombing format were juxtapositioned in relation of one to the other. Please refer to mission #3 and the "bomb run" if you require a refresher of what it was like to fly a combat mission. The low level incendiary raids were a totally different concept. Though hazardous they didn't present the exposure to death with the same intensity found with the high-level precision bombing missions.

On our way to Muroc it was necessary to land in San Francisco. While there, Port (Porter, flight engineer who deserves the Medal of Honor) and I elected to head into town to see the sights.

I've got to set the stage for what is to develop in this segment. He and I were, without equivocation, two of the most innocent, inexperienced, naïve guys in the entire Air Force. We were also unconditionally committed to our wives. Most men were faithful to their spouses. Some were not.

While strolling the streets I spotted a zircon ring in a jewelry store display window. We went in and I made the biggest purchase I had ever made in my life. I spent $275 on that gift for my beautiful bride. She was something very special. Peggy still considers that little ring among her most treasured possessions.

Later that night we found ourselves in a bar lounge with all the amenities you'd expect. There was a little combo and vocalist adding to the pleasurable atmosphere. Over half of the clientele were service personnel, which is not big news. The whole motif was done in red leather and red velvet with gold accents. It was an appealing establishment. OK, OK, enough of that descriptive stuff.

Remember, Port and I were genuine babes in the woods. Also, we were not big drinkers in the conventional sense. Neither of us made a practice of getting "smashed out of our gourds" just for the fun of it or to prove what "He-Men" we were.

Comes now the meat of this episode. While seated at the bar a young man approached us and asked, "May I buy you men a drink?" We said, "Yes, Thanks very much." He was well informed about the tactics of the 20th Air Force (we had our 20th A.F. patches on our coats) and the successes of the fire raids. After awhile he inquired, "Would you like to join my wife and I at our table?" We replied, "Sure."

He was a good-looking guy about 25 years of age with an athletic build. His wife was appropriately dressed. Her dress was blue and form-fitting but in good taste. She was by any standard a classy looking young lady. From all outward appearances they were the epitome of an upscale couple.

After some light-hearted conversation and another cocktail, the guy and I excused ourselves to go to the restroom. Stand by, my friends, I'm about to don the shock of my life. While returning to the table, the guy took my arm and said, "May I talk to you at the bar for a moment?" Number one, I didn't appreciate the arm grab and, number two, I was confused by the innuendo. However, I replied, "OK."

His conversation commenced with, "How would you like to go to our house for a night cap and some fun?" My question was " how far do you live from here?" He replied, " oh, about a half hour. We'll drive you there and return you here. Incidentally, what do you think of my wife?" Now what did that jerk think I would say? He knew darned well she was a beautiful girl and no derogatory remarks would be forthcoming from me. I replied, "She's a great looking lady with a lot of class."

I'm compelled to insert, "All that glitters is not gold."

His comment was "Thanks, I think so too but I'll bet you'll be surprised to know she's a real nympho. Wow, that nearly knocked me off my stool. I must confess, at that time I had heard that word maybe ten times. It was just not part of the normal vocabulary. Even more, at that point I could not define or delineate the word and it's implications. In that conversation the implied connation was oversexed. I know to many of you adventuresome, sophisticated gentlemen (scoundrels) this would have been an invitation to a singular night of unbelievable lustful fulfillment.

Next, I asked of him, "Are you inviting us to come to your home and make love to your wife?" He gave me a very positive, "I sure am. I get my real kicks seeing her making out with other guys. She loves it and so do I." I'm sitting there like a dunce. I can't believe my ears. The world in which I was raised was incompatible with that type of behavior.

He was on a real roll now and couldn't quit talking. He continued, "she really loves being the meat in a sandwich." Good gosh, I had no conception of what that meant. Pretty dumb, huh? I'll bypass the description of that act because I decline to make this too graphic. Suffice is to say it was a script made for a porno movie. Though I was a confused neophyte, I stated in a tone not open to compromise, "Thanks, but I'm not into that stuff. Let's go back to the table and see what Port has to say." I knew he would have the same reaction as I. Just a reminder, this is '40s in which this has taken place.

When we sat down I made the comment, "These people want us to go to their home for an intimate involvement of an unusual kind." (Stated that way because we were in the presence of his wife) His immediate reaction was, "No way, let get out of here." Without further ado, we pushed back our chairs, nodded courteously, said the obligatory, "Thanks for the drinks" and left. I realize there's a certain percentage of you who will think, "Those guys were a couple of first class-jerks for having passed on such an unusual, once in a lifetime opportunity. Your analysis is correct on the "once in a lifetime" thought. It never occurred again.

Soon Port and I were headed back to the base. I recited to him the account that guy had given me relative to the unconventional, insidious activities they had contemplated with us. He was as shocked as I had been. He observed, "That woman made some insipid remarks while you guys were gone. She asked me, 'How long have you men been overseas?' 'Do you like to have fun?' and, 'would you like to stay overnight with us? We could all sleep together, etc.?" I said to Port "You know, Ol' Buddy, I think we just dodged a bullet of hot lead tonight."

Both of us have repeated many times, "We have no regrets for having passed on that un-orthodox invitation."

HUMOR AT MUROC

During WWII housing for many people was a critical issue. That problem developed because of the number of citizens displaced by military service, erection of new training facilities and the expanding production juggernaut.

It was common for people in the affected areas to convert their homes into "rooms for rent" or "rooms for rent with kitchen privileges." In the rural sections property owners who raised chickens or turkeys or the like would also convert their chicken or turkey coops, sheds, barns, garages, and out houses (no not those associated with no indoor plumbing) to "rooms for rent." Too often the odor of the previous occupants remained to remind the human tenants of the previous inhabitants.

One cannot exactly equate this situation to an earth shaking imposition. It did, however, impose on those affected a style of living not normally associated with that which is found within the confines of a metropolitan district. Complaints fell on deaf ears. In reality, for every disgruntled individual there were ten anxious people all too ready to endure the inconveniences and disagreeable environment in exchange for a place to park the body. Rents, too, were outrageous. That good old reliable American concept of supply and demand did flourish in this arena of shortages.

Peggy and I luckily found a home in Muroc, California, which had been modified to accommodate several military and civilian personnel. Lead Crew training was conducted at nearby Muroc Air Force Base.

The owners of this home had three sons in the service. The two bedrooms the boys occupied were converted to three very small "rooms for rent." During the '40s and long before each child required a separate bedroom and bed and sometimes bath, it was common for siblings to occupy not only the same room but the same bed. The "Great Depression" only amplified this manner of habitation.

Further, they modified one-half of their garage to accommodate two 9.5-by-9.5-foot bedrooms. A bathroom was affixed to the room Peg and I occupied. The interesting and, I trust you will find, humorous reason for including this period of military service in this book is because of the unusual and unique manner the owner fashioned the access to the bedrooms and bathroom.

Peggy and I occupied the rear bedroom which, as stated previously, was attached to the bathroom. The front bedroom was rented to another military couple. All of that seems quite normal. However, the unique arrangement of the rooms and bathroom makes for a touch of levity. The story is worth reciting.

The layout of the bedrooms and bathroom was such that in order for Peg and me to access our bedroom it was necessary to pass through the front bedroom. There was no dividing panel or hallway separating us from their bedroom. Such an unorthodox arrangement created implications of an uncommon nature. Conversely, when the folks occupying the front bedroom found it necessary to make use of the bathroom facilities they were required to pass through our bedroom. The same set of conditions as stated above were in play for them. This set of circumstances engendered some compromising situations.

Despite conscientious consideration for the others' privacy it was impossible to avoid some inappropriate timing.

I can recall how we would walk in on them at the most inappropriate time. The one thing that stands out so vividly in my memory is that we never discussed the unintentional, indiscrete encounters. Strange conduct to some of you, I am sure. Sometimes we would mute our laughter or snickers under our breath or nearly gag trying to suppress our embarrassed laughter. They, in bed, would be affected in the same manner. This episode still produces a smile on my face. When they found it necessary to use the bathroom the situation was reversed. We all went through the same contortions trying to control our amusement, embarrassment and laughter. Oh yes, when the offending party got to his or her room the chuckling became audible through the plywood paneled walls. Lead Crew training did have its brighter moments.

Rotation

I have by design and intention excluded all missions flown in a concerted effort to mitigate redundancy. I trust you will appreciate the logic in not belaboring the point. Dwelling on the subject only exacerbates the negative. Further, I've made a conscious attempt to avoid overstating our exposure to death.

Mission #3 reflected the most severe damage we sustained on any mission. Again reading the details of that encounter and the overview provided in the segment titled "The Bomb Run" will instill in your mind a mental picture of what a flying combat crewman absorbed during his tour of duty. Each mission carried the same exposure, the same risks, the same hazards.

The degree of severity was materially lessened with the capture of Iwo Jima. Further, the strategic importance of the seizure of Iwo to the success of the B-29 program cannot be overstated. It provided an operational base from which to launch the P-51 fighters. The cover created by the P-51's greatly influenced the significant drop in B-29 losses.

USAF

P-51: Best of the best WWII fighters

During one of our April missions when I was flying co-pilot (pilot) I experienced the thrill and surge of pride of a lifetime. Imagine just how vulnerable we airmen felt plodding along, unable to do any evasive action, holding the bomb line regardless of the flak and fighter (Zeros) attacks. Truly we were sitting ducks. As we approached landfall there appeared out the side of my right-hand window the most beautiful, dramatic sight an often shot-up pilot could experience. There for all to see was a squadron of magnificent P-51 fighter planes.

They were among the first to fly out of Iwo Jima. Ahh, Thank God for those gallant Marines who took Iwo. It was a feeling much like that of a child and his security blanket, because these guys were going to keep those rabid-ass Zeros off our butts. The pilot in the plane nearest to us moved in closely and gave me a big thumbs up. God, what an emotional uplift. I returned the big thumbs up as he did a wing up and pealed off. I cannot express the pride I felt in being an American and a part of this superb group of men. This experience still gives me the chills.

Also, Iwo supplied an alternate, convenient haven for battle stricken B-29's. Obviously, many B-29's and crews were saved as the air war intensified. Once we landed on Iwo due to engine malfunction. Anyone who was there continues to give thanks to those Marines who absorbed the hell and horrifically high casualties that the taking of Iwo entailed. It was one bloody mess and deserves to be remembered for what it was. Almost every crewman who writes about Iwo will render a similar evaluation.

By the end of June 1945 the B-29's and P-51's had established overwhelming superiority in the skies over Japan. This is best exemplified by the general order of the day which modified the number of combat missions required for rotation. Suddenly, 35 combat missions were necessary for one to become eligible for an excursion stateside. Yes, there were some very unhappy campers when this order was posted. However, it was by any unit of measure fair. The order merely revealed conclusively how absolute our control of the skies had become.

I remember the horrible, emaciated condition of our 6 P.O. W's who survived their ordeal out of the 215 we lost from the 500th bomb group. Besides being beaten, tortured, and starved, they were also stripped and displayed naked in cages and put on public display by their captors. Our loses in the 500 bomb group ended up at 41%. This was the highest loss ratio in the 20th Air Force.

I will never forget my shock when we broke out of the smoke and up and down drafts, on the first fire raid ever over Tokyo. If ever there was a hell on earth, that was it. Now, I cannot permit myself to even imagine the agony and suffering these fire raids caused. War is truly hell, but it had to be done. Seeing our returned POWs convinced me of that.

Glenn McClure photo

Three Very Special Men

It is this photograph that is burned in my memory banks which has given me solace when my conscience needs and explanation.

When these men were returned to us on Saipan I was shocked to my inner soul by their appearance. I could not believe they were the same people I had seen just a few months earlier. They looked so emaciated, so wasted.

The depraved individuals who were their captors inflicted on them and other B-29 crewmen atrocities that defy all humane reasoning or explanation. I make mention of these despicable acts elsewhere in this book in greater detail.

In this book I have placed Col. Robert Goldsworthy's story in the pre-eminent position in this book. His story you will find number one in Part II. When you read his account of his captivity you wonder how he and very, very few others survived.

Homeward Bound

After Japan surrendered, I was selected to fly a B-29 and crew and 10 other veterans home (Mather Air Field, San Francisco). Before we reached "the point of no return" (Hawaii to San Francisco), we lost #2 engine with a blown "stack." So what's new? A typical happening with Wright engines. Since we were within a half hour of "the P. O.N.R.," I elected to continue on. Motivating the thought process were these considerations: I knew we would be in Honolulu 6 to 9 months waiting for a new engine. This was unacceptable because each man on board wanted to be stateside, S.A.P. Mine was a beautiful bride. I did not consider the impending catastrophic consequences of attempting to land this B-29 with potentially two engines out on the same side, in a strange environment, and with no experience and very little expertise in handling any plane with two engines out on the same side.

When a "stack" blows on a Wright engine, it seems like the whole plane's on fire. That's an illusion, of course. However, it's a very terrifying situation for anyone and particularly those who have never seen fiery pieces of metal flying from an engine. I can tell you we had panic on the plane.

Certain of our passengers went bonkers. One of the gunners advised me of this situation over the intercom. I informed him I'd be back there as soon as I "feathered" the prop and trimmed the plane to fly with #1 engine up. Before I started back through the pressurized crawl tunnel, I called the gunner and told him as soon as I appeared in the rear compartment to shout, "ATTENTION" loud and clear. He did, and it had the anticipated effect. The panic was quashed.

I explained the situation and pointed out that the now "feathered" engine was producing very few pieces of burning metal. One passenger commented, "It looked like a meteor." I advised them to sit tight, that a B-29 flies as well on three engines as it does on four, stay in control, not to be ashamed to say a little prayer, and be prepared to land in the good ol' U.S.A. in 3 ½ to 4 hours.

I returned to the cockpit. My uncertainties began to manifest themselves, and I began to "sweat." What if we lost #1 (meaning two out on the same side) engine? What to throw out? How to handle the panic? Would there be enough fuel to get us home? Could we find Mather Field among all the city lights (the navigator was a combat bombardier, and I felt very insecure with him as the navigator)? Should I attempt to "ditch" along the beach rather than chancing a crash in a populated area? If we found Mather Field and #3 engine were running, should I pull a lower manifold pressure on #3 and #4 engines and a much higher manifold pressure on #1 engine while raising the left wing slightly?

Or should I throttle back on #3 engine and come up on #1 engine as well as #4 engine so as to fly almost level? Should I come in high and flare out the landing? If I could hear Mather Tower but couldn't locate the field, what could I do to find it? The co-pilot (pilot) had far less expertise and experience than did I. No help there. The approach had to be good. I could not "go around" on even three engines. I had to remember to trim out as I neared touchdown. So I "sweated" and "sweated" the forgoing all the way to landfall. However, before we reached landfall I made an irrevocable decision. If we lost another engine on either side I would "ditch" the plane along the shoreline. Upon reaching landfall, and it was a magnificent site, I really became concerned that all three fans would keep turning, that we'd have enough fuel to find Mather Field and the biggest of all was: What do I do if we are unable to locate the field? Thank God, I did spot it all about 11 o'clock low. Lord, what a sight, what relief. I said to myself (and I meant it), THANK GOD! I called the tower and got my landing instructions. I came in high with higher manifold pressure on #1 and #4 engines (#3 throttled back), did my flare out, and landed a little hard (about 5 on the Richter scale) just past the tower.

Mission complete.

Editorial Comment

Please note, this account of this mission (non combative) was done from memory as is much of my entire narrative. It was first published in "the booklet." I've included it here with few changes. However, I did finally locate my diary and discovered I had made a major decision prior to reaching landfall. That discovery is a part of this account. It was to "ditch" along the coastline if I lost another engine on either side. That was the proper plan of action. It endangered far fewer lives.

FINIS

B-29 Hanger – 1944-45

This picture provides a great illustration of the huge building that was necessary to perform routine maintenance on a B-29. It is noteworthy to point out the slot in the center facia of the hanger. It was necessary to design it in this manner to accommodate the B-29s vertical stabilizer.

B-29s in the Flak Jungle

Photos such as this ferment unpleasant memories. I hated that stuff. I'm confident no one in the air ever loved it. This picture portrays the embodiment of potential doom encased in Flak Alley. Each of the black puffs or spots represents a "bomb bursting in air." They had a devastating effect on man and plane. The one compensating factor was the fighter attacks relented while we were engaged within the Flak Jungle.

Gunners Blister

This revealing photo (courtesy of Boeing –Wichita) of the right gunners blister and gun sighting mechanism is indigative of another innovative system on the B-29. You're doubtlessly becoming a bit bored with my constant ramblings concerning this state of the art flying machine. I'll let up after this.

Please note the "scanner" (gunner) holds no gun. Remarkable, yes, with an explanation mark. He sights his target within his scope, frames it and then depresses the soft trigger (like a automobile horn) to remotely fire the guns.

Further there was a CFC (Central Fire Control) "scanner" (gunner). He could control and or assign all gun turrets to the position generating maximum effectiveness. Really, is that great – or what?

Another important aspect of this photo is that it provides such a clear picture of the "blister." When you read Frank Reynolds story #1 you'll want to refer to this photo. I'd like to describe it here but that would ruin the story. The fact that he survived is one of those "divine interventions." Or may I add, "a miracle among miracles."

McClure photo

A B-29 with Two Engines Out

This photo depicts a remarkable achievement. "Pride of the Yankees" flown by Lt. Carrico of the 500th Bomb Group, 73rd Bomb Wing was the first B-29 to return to Saipan with two engines out on the same side.

Captain Pearson from my outfit, the 881st Squadron, accomplished the same feat. However, he had a prop come off and partially severed the plane in two. Flying that plane, in that condition, for approximately seven hours had to be the most harrowing, nerve shattering experience any airman had anywhere. The men on that plane knew the potential for disaster was eminent. The grating of the two sections was a constant, irrepressible, audible reminder. Once again the word "Guts" as in the book title is appropriate. I salute my friends. Another B-29 from our wing returned to Saipan with two engines out on the same side. It was flown by Captain Feathers. Bringing the B-29 home in that condition was a commendable accomplishment. All three of these pilots displayed remarkable expertise.

Front of B-29 after Crash Landing

This photo is another example of the superior structural design of the B-29. Boeing Aircraft does build a great airplane. The men alive at touchdown on this plane undoubtedly survived this crash. Just above the ground crewmen standing in the foreground is the flight engineer's window.

Radar Station

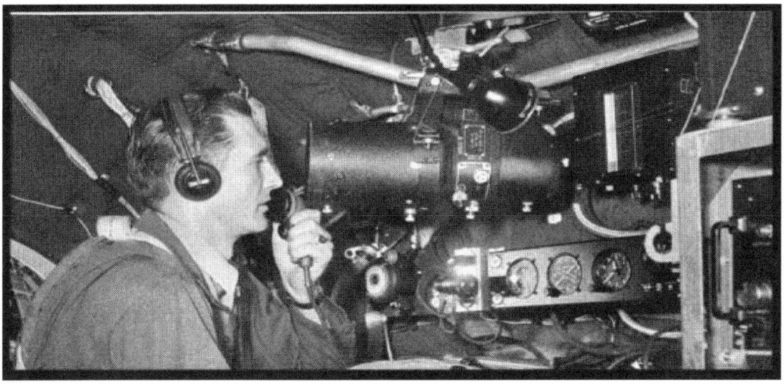

In this photo (courtesy of Boeing – Wichita) you are privileged to examine the radar crewmen's station. The airman has his eyes focused on the scope and appears to be relaying his findings to the pilots or navigator or flight engineer.

It is evident his accommodations are not spacious. However, I can, without concern for contradiction, assure you he's operating state of the art equipment.

Engineers Station

In this photo (courtesy of Boeing – Wichita) the flight engineers control panel is almost fully displayed. Almost all functions of the aircraft were monitored here.

This station was another unique innovation incorporated in the functional design of the B-29. The flight engineer was a specialist. No other aircraft required such a highly trained individual. His duties were many. His responsibilities were awesome.

His preflight checklist was more detailed and inclusive than that of the airplane commander or the pilot. Starting and shutting down the engines were his responsibility. That starting part was no easy task. During takeoff he controlled the cowl flaps as well as on cruise. At all times he monitored engine head temperatures as well as oil and fuel to all engines.

Two other functions required his undivided attention. During the long, tiresome, and boring segments to and from the target he was engaged in generating the most efficient use of every gallon of fuel on board to accomplish the demanded constant fuel air ratio mixes. Further, he was engaged in keeping the optimum rpm and manifold pressure settings operating at maximum efficiency. This was commonly known as flying on "The Step."

Lastly, he kept a scrupulously accurate fuel log of the plane's gas consumption. This one factor enabled the pilots to render better-than-average decisions when it came to "crunch" time. That is, to ditch or not to ditch.

As you can see, the flight engineer was a key element in any B-29 crew.

More than coincidentally, the poor guy had the unenviable distinction of being the only man on the crew who was not permitted even a few moments of "shut eye." Twelve to fifteen hours under that kind of pressure had to be tough.

A Salute to the Marines

The strategic importance of the capture of Iwo Jima to the success of the B-29 program cannot be overstated. It provided a base from which to launch the P-51 fighters. The cover provided by the P-51's greatly influenced the significant drop in B-29 losses. Also, Iwo provided an alternate, convenient base for the combat damaged B-29's. Obviously, many B-29's and crews were saved as the air war intensified. Once we landed on Iwo due to engine malfunction. Anyone who was there continues to give thanks to those Marines who made the supreme sacrifice. Even now, when I encounter a Marine, I salute him.

Crawl Tunnel

You see in this photo (courtesy of Boeing – Wichita) the much discussed crawl tunnel. This connecting link between the front and rear compartments (cabins) was a real creative innovation. Both cabins were pressurized (like the airliners of today) as was the connecting tunnel. All other aircraft of those days incorporated no such luxury.

The tunnel passed over the bomb bays. It did not adversely affect the bomb load. Further, where missions of great distance were involved the front bomb bay could be modified to accommodate an auxiliary fuel tank.

The rear bomb bay had the capacity to handle a viable bomb load. There, again, the flexibility of this remarkable plane was demonstrated.

Oh yes, that tunnel made an ideal "sack time" lounge. It could provide room for a man on each end with plenty of footage to spare. Such comfort on a combat aircraft was without precedent. It was an unexpected perk for the B-29 crewmen. The "Lounge Area" was even padded.

A B-29 with Front Compartment Missing

This picture is unique unto itself. The entire front cabin has been severed from the fuselage. Since the front compartment is not visible it is impossible to make an assessment as to potential survivors. Obviously, those alive in the rear compartment and the tail gunner lived to fight another day.

Please notice the flak damage to the left wing and flap. The fact that this plane and many, many other severely damaged aircraft could make it back to Saipan (six to seven and a half hours) is unimpeachable evidence that Boeing Aircraft had designed and built another Superbomber-in the image of her sister ship, the indestructible B-17.

I have been critical of the engines throughout this book. However, I want to emphasize my complete, unshakeable confidence in the airframe and other components which made this aircraft the unquestioned "Queen of the Skies" (1945-47).

B-29s Drop Bombs and Leaflets

This example of compassion during wartime speaks volumes about America's desire to spare as many civilians as possible. I doubt any such consideration would have been afforded our people had the situation been reversed. Try Pearl Harbor as a reminder.

These leaflets read as follows:

"ATTENTION JAPANESE PEOPLE

Read this carefully as it may save your life or the life of a relative or friend. In the next few days the military installations in SOME OR ALL of the cities named on the reverse side will be destroyed by American bombs. The cities contain military instillations and workshops or factories which produce military goods. We are determined to destroy all of the tools of the military clique which they are using to prolong this useless war. But unfortunately, bombs have no eyes. So, in accordance with America's well-known humanitarian policies, the American Air Force, which does not wish to injure innocent people, now gives you warning to evacuate these cities named and save your lives.

America is not fighting the Japanese people, but is fighting the military clique which has enslaved the Japanese people. The peace which America will bring will free the people from the oppression of the military clique and mean the emergence of a new and better Japan.

You can restore peace by demanding new and good leaders who will end the war.

We cannot promise that only these cities will be among those attacked, but SOME OR ALL will be, so heed this warning and evacuate these cities immediately."

Two weeks later, for all practical purposes, the war was over.

EPILOGUE I
FRIENDS UNITED

Fast forward to 2004. Last year I had an opportunity to visit the Pima Air Museum in Tucson, Arizona. It was an incredible, awesome experience. Vintage Aircraft were everywhere. Among those present were President Kennedy's Air Force One (A Lockeed Constellation) and a totally restored B-29 Superfortress.

I stood in awe at the sight of that B-29. It had been almost 60 years since I had seen one. She was an emotional sight to behold. After all these years I was still amazed by it's size and intrinsic beauty. The first words I uttered, almost incredulously, were, "I can't believe I actually flew that enormous plane." The fellow standing next to me said, "Hey, I was a B-29 pilot too." He was teary eyed and I'll admit I was a bit choked up myself. The curator had overheard our comments and realized we were combat veterans. He ignored a rule I am sure when he invited us to climb up into the cockpit for a nostalgic trip back in time. I can assure you it was one superb, thrilling experience. Sitting at those controls again was more than I could ever have imagined or hoped for. And then there were our wives. They were an intricate segment of this entire episode. When we pilots climbed into the cockpit and commenced our checklist procedures they too were overcome with emotion and began tearing up. It seemed to them three old friends had once again found one another. Two pilots and a B-29.

Restored B-29 - Pima Air Museum - Tucson, AZ

Two Pilots and a B-29 w/curator

REFLECTIONS IN A BYGONE ERA

Last summer while on a trip to Minnesota I decided to check out the old Walker Air Force Base at Victoria, Kansas. You will recall, I took my B-29 training there. It was difficult to locate. It had been bypassed by I-70 (no news there) and was now isolated, hidden and deserted in the middle of nowhere. When I found it, as you can well imagine it was surrounded by acres of agricultural fields and flat land. The gate posted a sign on which were printed the words "No trespassing - violators will be prosecuted." However, I was drawn by a overpowering force (or was it desire?) compelling me to once again walk on those taxiways. I climbed the steel pipe gate with considerable apprehension and started walking on a dirt roadway toward a deteriorating B-29 hangar. As I approached that aged and weather blackened building an unusual, ghostlike feeling started slowly creeping up my neck. It was a sensation I had very seldom experienced. Approximately one half mile to the east was another decaying B-29 hangar. These structures and two lone brick chimneys are the only evidence left standing on this once bustling air base.

One of the two deteriorating B-29 hangers at Walker Air Force Base.

As I turned my attention from these relics of the past I found myself literally in a sea of concrete. Weeds had sprouted in the seams of the 12 ft. x 16 ft. slabs which formed the basis for the endless taxiways and runways. I stood there in reverent silence. I was consumed in the wonder of the moment. My senses told me I was becoming engulfed in a surrealistic environment, something akin to a spiritual aura. Those last few sentences sound like I was on a real trip. However, the best was yet to come. I visualized buildings starting to form in the bluish, gray haze. Next, the taxiways and runways emerged free of any weed growth. Then the majestic B-29's began to appear followed by the ear-splitting roar of 2200 horse power engines. I could detect the unique odor of the burning aviation fuel. People now became a part of this dreamlike scene. I was unable to distinguish their facial features. I noted a controlled urgency in their every move as they performed the duties normally associated with the operation of an Air Force base. Now B-29's were airborne practicing running takeoffs and landings.

Though hours seemed to have passed, only a few minutes had elapsed. As the base began to return to the real world I recognized the fantasy was ending. I must tell you this realistic illusion will be with me forever. It was an overpowering segment of my life. I have been told that an out-of-body experience is much like this. I wonder???

The taxiways as they look today.

B-29 Memorial Plaza Concept

In the fall of 1997 the B-29 Memorial Plaza Committee was established to design and build a memorial to the men and women who made the B-29 project a success. The concept to build a memorial came from Bob Kilburn a veteran of the 20th Air Force. Bob visited the Great Bend Army Air Field in Great Bend, Kansas, and was dismayed to find little reference of the historic role of the airfield. He inquired about other B-29 airfields-Smokey Hill, Pratt, and Walker-and found they also were not recognized. He suggested a sign be placed at the sites and a plaque be dedicated to the men who gave their lives for their country. From Bob's suggestions came the concept of a memorial.

Great bend was chosen for the memorial site due to the number of original base structures that still exist, and it is typical of the World War II airfields. In addition, the city will donate the land and help maintain the memorial.

Veterans Richard Bergen and Gene Hilde have designed a dramatic and symbolic concept for the memorial; a plaza accessible to the public. From the ground, the intersecting arches represent the emblem of the Global 20th Air Force. Looking up 16 feet, through the arches, gives one the feeling of looking through the nose of the B-29. The Centerpiece will be a B-29 sculpture cast in stainless steel. The memorial will be lighted and will be visible for two miles. Groups (e.g. bomb crews), as well as individuals, will be honored with bronze plaques and inscribed bricks to be placed within the memorial's walls and brick paths.

Even though the memorial is dedicated to a past era, it represents a look toward the future. It will remind tomorrow's generations of the sacrifices that were made to keep the United States secure. Those sacrifices will never be forgotten.

B-29 MEMORIAL PLAZA

For more information contact:
B-29 Memorial Plaza
245 NE 30th Rd
Great Bend, KS 67530
(620) 792-9251

World War II Memorial

The much anticipated and long overdue National World War II Memorial was officially dedicated on Saturday, May 29, 2004 on the National Mall in Washington, DC. The memorial honors the 16 million who served in the armed forces of the U.S. during World War II, the more than 400,000 who died, and the millions who supported the war effort from home.

Symbolic of the defining event of the 20th century, the memorial is a monument to the spirit, sacrifice, and commitment of the American people to the common defense of the nation and to the broader causes of peace and freedom from tyranny throughout the world. It will inspire future generations of Americans, deepening their appreciation of what the World War II generation accomplished in securing freedom and democracy. Above all, the memorial stands as an important symbol of American national unity, a timeless reminder of the moral strength and awesome power that can flow when a free people are at once united and bonded together in a common and just cause.

The National World War II Memorial design by architect Freidrich St. Florian recognizes that the site itself pays special tribute to America's WWII generation. Nestled between the Washington Monument and the Lincoln Memorial, the vistas along the National Mall and the site's park-like setting are preserved, and the double row of elm trees that flank the memorial will be restored. Above all, the design creates a powerful sense of place that is distinct, memorable, evocative and serene.

The memorial's entrances are marked by two 43-foot arches, with two flagpoles framing the entrance at 17th Street. Twenty-four bas relief panels tell the story of America's war years. American Eagles perch atop four bronze columns, holding a suspended victory laurel. The WWII victory medal is inlayed at the base of the arches, surrounded by words "Victory on Land," "Victory at Sea," and "Victory in the Air."

The memorial also features 56 granite pillars, representing each of the states and territories from the era. A commemorative area on the memorial's west side recognizes the contributions and sacrifices made by members of World War II generation and allies. Semi-circular fountains at the base of the arches and waterfalls complement the natural water elements. Ramps allow access for handicapped visitors, and seating is available on the circumference of the Rainbow Pool.

The Pacific view of the Memorial.

Missions using Mt. Fuji as I.P.

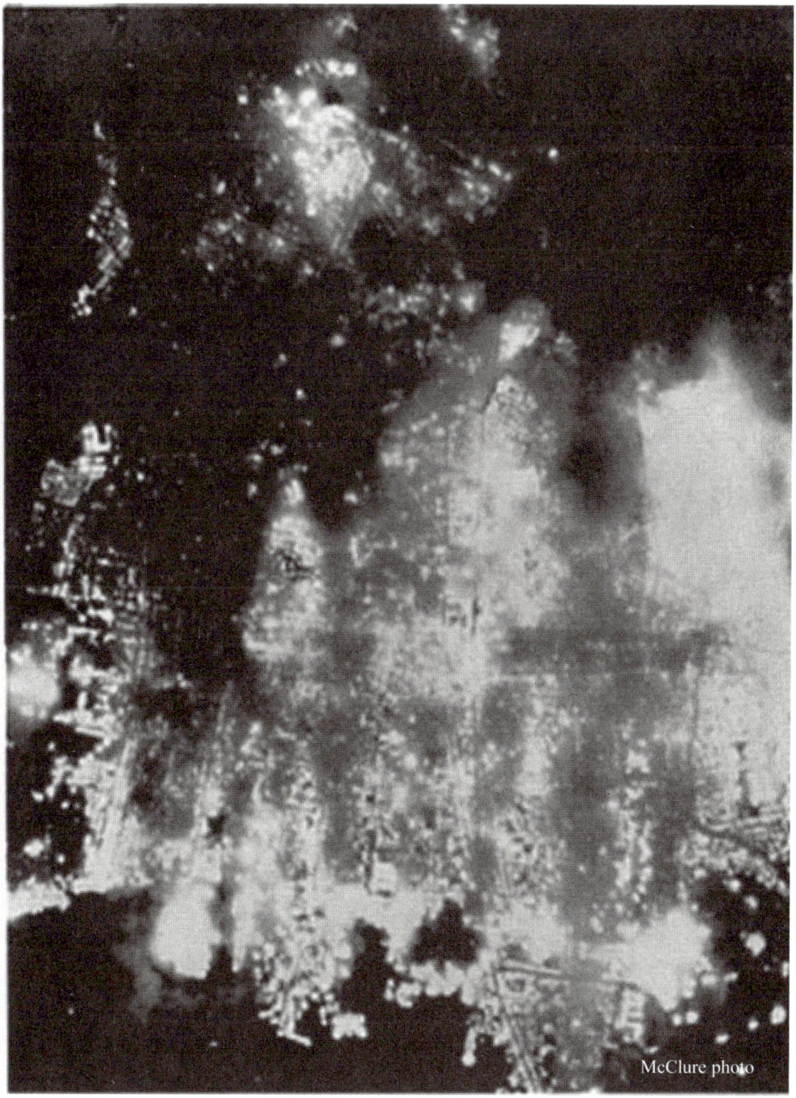

Toyama "burn job" of 1 August 1945. This Japanese aluminum producing city had a prewar population of nearly 128,000. Above photo shows 90% of area aflame. Later reconnaissance indicated a total demolition of 95.6%.

Part II

This section is Part II of my two-part book. It features a variety of experiences that will captivate your interest. Some elicit hair-raising accounts of heroic deeds performed by B-29 airmen. Others dramatize the challenges presented to the airmen before, during and after their death-defying missions. Some humor is appropriately inserted to relieve a bit of the tension which makes for more enjoyable reading. The POW stories are of particular interest. The cruelty our men absorbed will astound you. This book has achieved a unique balance between historical, informative, and nerve-wrenching combat content. It has provided a venue for the men who lived the experiences to present them in their own words.

Special Note : I've not included Hap Halloran's stories because they've been so extensively covered elsewhere. Hap was a POW with Col. Goldsworthy. They supported one another throughout their internment. Hap happens to be a remarkable American whom I greatly admire.

Introduction
Col. Robert E. Goldsworthy

Airplane Commander of the highest order-par excellence. His ready smile, wit, and solid professionalism made him liked and admired as a senior officer of the 881st Sq., 500th B.G., 73rd B.W. We junior officers seldom found solace in our superiors. Col. Goldsworthy was a notable exception.

His story, which I am placing in the pre-emanate position in this book, is convincing testimony to the high esteem in which I hold this superior man.

After reading his account of having his plane shot out of the sky and his parachute trip to earth you'll get an idea of what I mean-then his capture and internment. When you've completed that horrific episode you too will acknowledge Col. Goldsworthy a true, bona fide American Hero.

The Robert E. Goldsworthy Story
An American POW Hero

Major Robert Goldsworthy, A/C, 500 BG was shot down over Tokyo on Dec. 3, 1944, and captured by the Japs. He was incarcerated and inhumanely treated in the brutal Kempei Tai. A military torture prison of the Japanese secret service.

The morning of December 3, 1944: Saipan on the Mariana Island was clear and hot. My crew and I had received our final briefing and we were delivered by truck to our B-29. We were making our third bombing mission to Tokyo. Our target was 357, the code for the Musashino Aircraft Engine Works factory out of Tokyo.

The flight to the target was long and uneventful. We hit Mt. Fuji, our initial point, and made our bombing run on the target. I was leading the formation of B-29s belonging to the 500th Bomb Group.

We dropped our bombs and made a turn to the north of Tokyo to evade the heavy anti-aircraft fire that was concentrated around the Tokyo area. We were not worried about Japanese fighter planes as our intelligence had briefed us that the Japanese fighters were not effective at our altitude, which was 33,000 feet. How mistaken they were. Shortly after leaving the target, we came under attack by the Japanese "Tony." The first fighter made a head-on pass. We were shooting at it and I saw smoke come from the plane as he rolled underneath me. But he had inflicted damage on our plane. My right gunner called and said we were losing lots of gas out of our right wing. I had a great sinking feeling as I knew right then we were not going to make it back to Saipan.

I had the radio operator send out a call to the submarines that were part of our air-sea rescue service to inform them that we would be ditching somewhere between Japan and Saipan.

I don't know if the message ever went out as my B-29 caught fire. The right wing was burning and a fire had started inside the front of the airplane. We had no choice but to bail out. My intercom was shot out and the control cables were greatly damaged. I couldn't talk to the members of my crew who were in the back of the airplane, but it was evident that the plane was going down.

I had aboard that day two full colonels. Col. King was my group commander and Col. Brugge was the operations officer of the 73rd Bomb Wing. My regular co-pilot was replaced by Col. King and, luckily for him, was not on the mission.

In my excitement I had neglected to hook up my emergency oxygen supply that was used for high altitude bailout. I remembered this as I left the airplane and fell free for about 20,000 feet so I could get low enough to have oxygen to breathe. The day was clear, and all of Tokyo was spread out before me. I was fearful of landing on a power line, trees or on a house, but luckily I landed in a small clearing. It had been rather peaceful under the parachute at that altitude. There is no feeling of falling or motion until getting close to the ground. Then the falling seems to come rapidly and the panic sets in. I knew the Japanese were not going to like me very well and I was sure that I was not going to like them.
I landed in a little clearing and I made a short prayer. I said, "God, I am in great, great trouble. Give me the strength to endure." I saw now that my hands had been burned by the hot fire in the airplane. In the short time before I was captured, I had plenty of time to get in my emergency first aid kit and get out the sulfa powder to treat my burns but I had been too excited to think clearly. I was to regret this oversight, and my burned hands went untreated for some time.

It was not long before a squad of soldiers found me. They tied me with ropes, knocked me down and marched me down the road. After two or three miles I was placed in a little clearing and blindfolded. There was a large crowd around. I could hear them shouting and laughing. I would have given anything to have been able to understand Japanese.

I had been shot down about 2 p.m. and now it was evening and getting dark. I had been tied and blindfolded all that time. Finally a truck drove up and I was put in the truck bed. It was to be a long, long ride. Some Japanese guard kept hitting me over the head with a knotted rope. Others held my legs and burned them with lighted matches. I still have slight sears from those bums. I hate to be blindfolded because I get claustrophobic. Fortunately, because I was tall, they could not tie my blindfold securely and I could usually look down and see my feet and the ground.

During that ride the truck picked up two other members of the crew, Col. King and Col. Brugge. We were taken to-what, I found out later, was the headquarters of the Kempei Tai. I was taken to a little room and questioned by a Japanese officer. I couldn't understand him very well and I refused to answer any questions. After knocking me around for awhile the officer tried to take the belt off my flying suit. It was sewn on and in trying to get it off, he ripped my flying suite from the neck to the waist. The rip in the back of the flying suit was to cause me misery by letting in the cold. The temperature on Saipan was semi-tropical and I had foolishly worn a summer flying suit. Our cells were unheated and it was to be a very cold winter. If only I had worn winter flying gear I would have survived the winter much more comfortably.

Taken to a cell where my shoes and socks were taken away, I was given four little blankets. The doors to the cells were only about three feet high and I had to crawl in on my knees. The guards always helped with a really strong kick. I learned to go in backwards.

My first night I had a cell mate. A Japanese prisoner was in the cell wrapped in his blankets. I tried not to sleep because I thought he might be there to kill me when I slept. However, I survived the night and he was taken away in the morning.

When daylight came, I was told to fold my blankets and sit in the middle of the cell. No movement was allowed. After sitting cross-legged for a few minutes I thought my back would break. The guards watched and if I made a movement they would come in and slap me around.

Later that day four other members of my crew were brought into the cellblock. These were Col. King, Col. Brugge, Cpl. Schroeder and Sgt. Goeffery. Out of the twelve people on my aircraft these were the only ones I had any contact with.

Our cells were wooden, about eight by ten feet, and absolutely bare except for a small hole in the corner which I learned was the benjo or latrine.

I had eaten breakfast that morning on Saipan. We carried an in-flight lunch but I always saved mine for the flight home. I had nothing to eat the first day in captivity, nor was I given anything to eat the second, and it was not until noon of the third day that they brought in a little box of rice. It didn't look very good to me. I did not know that it was all I was going to get or that this was going to be my typical daily diet until the end of the war.

So I had been a prisoner of war for three days and I took stock of my situation. My hands were burned. My feet were frostbitten from the extreme low temperatures when I bailed out. My legs were burned. I received several hard beatings and I had received very little food. I was sitting in the middle of a small, freezing cell and my chances of survival were very questionable.

There is no worse life than that of a Prisoner of War. Your captors can do anything to you that they want. There is no appeal, no one to complain to, you have no friends and are surrounded by enemies who have absolutely no compassion. I knew that America would win the war, but I did not believe I would be kept alive to see the war's end. I did believe I would be kept alive for extensive interrogation. This worried me. I was required by the Geneva Convention to give only name, rank and serial number. However, I knew that Japan had never signed the Geneva Convention.

The fourth day I was taken out of my cell and into the main building of the Kempei Tai Headquarters. I knew my ordeal was about to begin. I had an armed guard on each side of me. I was taken to a room that had a table and several chairs. A Japanese officer introduced himself and introduced a civilian who was to be my interpreter. The officer was very nice to me and offered me a cigarette. Then they asked me about my wing, group, squadron and about my senior officers. I had already given them my name, rank and serial number and I told them that was all I was required to tell them. The officer laughed, slapped me once and I was taken back to my cell. Things didn't look so good and I didn't like the sound of that officer's laugh.

The next day things got a little worse. I was taken to the same room and slapped around. They beat me with little short bamboo clubs about three or four feet long and approximately one inch thick. I learned later that these clubs were used in the practice of "kendo," which I had never heard of. After a time I was told to sit down.

They started to ask questions about the B-29. We were never to discuss the B-29, as it was a "state of the art" airplane and quite secret. When I refused to answer they pounded me around some more and I was beginning to hurt. Then the officer showed me the technical records and the operating manuals of the B-29. Not just copies but our actual manuals! Where they got them I have no idea. Anyway, it showed me that they had all the information that they were trying to get out of me. Why they did not make this information known to me I will never know. Why knock me around when they were going to show me the manuals? It was evidently a planned action but for what reason I never knew.

That night I was given my little box of rice. I had much to think about. The officer told me that I would be asked questions to which they knew the answers to see if I was truthful. I came to the conclusion that they, in time, could beat almost anything out of me so I thought of a way to help myself. The next day I was seated at the table and when asked a question I thought of the biggest lie and told it to them as the truth. And I got away with it. From then on it was a game. I told them some whoppers. Sometimes I would get caught and beaten but many times I got away with it.

They asked me to draw a picture of the landing strip on Saipan. I drew a picture of a commercial airport in New York City. They brought out a large glossy photo of the air base and the living area of the 73rd Bomb Wing. It was a great picture. I could pick out my quonset hut and the mess hail and the little field where we had played a softball game such a short time before. Of course they compared the photograph with my picture and I ended up getting a good beating. The officer asked me to identify the commanding officer of the 21st Bomber Command. I didn't know -- I really did not know. After I was slapped, they brought out a glossy picture of General Hansell, who was the overall commander. Now where did they get that picture? Years later I told that story to General Hansell and said that the picture looked like it could have been taken at his high school graduation.

I was having much trouble with my hands. They had become badly infected. My feet were swelling and becoming very painful at night. The four small Japanese blankets did not adequately cover me and it was impossible to keep warm. But my hands were a complete mess. All I could think of was gangrene and the eventual amputation of my hands. So I was happily surprised one morning when a doctor and nurse came to my cell. We went to another room where the doctor took one hand and the nurse the other.

The doctor was very gentle. He carefully took all of the infected skin from my hand with tweezers and scalpel. The nurse was not so kind. If looks could kill, I would have been a dead man. She took the tweezers and ripped the bad skin and the good skin alike. She would take the scalpel and cut into healthy flesh. Man! Oh, man! Did that hurt! The doctor spoke sharply to the nurse. I didn't know what he said, but she got a little more gentle. However, she kept giving me that icy stare of wishing I were dead. Well, I didn't blame her. I had dropped bombs on Japan and when she was working on me I must have smelled like a pig and looked worse. I had seen no water to wash with and would not until late the next summer. The doctor tried to talk to me but he did not know enough English for me to understand him. He said something about the Japanese gift of life. I would have given anything to know what he was saying. He was a kindly man. I wished no good to come to that nurse. They soaked my hands in some disinfectant and wrapped them in bandages.

My interrogations went on and the game kept on being played. I told the truth on many things; I lied about many things and I was constantly being slapped around or hit with those little short bamboo clubs.

I noticed that my mind was always dwelling on food. I was getting very, very hungry. My ankles and knees were swelling which, I learned later was beri-beri. We all suffered from beri-beri because of low nutrition.

December 24, the day before Christmas, was a very exciting day. I was taken from my cell by the civilian interpreter and a couple of guards. My feet were so swollen that I had a hard time getting my shoes on, but I was taken out of the prison and put into a car. The sun was shining and the inside of the car was rather warm. We drove to what I think now was Yakota Air Base. There they had a B-17 and I was to be questioned on how to fly it.

There was a Japanese pilot sitting in the right seat. I was put in the left and the interpreter stood in between us. I wondered if that Japanese pilot was the one who shot me down but I did not ask. Some planes were taking off and landing and I watched them for a second. The interpreter slapped me a couple of times to get my attention. Then they asked me all about the position of the instruments for taking off that B-17. I told them everything backwards — low RPM, superchargers off, fuel pumps off, full flaps, cowl-flaps closed, everything just backwards from the proper position for take off. Now Japan had some great pilots, so I cannot imagine anyone following my instructions. Later I worried greatly that I would be severely punished for lying.

The best was yet to come. Lunchtime came and I was taken to a building and given the same lunch as the Japanese. It was rice but included two slices of bread. There was a little charcoal brazier with a couple of little chunks of glowing charcoal. My interpreter put my bread on one and toasted it. It tasted like cake. A lot of Japanese girls crowded around the door to the room staring at me. I must have looked like someone from outer space.

It had been an interesting day but it all fell apart when I was returned to my cell. Col. King in the cell to my right whispered and wanted to know where I had been. I tried to whisper back but we were caught by the guard. We were not supposed to talk. The guard grew very angry. He made me stand at attention for two hours. The warm car ride had helped to get a little tingle in my feet but now, standing barefooted on the freezing floor put me back to "square one." The guard kept pointing his pistol at me and clicking the trigger. Every time he did I would jump. I swore that I would not jump as I knew he would not shoot me, but every time that gun clicked I jumped. My feet hurt all night long so that I could not sleep. And the next day was Christmas Day. I felt terribly alone.

Christmas was always such a special time for my family. But, as I sat there in the freezing cell, I wondered about "Peace on Earth and Good Will Toward Men."

There was no special Christmas dinner as I had hoped. I had really thought there might be a little something extra.

January 1 , 1945, I was taken again to the B-17. This was a tough trip. The day was cold and snow was falling. The car was cold. A guard kept hitting me in the ribs with his rifle. There was no lunch, just a lot of shouting and slapping. They were asking questions about the radio equipment. I lied about the operation of the radio loop antenna, but who was I kidding?

Their planes were equipped with rotative loop antennas. I don't know how they could have been unaware that I was lying and I was constantly fearful of great punishment but, other than the usual beatings, nothing special was done in the way of extra punishment.

About this time Sgt. Goeffry was taken from his cell. He was taken out right in front of me and I could not tell that he was injured in any way. He was never seen again. I tried, after the war, to find out what might have happened but I never got a clear story. Sgt. Goeffry's cell was empty but not for long. A new prisoner was brought in.

Col. Brugge, in the cell to my immediate left, started to hallucinate. He had terrible dreams at night and was often out of his head. He asked me once through the wall, if I would tell his wife to take out a separate checking account. I said I would but why didn't he do it himself. He replied that they wouldn't let him. We both got beaten for that exchange but I don't think he knew it.

January was a very cold month. My interrogations were slacking off. The days were endless. Up at 5 a.m., breakfast at 7 a.m. Sit in the middle of that cell until noon when the noon rice came in. Then sit until around until 5 or 6 p.m. Roll into our blankets at 9 o'clock. A small light burned in the cell day and night. There was a small window high up on the wall but it was covered with paper.

I was very hungry and losing lots of weight. My burned hands were getting well. They were red and scabbed but I didn't worry anymore about losing them. The doctor had put some bandages and tied them around my wrists and ankles. This was to keep the cold out. I couldn't do anything about the long rip in the back of my flying suit.

In January I was taken out of the cell and interrogated by two naval officers. This was interesting because both had graduated from schools in America. In fact, one had graduated from the University of Washington and was attending the university at the same time I had been a student at Washington State University. They didn't ask me much. They were more interested in conditions back in the USA. They wanted to know if you could still buy chocolates and candy. Did I have a car? Could I buy tires for my car? I told them there was no lacking in consumer goods. Everything was in plentiful supply. And that America was so close to winning the war most armament factories were starting to convert to higher production of the things that the civilian community would require

for comfortable living. They were more interested in the chocolates than anything else.
They must have remembered the good life in America.

The U of W grad asked me why our navy didn't come out and fight. I figure this was a loaded question, but what the heck. I took a chance and told him that our navy would fight if Japan still had any ships afloat. We had sunk them all already. I thought sure I would get a beating but they just smiled at me like I was some kind of an imbecile. I did not know what was happening in the world. My world was the inside of that small cell. I could hear more and more airplanes as the days went by so I knew the B-29s were pounding Japan. Coming home from the first B-17 visit I asked my little civilian interpreter what was happening with the war. He, of course, said Japan was winning the war. He asked me one time who I thought would win the war. I said there was no way that Japan could win. That was the only time the war was ever mentioned to me.

I had several different men who acted as interpreters. Several were officers who spoke good English. The little short civilian was with me quite a bit and there was one officer, a captain, who sat through many of my sessions. He wasn't a bad sort but he is the one that told me they had heard from the Red Cross that my wife had been killed in a car accident. I didn't know whether to believe him but it was a constant agony in my mind.

I knew that we had not been reported as POWs and that I was not considered a POW. I was told right from the beginning that I was considered a war criminal and would be tried as a war criminal. Late in January I was shown several pages of paper which they told me was an account of my criminal acts and my confession to bombing civilians. Two of my three missions to Tokyo were over the target #357. One mission was a radar run on the Tokyo docks. I am sure that civilians could be hurt just as civilians were hurt at

Pearl Harbor, but we had strict orders not to bomb unless we were sure of our target. And we were not to let any bombs land near the Emperor's palace.

The captain said my trial was proceeding. I would hear more about this later.

My hands were healing but my feet continued to be very painful. My clothes were filled with lice. I wondered if I was to die in that cell. I dreamed of the day I would be taken out to a prison camp. I imagined the prisoners having the freedom to organize themselves, to have a baseball diamond and to have hot water. The barracks would be warm and there would be more to eat.

My diet still stayed the same-small amount of a rice and barley mix. Once in awhile I would get a cup of some sort of soup, and once in a great while a fish bone with a little piece of fish. I would keep the bones in my month trying to soften them up enough to chew. Usually the bones just stuck in my gums causing the gums to get sore.

We got a cup of hot water a couple of times a day. It had been boiled and it was
absolutely wonderful to hold that cup of hot water. If I drank it immediately sometimes I would get a second cup. Many times I burned my mouth trying to get that water down so that I might get a second cup.

The guards were not members of the highest intellectual order of the Japanese army. Some of them ignored us. They would walk their tour and not pay too much attention. One tall guard used to read a paperback book. He was very careful that no one saw him. One guard that we had for a short time spoke very good English but he refused to say much or to do any visiting. All too many of the guards took delight in tormenting us. One day a guard came in my cell and, for no reason that I could ever figure, kicked me in the face. I thought my jaw had been broken. Fortunately it was not. I had to swallow my rice unchewed for several days.

I was always tied and blindfolded when taken from my cell. The days were endlessly long. I tried to keep my mind active. I tried to remember the words to songs. I tried to remember poems that I used to know. I would sing to myself. I would start out in the morning singing "Oh What a Beautiful Morning." One morning I sang in a loud voice to one of my guards, who had been aggravating me. I sang "You Are My Sunshine."

He just motioned for me to shut up. I recalled all the events of my childhood and of my growing up on the farm; of my days in a little country schoolhouse. I tried to do out-of-body experiences and tried to actually put myself back at the farm where I grew up.

I thought of Jean and all the fun times we had over the years. I met her first when she was freshman in high school and our lives had been one of togetherness from that time. I would sing the song "Smile" and imagine Jean smiling every smile that is mentioned in the song. "There are smiles that make you happy, there are smiles that make you blue," etc.

I thought by wishing hard enough I would get out of that cell. So I sang "Wishing Will Make It So." I tried to bargain with God "Get me out of here and I will never be bad again." I could hear my mother saying "You can't bargain with the Lord," but I tried!
February 3 was a big day. Some guards with officers took another prisoner and me out of our cells. We were blindfolded and taken outside the prison and put in a car. I thought that at last we were going to the prison camp, but it was not to be. We drove to some other part of Tokyo and stopped at another prison. We were taken to a room where I had my first look at my trip companion and crewmember. I

did not recognize him at first. I could not believe that he was Cpl. Schroeder. When I did recognize him I asked how he was and I promptly got knocked flat. Later I found out that he had not recognized me either.

We were taken to the back of the prison, down a couple of steps, and put in cells much like the ones we had left. They were a little smaller, dirtier. This was a bad prison. The food ration was smaller than back at the Kempei Tai Headquarters. The cell had a small, covered window and a small light bulb in the ceiling. The main change from our past routine was that we had to empty our own benjo box every third or fourth day. This meant going outside behind our cells, taking the box out and emptying it in a pit. The ground was covered with snow and ice and each time I was taken out I thought I would never be warm again in my life. How I wished I had flown my last mission in winter flying clothes.

The guards in this prison were more attentive to us. I found it hard enough to sleep at night because of the cold but some of the guards would see to it that our sleep was constantly disturbed. There was a long bamboo pole that the guards would use to stick through the cell bars and jab us in the head or face during the night. There was one thing that was very positive in my cell — the sides of the cell had two by four braces running from the floor to the ceiling. I could sit beside the wall and hook my shoulder blade on the 2 by 4 and lean back. How wonderful that was!

One day we had some excitement. The man that was moved into the cell next to me was Olinto Lodovici. Everyone called him "Shine." When we could whisper through the wall he gave me news of the war and what was going on in the outside world. He asked "Were you the guy who sang 'You Are My Sunshine' to the guards?" When I answered yes, he said it gave him quite a lift.

Then came a terrible time. I was blindfolded, tied with ropes and taken from my cell. I was taken to a small room that was crowded with officers and prison personnel. I was told that my trial was over and I was given the death penalty and the rest of my crew was given life imprisonment. Since the war would soon be over they would be released, but the realization came to me that I would not be there to see it.

After a couple of hours I was taken out again. In my mind I knew I was going to be shot. It had happened to many others. Strangely enough, I was not terrified at the prospect. I was starving, freezing, hurt, and the prospect of release from this did not seem too unpleasant.

Then came one of the longest days of my life. In March there was a maximum effort by our naval carrier planes. The raid was to last most of the day. Usually during the air raids the guards would leave, but this time I was taken out of my cell, allowed to take two blankets, and taken across the street to a small air raid shelter. This shelter was dug along the side of the street a little below ground and open on both ends. The floor was covered with snow and frozen mud. The guards took my blankets and wrapped their muddy feet in them. I sat there praying for the "all clear" to sound but the raid went on most of the day.

I thought that day would never end. I was not given my noontime rice. I think it was the coldest I have ever been. When I thought I could not stand it any longer the planes left and I was taken back to my cell. My two blankets were muddy and wet. I quickly changed them for two dry ones from the pile in the corner. Luckily I didn't get caught.

On April 3, I was put into the bed of a truck which was already filled with other prisoners. I knew I was going to a prisoner of war camp. We were all blindfolded, but I could see below my blindfold and I could see many feet, some in flying boots and some with shoes like I wore. We drove down the highway toward Yokohama (I found out later). Finally we turned off the highway, went across a bridge spanning a canal and into the gates of the Omori POW Camp.

The prisoners in that camp did not even look at us. They didn't say a thing. Later we learned we were to be special prisoners, still considered war criminals, and were not to be approached or acknowledged.

Seventeen had been in that truck. We were unloaded and herded into two cells in the guardhouse. These cells were just like the ones we had left. We were finally allowed to speak. One skinny POW came up to me and said "Hello Goldy." I realized it was Col. King but I didn't recognize him. He had stayed in his cell in the Kempei Tai but after Col. Brugge died he was taken to a hospital for a short time. He glowed when he said they had even given him some ice cream.

After a couple of weeks we were taken from the cells and put into a barracks and were united with more special prisoners. Most of us were B-29 personnel but we had some Navy and Marine airmen and a B-24 pilot that was captured in China. There were 36 of us in this barracks. Our barracks had a dirt floor with 2 platforms running the length of the barracks on each side. We were given 4 blankets, a cup and a bowl, and a straw mat. We each had about 3 feet of living space. Col. Richard Carmichael, a wing commander of a bomb wing based in India, was our appointed leader. We soon got ourselves organized and for a few days just had a wonderful time meeting everyone. Some of the most recently shot down could give the rest of us what news they had of the war. It wasn't much but at least we knew that our forces were on the offensive and that our Marines had taken Iwo Jima. We started saying "Home alive in '45." I surely hoped so. I do not think I could have lived through another winter.

Kono San was the Japanese in charge of us. He spoke very

good English and he gave us a briefing regarding camp rules. He told us how to salute the officers and how, if anyone tried to escape, all would be punished. Escape? Where would we go?

Kono San asked us if we wanted to work outside. Of course, we did. It would be wonderful to get out of that barracks and we, of course, thought we would get worker's rations. On May 3 we were marched out the front gate, across the little bridge and onto the number one highway that linked Tokyo with Yokohama and to the area where we were to plant gardens. The area had been badly bombed, the houses had been destroyed, and we had to clean the rubble and then break the ground for the vegetable gardens. The ground was very hard and our garden tools were quite inadequate. We ended up scrounging what we could and making our own hoes, rakes and picks.

We were happy to be outside. It was my first really good breath of air in five months. The work was hard going but the biggest disappointment was that we did not get an increase in our rice ration. One nice perk was that we were allowed to build a fire. This was primarily to get rid of trash and debris of buildings, but it also gave us a chance to warm ourselves.

Summer of '45 finally brought the hot weather. I was still cold. Lots of the prisoners took their shirts off while working outside, but I could not make myself do that. With the warm weather came mosquitoes and flies. I figured I was so skinny the mosquitoes would have a hard time finding a place to draw a little blood.

I developed a great friendship with Raymond "Hap" Halloran. He was a B-29 navigator from a different group of our 73rd Wing. His plane had been shot down in January and he had spent time in the Kempei Tai cells. There were days when I didn't think I was going to make it, and Hap would help me over the rough time. There would be times when Hap was down, and I would help him. After the War, Hap and I returned to the States together and kept in touch. Now we call each other and write and get together a time or two every year. If I live to be a ripe old age, I will know it is because Hap was there during the bad times to help me along.

The vegetables in our gardens were growing. It was a great temptation to steal a carrot or a dicon, but we did not dare eat anything uncooked. Hap and I would clean around the houses in the little village of Omori. People were becoming more friendly. Sometimes a lady would slip us a little rice ball. One lady gave us a bucket of hot water and a little piece of soap. We stripped down and scrubbed ourselves. Another lady gave us a bucket of soy beans.

We always had sickness and physical disabilities among the special prisoners. We had recurring problems with beri-beri. A Navy pilot prisoner had badly infected shrapnel wounds in his legs and knees. A Japanese corpsman came in and cut one badly infected wound with a scalpel. It was terribly painful but the wound finally healed. The pilot survived to later become a doctor.

The air raid horns were going off more and more, and it got so that we were not taken back to camp during the B-29 raids unless they were close to our area, We could see many Japanese planes leaving flying south. Later we learned of the battle for Okinawa and figured that was where Japan was sending their air power. We could see so much damage from the air raids on Japan that we could not see how the war could go into another year.

In August we were feeling that great things were happening. We were beginning to see friendly single-engine fighter planes over Japan. An American P-S 1 came right over our camp, and Navy carrier planes were overhead. One morning we heard many engines overhead. Finally the overcast started to break up and we saw this Navy dive bomber come through a hole headed straight toward us. The pilot could not know that we were a POW camp, but we looked like a good target. We all ducked for cover and the bomb hit right outside the fence of our camp, knocking out some windows but injuring no one.

We were rather excited and it was hard to sleep. Hap and I used to sit outside the barracks in the very early morning hours and look at the sky. At one time that would have not been allowed, but now the guards did not seem to mind. I remember telling Hap that in my bones I thought August was going to be a very big month. He reminded me of that a little later when the war was over.

August 15 was a day to remember - for good and bad. The bad happened that morning when we were in the garden area. A B-29 gunner named Harry Hedges was caught stealing a carrot. He was given a terrible beating by Horseface and more by some officers from the camp. It seemed that they all were taking their frustration out on Harry. It was the worst beating I saw any man get. We had to carry him back to the camp, but he did survive.

After noon rice, we were started out to dig more in a tunnel 3 or 4 miles away being built to store food. Hap was beside me as we were marching out and he said, "Goldy, I don't think I will come back from the walk today." While we were stopped at the prison gate the regular prisoners gave us the sign, "She is over!" I can't explain the feeling. The war was over, and we had survived. Then the roof caved in on me. I came down with amoebic dysentery and to cap the whole thing, I got yellow jaundice. I was a real sick dog for a couple of weeks and didn't care if the war was over or not. The American doctor in the camp was able to treat me. He did not have much but he gave me a shot in the back to help my amoebic dysentery. The yellow jaundice ran its course.

One positive thing – it got me out of camp quicker.

When the rescue came on August 29 I was evacuated out to a hospital ship on the first little landing craft boat to leave right from our camp. We were on a land fill in Tokyo Bay. We pulled right along side of the hospital ship, The Benevolence. There were steps to climb to the deck. I made it about halfway up and my legs gave out. My legs just would not function enough to make the last half. Two sailors immediately came down and grabbed me. They may have been medium-sized guys but they looked like good giants to me.

When I got on the deck I breathed my first breath of free air. I could see Omori POW camp off in the distance. I went to the rail, shook my fist, and said, " All right you bastards, I beat you! " There were many people on the deck of The Benevolence watching us come aboard. I heard some of them clap and cheer.

We were immediately taken down to the showers. My flea- and louse-infested flying suit was taken away and I got in the wonderful hot shower. They had a hard time getting me out. Then I went to a quick inspection by a team of doctors. I weighed 85 pounds. Man, oh man, did those nurses look clean in their whites? They smelled so good. They all looked so beautiful. The food was so good even though I threw up the first few meals. I can't describe what it felt like to lie down on clean sheets; no fleas; to hear a language I could understand; no one shouting at me; no beatings. How clean and gentle everything was. I beat 'em!

I am sure that those few of us, who, by the grace of God and the heroic efforts of our comrades, came back from our Last Missions have a greater appreciation of that liberty which we lost for a time. I like to think that we have a greater determination to protect that liberty here at home. God bless America!

Robert Goldsworthy

Editorial Comment

My friends, isn't this a heart-wrenching story? Bob's (Goldy) ability to absorb that kind of degrading, animalistic type of treatment is a testament to the strength of his character. Thankful you made it, Bob.

The Raymond A. Porter Story
Part I

Ray Porter's Friday the 13th Bomb Bay Experience
April 13, 1945

It was a beautiful day when Crew 112, 881st Squadron, 500 Bomb Group took off from Isley #1 Airfield, Saipan, Marianas Islands on Friday, April 13, 1945. The crew was in good spirits. Keeping spirits high took real effort. The horrific losses incurred on the crew's previous high altitude missions to Japan were still fresh on their young minds.

On this particular mission, the plane assigned to Crew 112 was Z 10 named "Punch 'N Judy." Their usual plane, "There Will Always Be A Christmas," had been lost on its previous mission. Crew 112 had shared this plane – as well as a Quonset Hut – with Major Luman's crew who, along with the plane, never made it back to Saipan following that mission.

So Crew 112 took off on April 13 in a different plane than it was accustomed to. It was also a plane that had had its bomb bay modified in a way that would put the crew in harm's way.

The crew that day included:

A/C	Ray W. Taylor
Pilot	Ray W. Clanton
Navigator	William Vint
Bombardier	Robert Troop
Flight Engineer	Raymond A. Porter — 0868658
Radar Operator	John Hogg
Radio Operator	Torn Corlew
Ring Gunner	Robert Bouchard
Right Wing Gunner	William Bramble
Left Wing Gunner	Nate Gladke

(replacement for Henson)
Tail Gunner Charles Zetterstrom

The Ack-Ack started when Punch 'N Judy reached Japan. It was heavy and intense. The plane took several Ack-Ack hits, but the crew thought they had escaped serious damage. They could find no visible damage, at least initially, other than the entrance holes from incoming fire.

So the crew proceeded to drop its bombs on the designated target. While the head wind was high, Porter and Vint calculated that the plane had sufficient fuel for its return trip to Saipan. So the plane headed home.

During a routine fuel check a little while later, however, Porter found that the plane was showing unusually high fuel usage. Vint's check on the remaining flight distance and Porter's calculation confirmed that the plane did not have sufficient fuel to reach Saipan — or even Iwo Jima, for that matter, unless they were able to reduce their fuel consumption rate.

After checking the fuel consumption, Porter, with the help of Bramble and Gladke, visually checked to be sure that no fuel was leaking from the wing tanks. Clanton confirmed that the plane's controls were responding as expected, that there was no visible damage to the engines, and that all the flaps were up. Porter then surmised that the bomb bay doors must be open. A visual check confirmed his hunch. The extra drag of the open rear doors was not acceptable. Porter asked Troop to close the doors while he observed them.

The front doors closed. The rear doors closed — and then they popped open.

The problem had to do with a earlier modification made to the plane. At the beginning of the raids on Japan, it had been discovered that it was taking too long to open both the front and rear doors to make accurate bomb runs. The doors were then modified so the rear doors were opened by air pressure when the front doors started to open. This was accomplished by using cable to connect the front door to the rear door air valves.

After several trials, Porter determined that the cable would need to be cut if the crew was to avoid ditching in the ocean. All flight engineers carried an emergency repair kit that included a selection of screwdrivers, wrenches, pliers, sockets, other tools, and fifty feet of rope. Porter's kit included a pair of wire cutters, sometimes called dikes.

Remembering where the cable was located. Porter asked Clanton to reduce altitude to 8000 feet. He tied one end of his rope around his waist and gave the other end to Zetterstrom and Bramble to hold from inside of the gunners compartment. He entered the rear bomb bay and crawled along the narrow catwalk on the side wall until he was able to see the cable. Even laying down and leaning into the open bay from his waist and extending his arm, he could not reach the cable. Some one would have to be lowered down into the open bomb bay to do the job.

It didn't enter Porter's mind to ask for volunteers to perform the cutting. Repairs or adjustments of damaged items in flight were the responsibility of the Flight Engineer. It was his job to do. If he succeed, 11 men would return to Saipan to fight again. If he failed, those 11 men would have to ditch in a hostile Japanese-controlled Pacific Ocean.

Porter checked the rope knots on his waist and ordered Bramble and Zetterstrom to lower him into the bomb bay. The cable came within his reach. He was able to maintain his head-down position with one foot touching the catwalk. With just a single pair of wire cutters at his disposal, he had to use both hands to keep from accidentally dropping the wire cutters. This kept him from using his hands to position himself in the bay.

Porter found that he would need to cut through several small, hardened steel cables that had been wound together — all with a small pair of malleable wire cutters. Porter accomplished this feat hanging head-down at 8,000 feet in a cold and open bomb bay. To clear the blood rushing to his head, he had to pull up to head-above-heart position several times and then return to cutting the cable. The entire process took an estimated 30 minutes or more.

Once the cable was cut, Porter asked the Bombardier Troop to close the bomb bay doors. They stayed closed on the first try. It was in this moment that Porter, cold, bruised and scratched, realized what he had actually done. He was shivering as he gave thanks to God and climbed back into the gunner's department.

The 11 men in Crew 112 returned to Saipan with a small amount of fuel in the tanks.
They continued flying missions over Japan and bombed the Army Arsenal in Osaka on
August 14, 1945 after the surrender of Japan.

Porter was subsequently promoted to first lieutenant and 500th Bomb Group Flight Engineer, MOS 1028. He completed 30 missions over Japan and was awarded the Distinguished Flying Cross and the Air Medal with three oak leaf clusters for them.

Porter saved bomb pins from most of his flights. These pins were removed from each bomb by the Bombardier Troop to arm the bomb. Each pin had a tag attached with string, where Porter would write the date, destination, plane, duration and any unique circumstances about the mission. On the pin from this mission, which he still has, it is written:

Tokyo Z-I0
April 13 Friday
14 hrs.30 mins - night
Intense Flak
Bomb Door Open

At a surprise birthday party for Clanton in California several years ago, Zetterstrom and Bramble called Porter aside and informed him kiddingly that they considered dropping the rope with him on it, but were glad they didn't since his actions had saved their butts. That was good for a great laugh.

Raymond Porter

Editorial Comment

Part A of Port's story reveals a deed of heroism with meaningful results. However, it does not mention the potential for encountering an air pocket or "bump in the air" which would have caused him to fall to his death.

His unselfish, fearless actions saved his fellow crewmen's lives as well as his plane.

Because of his bravery, it is my opinion, he is deserving of our country's highest military honor, The Congressional Medal of Honor. To that end I have submitted his name to the proper authorities in order to accomplish this long overdue recognition. It was an honor to serve with a man of this stature.

The Raymond A. Porter Story
Part B

High Altitude Bombing Mission Nagoya Japan — January 23, 1945 73rd Bomb Wing, 500th Bomb Group, 881st Squadron, Crew 112

This mission received the Presidential Unit Citation and is described in the award order.

I recall that day as follows:

Before we reached the coast of Japan, our gunners had downed at least two of the Jap fighters and exhausted our ammunition. We were sitting ducks from the coast on to the target, During this time we received 265 incoming holes in our plane. Counting shells exiting, the total holes would be close to 350. These visible holes gave the ship a sieve like appearance. The only systems working on the plane were the manual flight controls. We had lost ability to pressurize the cabins. The shell that wounded Troop also caused a sudden depressurizing of the cabins. The temperature dropped from 70F plus to a minus 50F. in a matter of seconds. Crew 112 survived for just one reason: the Grace of God.

At about the same time, we received a cannon round from a Zeke which Porter and Clanton saw as it was fired and felt it hit the right side of the plane. Porter felt a shell hit the back of his seat and felt blood running down his back. He called Clanton and advised that he had been hit. Clanton replied that so had he. Porter felt no pain and neither did Clanton. A shell had come between Porter's and Clanton's seats that were back to back with about a six-inch clearance that the shell had entered. The blood was actually spontaneous sweat running down their backs.

This same Zeke most likely hit radioman Herb Schoenecker in the hand and left it a bloody mess. Two other gunners were wounded in the back cabin. They were able to treat the wounds themselves and none were life threatening.

Vint who was nearest Shoenecker, put a tourniquet on his arm to staunch the bleeding. Clanton was flying the plane as the autopilot was inoperative and controls had to be man-handled to keep in control. This was no small feat. As soon as possible Taylor, Vint and Porter checked out the wound and realized that we should give him a blood transfusion. His veins were too small to find and it was decided to use the sternum transfusion method. About this time Taylor couldn't stand the bloody mess, left the scene and retired to his seat. With Vint taking the lead, he and Porter were able to get the transfusion going into the sternum. With Vint's constant attention Schoenecker survived the seven-hour flight back to Saipan.

Editorial Comment:

In my description of this mission I neglected to mention that 20 M.M. shell passing through that six inch space separating the backs of our seats. Reason: I had forgotten that "insignificant" detail. When Port reminded me of it about 8-1-04 we had a hearty laugh over the blood and sweat concept.

Incidentally, we had a rough time man-handling the sky giant all the 1500 miles to Saipan. She just did not respond to the controls in the normal manner. I say again, its more than a monumental miracle one of those rounds didn't sever something essential to remaining airborne. We earned our flight pay that day.

The Stanton "Bud" Child Story

1st Lt. Stanton "Bud" Child
Pilot
482nd Sq. 505th Bomb Group

"To Err is Human"

Although I was a member of one of the best crews in the 505th B.G., I did see some mistakes made while I served on the island of Tinian. Our B-29 was the third plane to arrive on Tinian on the 22nd of Dec. 1944. I was the last member of the crew to leave the island in Oct. of 1945.

The reason for my late departure from Tinian was because I had been sent with another crew to Lead Crew School at Muroc Army Air Base in June 1945. The rest of the crew finished their 35 missions in early Aug. 1945.

Now to get to the point of the story. We had gone on a night incendiary mission on May 16th. The early part of the flight was routine with a normal take off and the steady drone of the engines for six plus hours on the way to Nagoya. As the plane was being flown on auto pilot, there was not too much to do except keep an eye on the engine instruments and occasionally make a slight course correction. I passed the time by staring out the window at the total black darkness of the sky and ocean. The only thing to break up this monotony was to watch the flame coming from the # 3 engine exhaust. This reminded me of when one of my fellow cadets had bailed out of his
BT-13A on his first solo night flight when he thought that his plane was on fire. As it would be a long 1500 mile swim in the Pacific, I decided to stay with the plane.

As we were approaching the Japanese coastline after midnight, we could see the flames from the city of Nagoya. At this time everyone on the plane was on the alert and ready to do their assigned jobs. Sykes, the navigator, gave us the final course correction to bring us to our IP. Ebright, the bombardier, started getting his bomb sight ready for the bomb run. On the final bomb run, Higgins the A/C was flying the bomber, and this left me with nothing to do except watch the flames, the many search lights and the bombs bursting in air. At times like this I crossed my fingers to put a double whammy hex on the flack gunners and the night fighter pilots.

The Japanese night fighter pilots usually flew with a blue light in their cockpits, so all of us were on the look out for one or more of these blue lights. About the time that we were leaving the target area one of the side gunners spotted a blue light in the distance off the left side of our plane. We wanted to keep the fighter plane at a distance so I gave the order for Lubisch, the left side gunner, to fire a few tracer rounds to keep the Jap at a distance. The blue light kept following us and Lubisch kept firing a few tracer bullets. This situation continued for a half hour or so, and it finally dawned on all of us that a fighter plane could not follow us for this long a period with out running out of gasoline. Then the truth of the whole blue light came on all of us at the same time.

We had been trying to shoot down the planet Venus. Fortunately, we missed and I still see Venus when I go out after dark. But, I always think of this night over the Japanese Empire.

Stanton "Bud" Child

Editorial Comment

Bud and I met in the 7th grade and became instant friends. We remained so all through high school, in combat and throughout our lives. He possesses a great sense of dry humor as evidenced by the story he chose to recite for this book. He encountered the identical death defying experiences I did. However, he preferred recounting a little humor. It is so typical of his personality.

The Bob Wetter Story
A-B-29 Experiences

I would like to relate an experience I had as a 20th Army Air Force B-29 Central Fire Control Gunner (CFC) whose home base was located on Saipan, an island in the Marianas chain, just north of the Equator in the Western Pacific Ocean.

It was not a well-know fact, that the B-29 was a rather comfortable aircraft when compared other heavy bombers of WWII (B-I 7 and B-24s). The B-29 was the only pressurized aircraft, which meant that it was just like the present-day airliner: no oxygen mask or heavy winter clothing was required at high altitude, to keep warm and comfortable. Oxygen was always a requirement (backup) when an aircraft came within range of enemy territory.

Another feature of this long-range B-29 (greater than 3,800 miles), high altitude (above 30,000 feet), rather fast (350 mph), very heavy bomber (VHB) was a computer which controlled five turrets with a total of twelve 50-caliber machine guns. The computer was a top secret, electromechanical device (the first real aircraft computer). The gunners were located in sighting stations, which were divorced from the gun turrets, some by 44 feet. These five sighting stations were related to the guns (turrets) via the computer, which digested the information the gunner at each sighting station fed into the computer via an electronic gun sight located at each of the gun sight positions.

The computer processed this information and adjusted the related gun turret or turrets accordingly (lead, deflection, range, speed and size of the attacking aircraft), taking into account the B-29s airspeed, altitude, temperature, and cross wind. The job of the (CFC) gunner was to assign turret/s (through a switching device, to a sighting station, while manning his own top sighting station, where it was possible to control two turrets at the same time and on the same target. It was also possible for either side blister sighting station to control as many as three separate turrets at the same time, (lower front, lower rear and the tail gunner's turret). Where again the computer had the capability to make the proper target lead, deflection, etc., for that same target, for each of the turrets, the tail gunner had the ability to control just the tail guns. It was an amazing, fast and accurate gunnery system, which the Japanese pilots quickly learned to respect.

One rather gratifying incident I would like to share with you is the "Prisoner of War" (PW) missions carried out by various B-29 Squadrons. The war was coming to a close an the B-29 flight crews were informed to report to assigned B-29s at 1900 hrs (7:00 pm), to pack special clothing and canned foods, in special containers. The special containers were fitted with parachute harnesses, and the containers were loaded into the bomb bays of the B-29 and attached to the bomb release shackles. Our "Prisoner of War" assigned target was a "PW" camp near the city of Nagoya, Japan, on the Island of Honshu. The Swiss government, acting on behalf of the Japanese government, had agreed to inform the various Allied governments (American, British, French and Dutch), the location of each "PW" camp and the number of prisoners held. In addition each "PW" camp would erect/construct a sign with the letters "PW." The six-foot high white letters were on a black background and orientated so as to be visible from the air. We took off from Isley Field on the Island of Saipan at 0600 hrs. (6:00 am) with a full load of fuel, 8,900 gallons of aviation gasoline and headed for the Nagoya area. On the way we passed over the Island of Iwo Jima, and arrived over the city of Nagoya about 1100 hrs. (11:00 am). All we knew was the location of the "PW" camp was near the City of Nagoya, not northeast of southwest, just somewhere around the Nagoya area.

After three hours of searching and becoming concerned about our dwindling gasoline supply, we sighted the "PW" camp with the 23 French prisoners of war.

We "buzzed" the camp a couple of times at 200 feet just to let them know we saw them, do not know who was happier to see whom, as they were waving their arms so hard and fast I thought they would fly. We climbed to 400 feet and salvo (dropped all the supplies) at once from the rear bomb bay.

The containers were attached to shroud lines, which were hooked to the bomb shackles (a release device) in the bomb bay; when the containers were about 20 feet away the shroud lines opened the containers' parachutes.

We learned from the first drop that perhaps we were too low, as the chutes did not have time to open and that we had packed some of the individual containers incorrectly (we had put all canned goods in one container (too heavy).

We should have mixed some clothing and canned goods. The medical supplies were packaged in separate containers. One of the containers hit the small guardhouse and destroyed it (the guard was outside watching). We climbed to an altitude of 800 feet to salvo the containers in the front bomb bay, hoping to give the chutes more time and altitude to open. The results were the same - Parachutes were incorrectly packed. Either the parachute tore off or turned inside out. We were running low on fuel by this time and discovered we could not close either of the bomb bay doors. The majority of the shroud lines (a 20-foot webbed belt attached to the bomb release mechanism [shackles] and to the various containers) did not drop free when they were unhooked from the bomb shackles.

With the bomb bay doors open and the shroud lines dangling in the aircraft slipstream, and already low on fuel, we headed for the open sea and Iwo Jima at tree-top level over the city of Nagoya.

Climbing to 500 feet, reaching the open sea and having the problem with the open bomb-bay doors, our situation was becoming more tenuous by the minute. To the point that if we did not get the bomb bay doors closed, we would not even make it back to the island of Iwo Jima (600 miles). Someone came up with the idea of breaking the gasoline dipstick, and using it to dislodge the wedged shroud lines. In order to reach the wedged area it was necessary for the two smallest, lightest men, which were Pilot, 1st. Lt. John M. Hunter and myself, to shed their parachutes but keep our Mae West inflatable life vests on. We were to he held by our ankles by the two largest (hopefully the strongest) flight-crew members George Knowles and Ray Whitt. After about an hour both bomb-bays were free of the shroud lines and closed. Due to the long search and the bomb bay problem, we could not make it back to our home base Saipan. We were forced to land on the island of Iwo Jima with very little fuel remaining.

I feel I owe my life to the Marines who took the island of Iwo Jima at a staggering cost. The assault units of the Marine Corps and organic Navy personnel sustained 24,053 causalities, by far the highest single-action losses in the Marine Corps history. Of these a total of 6,600+ gave their lives so that we B-29ers could have ours. It was estimated that 2,253 B-29s (24,700 airmen) used Iwo Jima as an island of life.

Editorial Comment

This very informative, detailed analysis of the B-29 and the heroism displayed by CFC Gunner Bob Wetter and Pilot John Hunter is of significant importance. Together both these men accomplished deeds worthy of the Congressional Medal of Honor. They saved their crewmen and plane. I salute them.

The Stephen K. Atwater Story

Thought I'd mention another event from those WWII days. It's much like one you experienced, Ray. It occurred on our first mission, we flew loose formation all the way to Japan, instead of rendezvousing off the coast of Japan, as we did thereafter. This, we learned the hard way, it used up more fuel, so that on return, nearly everyone was very low on fuel; and was calling in to get a fix on Saipan, which thoroughly blocked radio transmission. The last hour our flight engineer spent transferring fuel from tank to tank to keep all four engines alive! The last half hour most of the crew was in "ditching" mode. "OB" and I had our eyes peeled for The Island and landing strip, it was night and pitch-black! We finally spotted the strip on Tinian, and "OB" banked steeply and put it down! At the end of the runway all four engines died...dry! They towed us in! We flew over to Saipan the next morning.

One other item which you may have heard of...about the "Irish Lassie." It was to be "our plane" (A-52), and our AC, Belah O'Brian Price, a good Irishman, got to name her. Well, on the mission of Jan. 27,'45, we didn't fly, and "Pop" Avery (AC) and Leonard Fox (Pilot) flew her. They were rammed twice, credited with 13 Jap fighter kills, yet managed to get her back to Saipan. This was written up in Colliers magazine, a copy of which I'll enclose. This was our most costly mission ...5 of 13 planes were lost from our squadron alone! It was also the most costly for Japan, with 34 aircraft lost, 7 probable, and 12 damaged ... again, from our squadron alone!

Excerpt from Collier's Magazine:

The Irish Lassie Gets Home

Superfortress Irish Lassie wheels in toward the coast of Japan at 2 o'clock on the afternoon of January 27, 1945, at

29,000 feet. The air over Japan is bright and freezing. Back at her base at Saipan, in the tropics, the day is hot. Below, a winter snow lies over Tokyo's streets.

Irish Lassie's crew is warm; they're flying pressurized over the target today and their oxygen masks hang down loosely to the left of their jaws. It is their eighth mission to Japan, though other B-29s from the 73rd Wing have been flying to Tokyo from Saipan for over two months.

In the blisters, in the tail, in the turrets, gunners squint anxiously through their Plexiglas, searching their arcs of sky. Someone shouts: "There they are – at 3 o'clock, high – God! About forty of 'em!"

Over the coast line now, the fight begins. Forty enemy fighters pile into this first flight of twelve B-29s, from above, in front, the sides, from the tail. Central Fire Control Gunner Jim McHugh swings his upper turret, lets fly with his four fifties at the attackers from 12 o'clock. One Tojo plunges through. McHugh's tracers riddle him, but still he doesn't stop. At 400 miles an hour he plummets in at the Superfort and crash! In a suicide dive the Tojo rams Irish Lassie, smashing into the left wing, tearing out great hunks of the No.1 engine nacelle and shearing off half the left aileron and flap. Her giant metal frame shudders, then recovers and heads on into her bombing run. The Tojo, spinning down out of control, blows up at 25,000 feet.

Despite the impact of the crash dive and the scores of hard-pressed fighter attacks. Bombardier Gage never budges from his sights. Delicately he twists the knobs, concentrates on the cross-hairs, whispers steadily into his throat-microphone. Deliberately his hand reaches out, closes over a toggle switch. "Bombs away! Bomb bay doors closed! Free to turn and for God's sake turn fast!" Twelve 500-pound bombs arch and tumble on their way down to the Musashino Aircraft Engine Plant, Tokyo.

Gage jumps back to his guns, blasts the canopy off an attacking Zeke, killing the pilot. Amidships, McHugh throws his four fifties onto another Zeke, attacking him from above, and shatters him. Alone and isolated in the tail sits Charlie Mulligan. He's been having a busy time back there, fighting off the attackers. Already Mulligan has chalked up three certain kills since 2 o'clock. Now it is 2:20.

The Nips still come driving drunkenly in at Mulligan, plunging through his fire to within a few feet and then pulling wildly away. Right above him now one persistent devil flies. The Jap turns in for another attack: at 30 yards Mulligan lets fly with everything. The Jap never stops-but tears smack into the tail in a full power dive, smashing his plane to pieces on the giant fin. He almost takes Irish Lassie with him. His suicide dive tears off the entire left stabilizer, the whole left side of the tail compartment.

Up front in the pilot's seat, Avery feels the nose drop away violently and every man in the plane feels the terrible impact of this second ramming in less than half an hour. The B-29 falls off into a creaming dive. Avery pulls back hard on the control column and kicks the rudders. Nothing happens: the plane persists in her dive. Copilot Fox is on the controls too. He thinks he's just helping Avery out, with his extra strength, but it turns out he is actually flying the plane alone. There is just one thin strand of cable left to the elevators and that belongs to Fox.

The B-29 continues to dive for 9,000 feet. Nobody expects to get out alive. Fox, using every ounce of his strength, manages to level the ship out at around 20,000 feet and it is a miracle that their meager control cable doesn't snap.

The 20 Jap vultures now close in for the kill on the helpless cripple. But the blister gunners are still on the job. When it is all over, Irish Lassie's total kill is 13 Jap fighters.

Off the coast, Avery lets down to 17,000 feet and depressurizes the cabin. Mulligan can't be raised over the interphone, so Leach and Meyer make their way aft to see if he is in trouble. Mulligan is in the worst possible trouble. Bleeding and unconscious, his head between his knees, Mulligan lies crouched in the wrecked tail section. Twisted metal, broken guns, smashed equipment and splintered glass are piled on top of him.

Working in shifts and with additional help from Gage and McHugh, Leach and Meyer extricate Mulligan and drag him inch by inch back towards the radar room. The temperature is subzero, the gale terrific, with the full draft and slip stream of the engines pounding directly in upon them.

The pilots are having their troubles. They have 1,500 miles to fly over ocean in a wrecked plane with scarcely more than a strand of cable to control it. In addition to their tail gunner being seriously wounded, their radar man, Klimczak, is badly shot up. In the radar compartments, Navigator Faubiom and Radio Operator Nellums are giving him first aid. He has been shot through the leg, back and arm, and he's bleeding profusely. They give him morphine and plasma, strip off his clothes and sprinkle his wounds with sulfa. They feed him full right oxygen and wrap him in blankets.

Then they got to work on Mulligan. Due to the extreme cold in the exposed tail where the unconscious gunner lies, all his clothes have frozen. His hand has been shot through and he is covered with deep gashes from the splintering glass and metal. They dress these wounds; difficult work, because the sudden warmth of the radar room causes the frozen wounds to bleed profusely. Mulligan is given two units of plasma, and all the crew except the pilots and navigator, who can't afford to pass out, go off oxygen so the wounded men may be fed it full right and continuously.

It is time for Engineer Watson to go through the plane and make a report on the damage. It isn't encouraging. No repairs will be possible in the air, he says. Chances of making a successful 1,500 mile overwater flight in bad weather and in darkness are slim.

There is nothing to do but fly and hope. The black night hours drag by silently, as if they are years. The men do not talk. But Avery is glad he has kept his altitude. He needs every inch tonight, for below them the weather is bad-rough rain clouds which would throw the ship around if it got in them. And he has just that one torn cable; any extra strain might snap it. Through the night they plow on, hesitantly, counting off the slow minutes and endless miles.

Now it is time for the letdown. Somehow they have made it this far and it is only a matter of minutes from Saipan. As they descended it gets rough: nothing to fear in a sound, tight ship, but something to dread in this wrecked bomber, held in level flight by that thin strand of steel.

Every few moments Avery calls the Saipan tower: "Bluegrass! Calling Bluegrass! I have wounded aboard and am in distress…Request permission to make emergency straight-in approach." Avery hears nothing but static in his earphones. His aerial has been shot away over Japan and he is unable to pick up anything farther than ten miles for the transmitting station. But one piece of good fortune has remained with him; he has his very high-frequency transmitter intact and he is thereby able to send out his distress message.

The Superfort flies closer and closer to Saipan. Gas is low, every gauge registers empty. The pumps are sucking up the last quarts and pints that swish on the bottom of the tanks. Four hundred precious gallons of gas were lost in the first ramming.

Then the tower comes through: "This is Bluegrass. You have permission to land. You are cleared for an emergency straight-in approach. Ambulances and fire trucks are waiting."

It is up to Fox. He alone has controls left. In the darkness he cuts down between two other B-29s in the traffic pattern. Approaching the field, power suddenly fails him and the seventy-ton bomber drops clear below the level of the cliffs. Fox hits the throttles full forward to maximum power and strains the last elevator cable to the breaking point as he hauls back on the control column. Miraculously he lifts the torn ship up and over the cliff, then he pushes the nose down.

Irish Lassie hits the runway with dead engines. The last ounce of usable gasoline has been pumped out of the tanks. She hits, nose-wheel first, at 180 instead of the usual 100. The nose-wheel folds up, crashing thought the fuselage and into the cockpit. The props chew into the coral, the ship smashes in two.

Avery's head slams into the instrument panel; he is knocked out. Meyer, Leach, Nellums and McHugh have packed their solid bodies around the wounded men for protection and the crash landing bruises and cuts them. Fire starts in No. 1 engine thinking she would burn, grab Mulligan. Still delirious, Mulligan fights furiously as they drag him stark naked from the clothing piled about him and out of the plane.

Klimczak is too sick to be moved. But help from the ground is there. They cut a hole through the fuselage and first-aid men gently load his wounded body onto a litter. From the runway, McHugh and Meyer look at the wreckage. Irish Lassie did not burn-there was too little gasoline left.

All but Mulligan and Klimczak returned to bombing Japan after a brief rest. All are alive today. Mulligan and Klimczak were hospitalized. Mulligan's hands had to be amputated. They had frozen while he lay wounded and unconscious in the subzero tail section. Klimczak shot in the arm, leg and back, also suffered a shattered pelvis and hip bones. And a baby was born to Mrs. Fox the night her copilot husband flew Irish Lassie back to Saipan.

Here is the cast of this terrific war drama of the substratosphere recorded at the time as an official Army Air Forces document but impounded until now for security reasons:

Pilot Lt. Lloyd Avery, Jackson Heights, Long Island, NY.
Copilot Lt. Leonard C. Fox, Emmet, Nebraska
Navigator Lt. John Faubiom, Ausin, Texas
Bombardier Lt. C.R.Gage, Wauwatosa, Wisconsin
Engineer Lt. Robert E. Watson, Pomeroy, Washington
Radio Operator Sgt. Walter S. Klimczak, Plymouth, Pennsylvania
Radio Operator Sgt. Lewis E. Nellums, Pensacola, Florida
Central Fire Control Gunner Sgt. James McHugh of New York City
Left Blister Gunner Sgt. Clarence O. Leach, Martins Ferry, Ohio.
Right Blister Gunner Sgt. Marvin E. Meyer, Boone, Iowa.
Tail Gunner Sgt. Charles D. Mulligan, Henderson, Kentucky.

Edited By Frederick R. Neely
Colliers July 6, 1946

Stephen K. Atwater

Editorial Comment

Thanks, ol' buddy, for submitting your story. You've given my book an even greater appeal. It is appreciated by all of us. "Keep 'em flyin."

The Mel Cash Story

The 505th Bombardment Group on Tinian.

Tinian, our home for the next year, was a little, green, flat, semitropical island formed by prehistoric volcanoes and coral animals. It lay just three miles southwest of Saipan, with its clearly visible harbor of ships and its high mountain, and about 125 miles northwest of Guam. Of the fifteen islands in the Marianas group, Tinian was one of the four largest. It averaged four miles in width and eleven miles in length. Heavy growth of cane greeted the Americans, but the vegetation was not tropical; the trees were evergreen, mostly pine. This is where we built our “Quonset hut’ and set up housekeeping by December 29.

The 313th Bombardment Wing was a unit of the 21st Bomber Command, later 20th Air Force, and forerunner of the Strategic Air Command. The 73rd Bombardment Wing had been operating out of Isley Field, Saipan, since October 1944, and the 58th Bombardment Wing operated out of China, but logistic was a problem from that location, so in May 1945 it moved to West Field, Tinian. About the same time, the 314th Bombardment Wing was established at North Field, Guam (later Andersen Air Force Base), along with 20th Air Force Headquarters. All these units were under the command of a Lieutenant General.

January 1945 was utilized by the unit as a training month; although we did include bombing missions on Truk, to the southeast of Tinian and Iwo Jima to the northwest. Our crew participated in the mission to Truk on January 21 and to Iwo Jima on the 29th. These missions to Truk, a bypassed stronghold, and Iwo Jima had a purpose. By keeping the runways at these bases torn up, it prevented the Japanese from staging suicide missions from there. This month Captain John T. Weir with Squadron Commander James A. Ferguson crashed 75 miles off Tinian. Squadron crews searched the area for days but could spot only one life raft, that of Corporal Estle Davidson, a gunner who was later picked up, after being in the water five days. Major Cyrus R. Lewis became the Squadron Commander, and Captain Horace A. Payne became the Operations Officer. I spent my 28th birthday in the compound with my crew.

A chronological listing of missions performed by me and the crew from Tinian is as follows:

Date	Mission	Time	Remarks
04 Feb	Kobe	03 :40	Abort, fuel transfer problem
10 Feb	Ota Air Field	15:00	Shot over target, ditched, purple heart
09 Mar	Tokyo	14:30	Fire Raid
11 Mar	Nagoya	14:45	Fire Raid
16 Mar	Kobe	14:50	Fire Raid
18 Mar	Nagoya	14:50	Fire Raid
30 Mar	Shimonoseki St.	15:00	Mines
07 Apr	Nagoya	14:20	Mitsubishi Acft plant
15 Apr	Kawasaki	14:20	Fire Raid, DFC
21 Apr	Kokubu AF	15:10	Destroy Runways
24 Apr	Tachikawa	15:15	Hitahi Aircraft Plant
27 Apr	Kokubu AF	03:35	Abort: Low oil all engines
30 Apr	Hamamatsu	14:15	Fighters failed Rdzv
05 May	Izumi AF	14:00	58BW acft engine fire
10 May	Kanoya AF	14:35	Lost sortie credit
07 Jun	Osaka	14:10	Fire raid
11 Jun	Shimonoseki St.	14:30	Mines
13 Jun	Niigata	14:55	Mines, Oil pressure gage
27 Jun	HagiHarbor	14:50	Mines,
01 Jul	Kure	14:20	Night Incendiaries
03 Jul	Takamatsu	13:50	Night Incendiaries
06 Jul	Shimizu	15:45	Night Incendiaries
12Jul	Tsuruga	13:10	Mines
19 Jul	Chosi Point	12:45	Mines

26 Jul	Kawasaki	14:50	Oil Center
01 Aug	Nagaoka	15:05	Night Incendiaries
07 Aug	Toyokawa Navy	13:15	DFC oak leaf
31 Aug	Takasaki	14:30	PW Supply drop
02 Sep	Tokyo Harbor	13:15	Battleship MO Flyover

To put these B-29 missions in perspective, some history of WWII occurring at the same time is useful. MacArthur had landed at Leyte Gulf on October 20, 1944, and continued the Philippine campaign well into 1945. Iwo Jima was captured by the Marines on March 17, 1945 giving an emergency landing base for the Marianas Island B-29's. Okinawa was invaded April 1 and captured June 21. The Japanese had established a Kamikaze force and were launching from air fields on Kyushu against American operations at Okinawa. Later model Kamikaze aircraft were rocket powered, 19 feet long, 16 foot wingspan, and carried 2645 pounds of explosives, a pilot with no parachute, and released from a bomber near the target. They were called baka bombs by United States forces.

At the outset, my crew was adopted by the 50th Seabee Construction Battalion, and some of them flew on our missions. We had meals with them in their compound, they had better chow than the Army. And among their many talented people was a sign painter who put the name 'Homing Bird' on the crew's aircraft. Our first mission against the Japanese homeland was supposed to be a high altitude bombing raid on Kobe, but ended in an abort because of fuel transfer problems. The flight engineers were briefed to empty the bomb bay and center wing tanks before target, and Stapher ended up pumping fuel into the aircraft bomb bay area, spilling fuel and filling up the aircraft with gasoline fumes. We returned to Tinian wearing oxygen masks and windows open for ventilation.

The second mission February 10 was not any better. Eighty-four B-29's were launched against the Nakajima Aircraft plant at Ota, just north of Tokyo. Major Julian Dendy, from Caribbean duty with me, led the Group and Captain Carmel M. Slaughter, Jr. led the high flight. Before continuing the narrative, an explanation of jet streams is in orders.

Crews had become acquainted with high winds at altitude while in training, but nothing like that encountered over Japan during the winter months. If you tried a crosswind bomb run, the drift exceeded bomb sight capabilities, and if you came down wind, you were past the target before you were synchronized. The other alternative was up wind, and that day we were at 32,000 feet in a horrendous jet stream going up wind.

It seemed like we backed up when the bomb bay doors were opened. This gave the antiaircraft batteries time to reload and continue firing. The 'Homing Bird' received a shell through the right wing. Gunners called out we were on fire, then changed it to losing fuel. About the same time fighters knocked out the number two engine, and it would not feather due to loss of oil.

Over the target, Captain Slaughter and Owen O. Barnhart ran their aircraft together and went down. As the formation pulled away, and we were being picked out as a straggler by fighters, we decided this was enough of being locked in air. We picked a target of opportunity, reversed course after bombs away, and headed east, seeking a lower altitude. Meanwhile, Stapher kept the #3 engine running by pumping fuel from the #2 tank, and I tried to throw the #2 prop to reduce drag. The gunners were giving the fire control system a work out and claimed three fighters on the way out to Choshi point, our exit from the Japanese mainland. Turning south, we tried to avoid the Japanese small islands.

Over the target, the co-pilot, Harry Wing suggested we head to Vladivostok and land in Russia, but I wanted no part of flying upwind across the cold Sea of Japan. We would instead take our chances with a night ditching in the warmer waters of the Pacific Ocean. The Radio operator, James F. Haley tried to establish radio contact with a United States submarine on station, but could not. It was just as well, for it was snowing. When the aircraft reached a lower altitude, it controlled fairly well with one engine dragging and one feathered so the crew made plans for the eventful ditching yet to come. Radio contact was established with Tinian and our intentions were made known. A superdumbo, a B-29 assigned to provide ditching support, was contacted and maintained course with the "Homing Bird." We were trying to make it to the Bering Strait, a navy vessel on station southeast of Iwo Jima, assigned the task of picking up ditched B-29 crews. A survey of the aircraft revealed we had flak holes in the crew compartment, but none of the crew received any hits. We discussed salvoing the empty bomb bay fuel tanks to lighten the load, but decided against it, especially if one shackle did not release. This would increase drag, and they would also provide flotation.

At 10: 15 PM that night the fuel supply was used down to five minutes, then we headed into the wind for the ditching. It was a fairly dark night, and with the experience I had gained from night submarine runs in the Caribbean, I knew there was always an horizon, and elected not to use landing lights which could blind, causing other problems. We had placed our gear near the exits, gone through the briefing as to what each member would do, and Radio Haley let out the trailing antennae to give me surface contact. We briefed the Super-Dumbo and headed down. Sure enough, when the aircraft got into ditching position, there were the waves, the horizon, and the swells could be distinguished. And as the propellers began clicking the tops of the waves, I cut the power and settled in.

The aircraft came to an abrupt stop, so much so that my head hit the bullet proof glass over the instrument panel, and the sliding window, which was opened for ditching, slammed shut: but not enough to stop the flow of water into the cockpit. It was eerie, here was this fluorescent water running in and I couldn't understand it at first, but opened the window and saw the wings still intact, and inflated the life rafts.

I took charge of the left raft and Harry Wing the right raft. Bombardier William T. Trivette dove out the engineer's window, and took a pounding from the aircraft wings due to the choppy sea. The two rafts became separated during the night. The crew was unable to off load a large box of survival supplies. I wanted to reenter the aircraft, but the crew talked me out of it and it was just as well, for the 'Homing Bird' went to the bottom of the Pacific Ocean around 5:00 AM the next morning.

I had purposely changed the course to the east of Iwo Jima to avoid being strafed in the rafts by any fighters that could be launched from Iwo. As morning came, three B-29's from the squadron flew over the spot we had radioed that we would ditch, and we established mirror contact with them. The hand cranked survival radio wasn't making any contact, not even with our target ship, the Bering Strait. But Tinian had told the Captain of our position, and a Navy B-24 took up cover over our rafts and stayed until around 4:00 PM that evening. Remembering the accident just 75 miles off Tinian, I was prepared and set up rations for a 14 day wait; since we were in enemy contested territory. And sitting there in the raft with the sun shining down, I made a vow that "I would live the best life I could for as long as I could." The "Bering Strait" came on the horizon around 5:00 PM and the crew was piped aboard. Here we found that two other crews from the group had ditched the same night. Lieutenant Lowry of the 484th, also had a badly shot up B29. He used landing lights and hit a big swell instead of a trough. The plane broke into three sections. The nose sank immediately, and the other sections filled rapidly. Lowry and three gunners went down with the plane. Lieutenant Jack Halloran, also of the 484th had better luck. He found the Bering Strait and circled it twice with his landing lights on. The ship gave him a heading, and also turned on its lights. Jack had about the same experience as I had when the plane came to a halt. The window also slammed shut, and his crew experienced the same problems we did in evacuating the plane.

Our crew was given soup and put to bed. The next day I met the Captain, Walter Deane Innis, later to be rear Admiral. And about 45 years after the war, his wife Pauline started a history of the Bering Strait. We corresponded and I gave her more details of that night, I still have to see the history. It took us another five days to make the surface trip back to Tinian aboard the Bering Strait, but after all it was much better than doing it in a life raft.

When we returned to Tinian, we found out the extent of losses from the February 10 raid. Lieutenant Edward Quay had crashed and burned on take off, Slaughter and Barnhart had gone down over the target, and of the 84 aircraft launched that day, 21 did not return, but the crews on the Bering Strait were saved. While the crew was being refitted, we spent the time going around to the other units in the 313th Wing explaining how to ditch a B29, since it was the most successful so far. My crew made recommendations that were later incorporated in the aircraft structure, like: shoulder harness for the pilots, and braces for the bomb bay bulkhead doors to keep water out of the crew compartment on ditching.

Joyce was pregnant. We had been corresponding on a regular basis, and this little incident would upset the schedule of daily letters, so I started out a string of daily letters, backing in the dates so she would not worry; and have a miscarriage and lose our one link with the future. And that future looked dim for me, since this was only my second mission against the Japanese mainland. At that time the number of missions until rotation to the United States had not been determined.

Lieutenant Odie T Smith and crew checked into the compound as replacements and were assigned to the Quonset previously occupied by my crew and that of Slick Slaughter. When he asked about our whereabouts and was told that Slaughter had gone down over the target, and Mel was still at sea, remarked “what a way to start a war.” About a month later, I was issued a new B29. Tail numbers were no longer important, but it was still ‘Skyblue 65’. At this time B29’s were built at three locations: Martin constructed their version at Bellevue, NE, the Boeing Wichita their version, and the Boeing Renton, WA their model. I was partial to the Renton version which I would keep until August when I was issued a new fuel injection-engined and improved radar model, since we were now lead crew status.

Sometime after the ditching and returning to the War, Major Robert E. Blauw and I took the 313th Bombardment Wing B24 to Guam without orders. The idea was to go to Hickham in Hawaii and pick up items that would make living on Tinian more bearable. On checking in with General LeMay at Bomber Command, he told us politely that a previous mission of that sort from our Wing had caused him embarrassment by raunchy behavior, and that we should just return to Tinian. As we left his office, we overheard him say, “Get General Davies on the phone.” We were considered ready to reluctantly return to war. And from then on, the Chaplain played a large part of our preflight and get together before boarding the aircraft. I prayed a lot in those days.

Since high altitude bombing seemed to be out of the question at this time of the year, and Japanese industry was spread throughout their cities, the decision was to go area bombing at night and at lower altitudes. General LeMay came out with the idea to download the bomb bay fuel tanks, offload the guns and gunners; and load up with incendiary bombs. So there began the historic fire raids on Japanese cities during the period 9 through 18 March 1945. The first raid was against Tokyo and my crew was assigned a drop area just north of the Emperor's Palace and at an altitude of 9000 feet. By the time we got to the target area in Tokyo, the city had began to burn, searchlights were putting their spot on B-29s so antiaircraft guns and fighters could knock them out of the sky. We dropped our load to add to the conflagration, and on withdrawal, Tokyo could be seen burning from 200 miles out. The 21st Bomber Command launched 279 aircraft of which 12 were lost, but more than that, one fourth of the city was destroyed killing more than 83,000 people -- more than was to be sustained by the atomic blast at Hiroshima.

Two days later Nagoya received the same fate from 285 aircraft, and on March 14 the same fate fell on Osaka, My crew and I did not make the Osaka raid for some unknown reason, but did make the raid on Kobe on the 1 6th and the final raid on the 18th for the second time on Nagoya. After these fire raids, things began to look better from a survival standpoint for B29 crews. About the same time, Joyce, in correspondence with Betty Slaughter, had learned of the fate of Slick, so I had to tell the true version of my experiences up to that time. On March 30 the 20th Bomber Command ceased operations in China for its impending move to Tinian, and we began mining operations against the Shimonoseki Straits.

In April my crew was picked for lead crew school on Tinian, and I was made A Flight Commander and issued my own Jeep. As lead crew it was necessary to train for a mission on the newly developed simulator. This gave the Bombardier Navigator, and Radar the opportunity to get a better view of what the target would look like from their perspective. The pilots controlled where the marking device would go on instructions from the nay team. After the simulator practice, a practice mission was flown in the B-29 before making the actual mission. This had the effect of taking a crew longer to accomplish its missions, which had by this time been established at 26. On April 7 I led a flight on the bombing raid against the Mitsubishi aircraft plant at Nagoya, and on April 15, it was back to Kawasaki for another fire raid, this time from an altitude of 13,000 feet. It was not our easiest mission. By now the Japanese were using Baka Bombers (the Kamikaze pilots) to defend their cities, and after we dropped our bombs, I purposely entered a smoke funnel rising from the burning city. It was pitch black, the burning stink entered the cockpit, and we came out the other side at 1 7,000 feet where the baka bombers could be seen following the bomber stream. Before climbing to altitude for the return to Tinian, a standard operating procedure to take advantage of the jet stream tail winds, we had to close the bomb bay doors by means of hooks we had constructed for that purpose when the compressed air system failed or froze. This flight earned me the Distinguished Flying Cross to go with the Purple Heart received after the ditching.

At this time in the war, United States forces were involved in the Okinawa campaign, and the Japanese were using airfields on Kyushu to launch bombers carrying the Baka bombers. The newly constituted 20th Air Force, which by now comprised the 58th Wing from China and the 3 14th Wing on Guam, expended 75% of their effort to deny use of these airfields. My crew led flights or squadrons on high altitude bombing missions during daylight using sensitive munitions -- some did not explode on surface contact but did when the Japanese tried to clear them. These flights were as depicted on the recapitulation chart to Kokubu, Izumi, Kanoya, interspersed with a daylight bombing raid on Hamamatsu when P-51 fighters from Iwo Jima failed to rendezvous (I don't believe we ever had fighter support, except one time we had to act as support for one that was lost and disorientated. After dropping our bombs, we escorted the P5 1 back to Iwo Jima, made the penetration because of weather, and watched him land. We had to do some serious talking to the pilot to keep him composed with his rough engine. This earned the respect of the fighter pilots and again I was commended.

On the aborted flight of April 27 against Kokubu airfield, I did not have my usual Skyblue 65 B29, and the aircraft used was war weary and made a sluggish take off -- it barely became airborne, and would not climb. I was afraid to salvo the bombs for fear of getting them back, so I let it continue. Finally, we made enough altitude to lift the flaps and headed North on course. But near Iwo Jima it became evident the aircraft would not make it to the target and back. The engines were all running out of oil, and I did not want another ditching, so we salvoed the bombs into the Pacific, feathered an engine, and returned to Tinian. On landing, we told maintenance to change all four engines. This they did to give new life to this war-weary B29. With victory in Europe declared on May 7, the United States turned all its attention to the Pacific.

On the Kyushu airfield raid to Izumi on May 5 when I was Squadron lead, we had two 58th Wing aircraft in the formation, and on coast out, one of them developed an engine fire and could not keep the engine feathered. Knowing the wing would burn off if not attend to, I told him to take it down and ditch if it did not improve, and assigned the other to act as Superdumbo. But on the way down the fire burned itself out, and the two continued back to West Field on Tinian after an emergency landing at Iwo Jima. That island saved a lot of B29's. On the flight to Kanoya on May 10 I was leading the high flight, and Japanese fighters were particular aggressive, and Ted Trivette had the pickle release in his hand and firing the nose guns at the same time. Copilot Harry Wing was changing altitude to keep from being rammed -- you could hear their engine roar as they went between the propellers -- and I was flying formation. We accidentally released early, and six other aircraft in the Squadron released also. This was embarrassing, and Ted and I lost sortie credit for that most difficult mission.

And, on May 15 our crew was granted a 10 day rest and recuperation leave and traveled to Hawaii by a Navy PBY5 aircraft. There on the beaches and in the restaurants we again found out what women were, even to applying suntan lotion to one lovely miss after I told her I was married. John Slevin, the navigator, and I were invited to spend a few days with Senator Rice and his wife at their ranch on Maui. The couple was very generous to John and me, taking us on a trip up the mountain to view the dormant Haleakala volcano and seven mile crater. From their front porch, you could look down under the clouds and view the island of Molokai.

On return to Tinian, it appeared that things had improved. After the Seabees completed the runways, they began constructing roads and had made a four- lane highway down the middle of the island and paved Riverside Drive. A hospital was being constructed to accommodate the expected casualties from the impending invasion of the Japanese homeland. Also, nurses began to arrive on the island, and a sister wing unit, the 509th Bombardment Group, which had been held back at Fairbury, Nebraska, and later transferred to Wendover, Utah, for additional training began to arrive on the island. Their group had tail insignia representing all the groups in the 20th Air Force, including the circle W of the 505th. And I had to give up my hardstand to make way for the Enola Gay. Later, on drives by my old hardstand, I noticed a 10-foot high canvass covering, with Military Police at 20-foot intervals and thought nothing of it except there must be some new classified weapon system. Our Group Commander, Robert A. Ping, had been assigned to Wing, and the Vice-Commander, Colonel Charles M. Eisenhart, later General, assumed command.

Harry Wing, my co-pilot took over a crew in the 484th Squadron, and from then on, the right seat of the aircraft was occupied by Wing, Group, or Squadron Staff. It was also used as an indoctrination flight for newly arriving Aircraft Commanders, as the pilots were now called. Traveling USO shows began to invade the island, tennis exhibition matches were staged by Bobby Riggs, and the 313th Wing had a professional baseball team with big league players, like Joe DiMagio, Pee Wee Reese, and Johnny Mize. So, our volleyball court and beach strolls were not the only sources of entertainment.

By this time in the war, the 20th Air Force was running out of choice targets, and on June 7, we went on another fire raid again to Osaka, when undercast required bombing by radar. Then on June 1 it was back to Mine laying in the Shimonoseki Strait, and on June 13 to Niigata on the north side of Japan, where the number two engine lost the oil pressure reading and Flight Engineer Stapher wanted to shut it down. He was overruled, since it would appear to be an instrumentation error. Then it was to Hagi Harbor on the 27th for more mine laying. The benefits of being a lead crew paid off, for on June 18 I was promoted to captain. The raids against the airfields on Kyushu helped the capture of Okinawa for it was declared won on June 2 1 , 1945.

The 509th Composite Group began flying training missions, but nothing important happened, except back in Virginia on July 12, 1945, Joyce gave birth to our first born, Carol Dean Cash, our link to the future. The Army Air Force had developed a policy of identifying which cities in Japan would be subjected to fire raids, and urged the population to flee their cities. There ensured a series of fire raids as depicted on the recapitulation chart of missions flown, with an occasional mine laying mission, like Tsuruga. On August 1 the 20th Air Force put up a maximum effort of 836 B-29s -- the largest single day's effort of the war. From then on, after each mission launch, the dump trucks used to build the runways were loaded with rock and placed on the runways until the missions returned. And, on August 6, 1945, some of the mystery to the things going on was revealed when Paul W. Tibbits and the Enola Gay of the 509th dropped the atomic bomb on Hiroshima. The city with a population of about 245,000, was the seventh-largest city in Japan.

Later, the papers gave this account: “At 8: 15 AM the Enola Gay (named after Paul’s mother and built at the Martin Bomber Plant in Bellevue, NE) appeared at 3 1,790 feet above the city center. Out of its bomb bay dropped a 8910 pound bomb, called Little Boy. The bomb exploded about 1910 feet above Shima Hospital. A blinding light blazed across the sky. Buildings vanished in a circle about 4290 feet around what became known as ground zero. People were vaporized, their shadows, imprinted on stones. No one knows how many died or how many, burned and saturated by radiation, were to die. The official Japanese estimate, up to December 1945, was 140,000 dead.”

The next day August 7, I was assigned Group lead on a high altitude bombing mission against the Naval Supply Arsenal at Toyokawa. We expected massive retaliation, but nothing occurred. From a bombing standpoint this was a very successful mission and I was awarded a cluster to the DFC. Apparently the Japanese still had a sufficient quantity of munitions in that arsenal for it blew sky high. That was my last bombing mission, for on August 9, another B29 dropped a second atomic bomb, Fat Man, on Nagasaki, killing as many as 70,000 people; again, no one would ever be able to calculate the actual toll. And the World entered the nuclear age.

On August 15 Tokyo time -- August 14, 1945, in the United States--Emperor Hirohito, speaking on the radio for the first time, announced that he was ending the war. In his long speech he didn’t use the words “defeat” or “surrender,” but he did mention “a new and most cruel bomb.” On August 3 1 I carried a load of Prisoner of War supplies to a drop near Takasaki -- at least the coordinates were near there, with people lined up in circles in the compound. It was eerie flying around Japanese gun emplacements looking down their barrels, when the occupation forces were not yet on the

Japanese mainland. And on September 2 I participated in the B29 flyover of the battleship Missouri anchored in Tokyo bay where the peace treaty was being signed by MacArthur.

Being one of the high point men on the Island, I was transferred to Saipan on September 30, 1945, for return to the United States. While there I was subjected to long chow lines, sleeping in tents, and went through a Typhoon with the tent flapping all night long. This did not worry me that much. I tried to get a cyst removed from my foot, but couldn't fit it in for on October 13 I boarded a Navy transport ship for the thirteen-day trip to San Francisco. I might mention that when I left the United States in December 1944 I weighed 170 pounds, and when I started the return, the weight was down to 155 pounds. Diet, anxiety, and exercise do have a way of taking off weight -- muscle and fat. We arrived at Angel Island on October 1945, having two October 13th's by crossing the date line again, and beating the Pacific slogan of the "Golden Gate by 48" by three years. While in San Francisco I visited the Mark Hopkins (Top of the Mark) and enjoyed some wonderful food in the many premier restaurants in the city, before boarding the troop train for the ride to Reception Station No. 4, Fort Bragg, North Carolina. I was somewhat of a troop train commander, but did little or no commanding, just let the train roll through Nevada, Utah, Wyoming, Nebraska, Missouri, Tennessee, and Carolina; arriving at Fort Bragg on October 30. The next day I was reassigned to the AAF Redistribution Center, Greensboro, NC, given 45 days recuperation leave, and boarded a bus up the mountains to Virginia, where I was met by Joyce and her mother at Highway 52 crossroads the next day in time for Halloween.

After I held our daughter, Carol Dean, examining her from head to toe, Joyce and I had some catching up, and planning for the future. Later, I learned that some of my crew beat me to the United States, since they were part of a three-ship flight of B29's using the polar route to Washington, DC. I sent my pinks and greens to the cleaners, and November and early December were spent in visiting with friends and relatives throughout Virginia. As time arrived to return to Greensboro, NC, I took the DeSoto, signed in on December 1 7 and took another 10-day leave for Christmas. This Christmas was special for Joyce and me. I gave Joyce a four-place setting of Towle Candlelight Silver flatware. Her parents gave us some Fostoria Crystal, from which we drank champagne for her 24th birthday.

Mel Cash

Editorial Comment

Mel Cash has written such a great, all-inclusive story. We're so very fortunate to have him share a part of his military life with us. His attention to detail and the manner in which he has presented it is modestly stated – more than commendable. Thanks again, Mel.

An Enola Gay Brief

Those of us on Tinian could sense something strange about the 509 crews and aircraft as they began arriving. The aircraft had a mixture of tail symbols including the arrow. Strange to have a B-29 Group with C-54 transport planes and its own, Security Polices Squadron. Also, I had to give up my hardstand and the adjoining one. As I passed it one day there was a canvas fence surrounding the hardstands with Security Police posted at 10-foot intervals. Also, at the end of July we noticed another unusual operation of placing Dump Trucks loaded with coral on the runway after we deployed mission aircraft for the night.

On Tinian, Tibbets continued the training of his crews, flying in three ship cells and dropping the 'Pumpkin' shapes. He told of an experience he had with General Davies after he was called to 313th Wing Headquarters after one of these missions. It seems The General assumed he could enter the hard stand, since the 509th was under his command. But the Security Policeman loaded the chamber and told the general he would have to shoot him if he proceeded. Tibbets fitted all the pieces of his story together, when he told of the Enola Gay Mission to Hiroshima on August 6th.

The "Enola Gay" carried an expanded crew. In addition to the regular crew there was an Electronic Countermeasure Officer, and Navy Captain Deak Parsons, who knew just about all there was to know about the workings of our bomb. One thing we had worked out; in case the aircraft blew up on takeoff and obliterate Tinian; was to arm it after airborne. Not to worry though, for the weather aircraft and those planes acting as observers and spare performed marvelously. As we climbed out to our initial altitude of 4500 feet, Deak Parsons entered the bomb bay to arm the bomb. By the time we reached Iwo Jima, the rendezvous point with Sweeney and Marquardt, we climbed to a new cruise altitude. After Iwo, we set course for the island of Shikoku, beyond which lay the city of Hiroshima - our target could be Kokura or Nagasaki depending on what the weather aircraft reported. Our orders were for a visual bomb run, as we slowly climbed to our bombing altitude of 30,700 feet.

The weather aircraft advised Hiroshima would be visual. The next thing to do was find the IP or initial point and proceed to the target. From a distance of 10 miles from the target, Ferebee suddenly said, ‘‘Okay, I've got the bridge." He pointed dead ahead, where it was just becoming visible. Van Kirk, looking over his shoulders, agreed. The T-shaped bridge was easy to spot even though there were many other bridges in this sprawling city, there was no other bridge that even slightly resembled it."

As we approached the Aiming point, I watched for the first signs of anti-aircraft fire or the approach of fighter planes. There was no ack-ack, which is usually ineffective at this altitude. As for interceptor aircraft, they were seldom sent up these days against planes that appeared to be flying only a reconnaissance mission. "We're on target," said the Bombardier as he flipped the toggle switch to activate the high-pitched radio tone. Exactly one minute after it began it ceased, and out tumbled "Little Boy." By my watch the time read 9:15 am in Hiroshima it was 8:15 am, as we made a 155 degree diving turn to the right, with a 60 degree angle of bank losing 1700 feet attitude in the process."

The flash came first, and as we were racing from the target we must have been 9 miles away when the shock wave arrived. It was violent and our B-29 trembled under the impact. As we viewed the awesome spectacle below, we were sobered by the knowledge that the world would never he the same. War, the scourge of the human race since time began, now held terrors beyond belief. And as we swung southward on the return flight to our base, the feeling of tenseness gave way to one of relief. Our mission, for which we had practiced diligently for so long, had been successful. All doubt about the mystery weapon had been removed. The frightful mushroom cloud that we left behind was still visible for an hour a half as we flew southward from Hiroshima. And when we landed on Tinian, I was not prepared for the reception committee that would meet us (practically all the ranking military brass that could be mustered in the Marianas at the time,").

Editorial Comment

Thanks Mel, for this "Enola Gay" short story. No book of this type would be complete without mentioning her.

The Uline C. Miller Story
An Accident In India
12/24/1944
58th Bomb Wing

Capt. Nicolas Van Wingerden's crew 58BW/444BG/676BS), consisting of Co-pilot 1/Lt. William C. Jennings, Navigator l/Lt. Wendell F. Geiwitz, Bombardier 1/Lt. Albert E. Woltz, Engineer M/Sgt. Uline C. Miller (my father), Radar Operator T/Sgt. Thomas J. Maxham, Radio Operator S/Sgt. Samuel E. Davis, CFC Gunner S/Sgt. Kenneth C. Carlson, Right Gunner S/Sgt. Rex T. Phelps, Left Gunner S/Sgt. Martin T. Warner, and Tail Gunner S/Sgt. Scott C. Baker, had come to the CBI in olive drab aircraft 42-6225, "Ding How," but had recently been assigned a new aircraft, silver 42-63458, which may have been named "Wing Ding." A week after the accident, an inquiry was conducted, and the dialogue with the three survivors, Aircraft Commander Van Wingerden, Flight Engineer Miller and Left Gunner Warner, is included in the accident report, as well as written statements by the crewmen and other involved parties.

THE STORY

It's about 5:05 in the morning (IST) of 24 December 1944 at APO215, India. Aircraft 458, under the command of Van Wingerden, readies for take-off to forward base A-3 in China with a load of 500-pound bombs. The aircraft is loaded with 6700 gallons of fuel, and the AC estimates the gross weight at 136,000 pounds. He likes this aircraft; it has just over 103 hours on it. In the control tower, Cpl. Louis F. Angelo gives taxi instructions. As they are taxiing, the AC calls the control tower for the last time to report that another ship is blocking their path but it is being towed out of the way. On the fire fighter line, Capt. Franklin C. David, Medical Corps, prepares to leave; it appears that this will be the last take-off this morning.

Flight Engineer Miller notices that the cylinder head temperatures are all between 180 and 190 degrees, so he closes the cowl flaps down to 12 degrees, enabling a take-off with head temperatures straight across at 200 degrees. At the near end of the N.E. runway, all checklists are completed. Take-off is made about 5:27, with the right landing light partially extended, the co-pilot watching the ground and the bombardier calling off airspeed. The engineer has closed down the cowl flaps to 4 1/2 degrees, and the cylinder head temperatures on the two high engines are not going over 235 and 240 degrees.

After using less than 6,000 feet of runway, the ship is airborne with an air speed of between 130 and 135 mph. The AC goes onto instruments and corrects a slow turn to the left. He observes the climb indicator is showing 500 feet per minute, and the airspeed has slowly increased to 150 mph. The flight engineer hears the landing gear going up. He checks his instruments; everything looks normal, and the rate of climb indicates 500 fpm. The left gunner reminds him to turn on the landing gear lights. In the control tower, Cpl. Angelo observes what appears to be a normal take-off; he can see the navigation lights of 458. From his position on the crash line, Capt. William F. Greene, Medical Corps, sees the plane rise and disappear from view.

After about half a minute, the co-pilot, Jennings, announces he is going to raise the lights. The AC notes an altimeter reading of 500 feet (240 actual) and calls for a reduction of the turbo boost setting to six. As the co-pilot starts to put his hand down to the controls, the crew experiences the sound and feeling of a bang or explosion as if blowing a blister. In the cockpit, the AC notices a flash of blue light reflected from the armor glass. Behind the co-pilot, FE Miller also notices the flash of light and starts to turn around to ask the pilot about it, but finds that he is still belted into his seat and cannot move, so he begins to make a check of his instruments: engine rpm is 2800 and manifold pressure is 50 inches, take-off settings. LG Warner calls to the right gunner without using the intercom, asking what the noise was. In the control tower, Cpl. Angelo sees a red flash come from aircraft 458.

Fearing he may have lost an engine, AC Van Wingerden wants to turn to the engineer but keeps his eyes on his instruments: the gyro compass is not turning, and airspeed is between 150 and 155. Before he can check the climb indicator, there is a shudder followed by crashing. Flight Engineer Miller is thrown back against the armor plate. Left Gunner Warner grabs onto a bundle of wires above him, holding on while the aircraft is bouncing. One of the engines has gone through a tree, and the aircraft comes to a stop amid clumps of brush and trees, with flames breaking out. From his position on the crash line, Capt. Greene hears a dull thud and sees red flames shooting up into the sky. He heads for base to get an ambulance. In the control tower, Cpl. Angelo notes that just one minute has elapsed since take-off, and notifies crash crew, fire station, base operations, group operations, base commander, AACS office and provost marshal.

Van Wingerden unfastens his safety belt and attempts to help the co-pilot, who appears to be unconscious and badly wedged in. Behind him, Miller tells him to get out quick, so the AC goes out through the nose, noting that the bombardier Woltz is not there. He has somehow gotten out of the ship. Miller tries once more to pull the co-pilot free, then goes through the opening in the nose after Van Wingerden. Meanwhile, LG Warner unfastens his parachute and tries to kick out the left blister, without success, so tries to go through the radar room, but is choked by smoke. As he backs up toward the right blister, he notices a hole in the ship forward of the right blister and dives out through it, head first.

The pilot and the engineer are only about 15 steps from the aircraft, which appears to be engulfed in flames. They see no one else trying to escape. On the other side, the left gunner is running away from the ship. There is then a loud blast, and Warner falls to the ground. Van Wingerden and Miller are knocked flat. Flames and burning debris shoot into the air. From his jeep, Capt. David sees the flash of the initial explosion and hears the concussion. He turns his jeep toward the crash site, and hears another bomb explode as he nears the jungle area.

About 150 feet from the plane, he finds the bombardier, Lt. Woltz, with a head injury and broken arm and leg. As Capt. David is administering to Woltz, another explosion occurs, sending a metal fragment across David's knee and leg. While David goes off to look for other survivors, Capt. Greene has arrived on the scene, and at 05:40, finds Van Wingerden and Miller about 200 yards from the wreckage. Shortly, the left gunner is found by other rescue personnel. These four survivors are sent to the hospital. The remaining seven men's bodies are identified. The bombardier, Lt. Woltz, succumbs from his injuries two days later.

EPILOGUE

The board of investigation, consisting of Col. William P. Brett, Lt. Col. Alvan N. Moore, Lt. Col. Winton R. Close, Capt. John Page, Capt. Edmund B. Sullivan, Capt. John L. Hardy and 1/Lt. Robert W. Libby, met on December 31 St. The board determined that power was reduced either inadvertently by the co-pilot or by malfunction of the turbo system due to an electrical failure, causing an unexpected loss in power. A later review of these findings by headquarters, dated 24 January and signed by Brig. Gen. Roger M. Ramey, disagreed, stating that pilot technique was a contributory cause of the accident. It was noted that aircraft landing lights should have been left on longer, up to a full 500 feet of altitude. It was also noted that the pilot, probably inadvertently, reduced power at a dangerously low I.A.S. (150-155 mph), while stall speed of the B-29 is about 128 mph. The review considered it doubtful that an electrical malfunction could have caused all turbo waste gates to open abruptly.

BOB SCHUMACHER'S MEMORY OF THE ACCIDENT

I wanted to share with you the recollections of a fellow flight engineer of my dad, Robert M. 'Bob' Schumacher, who witnessed the crash described in the original story. He emphasizes that "this is my personal opinion", but his explanation sounds very plausible in light of the fact that the engines were still running at full power when the ship hit the ground. I find it interesting that the "official" report mentions nothing of what Bob remembers.

"I don't personally think the turbo waste gates had anything to do with the accident. Those gates controlled the amount of engine exhaust that was diverted to the turbo superchargers on each engine. They were controlled by electronics made by Minneapolis Honeywell and each engine had it's own control system."

"Any airplane tends to rise a little as it approaches flying speed and often it will settle back a little and rise again as the lift increases. The B-29 had safety micro-switches to keep the landing gear from retracting while the struts were fully compressed while on the ground. Once the struts were fully extended, the circuits were completed so that the gear could be retracted."

"Having been born and raised on a farm, I had a habit of getting up early. I used to like to go down to the base and crawl up into the radio operator's position and listen to BBC and/or Tokyo Rose. The morning of the accident was pleasantly cool (for India anyway) and very bright as I remember it."

"On takeoff that morning all seemed normal but as the plane reached takeoff speed, the gear started to retract. The question arises as to whether there was a problem with the switch circuit (an electrical malfunction) or was the "gear up" switch in the "up" position while the plane was still speeding down the runway (a serious error by the co-pilot)? The plane settled back until the propellers hit the runway and all hell broke loose."

"The co-pilot was responsible for raising and lowering the Landing Gear and Flaps on orders of the A/C. The big question circulating thru the squadron was whether or not the switch might have been placed in the gear-up position during the takeoff run with the idea in mind that when the struts extended, the gear would retract and thus speed up the process and aid in keeping the engine temperatures down."

Mark R. Miller, son of Uline C. Miller, flight engineer, 58W/444G/676S provided the foregoing. This account was derived entirely from an accident report obtained from "accident reports" of Millville, New Jersey.

Editorial Comment

This is one unique story. Uline has stated it so eloquently one can literally ascertain what is happening, as though he were there. The epilogue contributes an insightful commentary on how a crash investigation functions. Bob Schumacher's recollections present more intriguing information. Thank you Mark for submitting your father's story.

The Wallace Van Eaton Story

1st Lt. 498th Bombardment Group
875th Bombardment Squadron

My story begins as a lad living on a farm in Northern Saskatchewan, Canada. On the wall of my parents bedroom was pinned a picture of "The Spirit of St. Louis", the plane that Colonel Lindberg flew, in his historic flight, across the Atlantic Ocean. I remember looking through magazines at the newest airplanes and thinking that someday I would have a plane like this or that, never dreaming of the metamorphosis the airplane industry would go through in the years to come, nor did I dream of the changes that came into my life.

I would become a World War II B-29 pilot, bombing the Japanese homeland. Japan was a far distant land whose people were fighting the Chinese in Manchuria. This was so far away I didn't realize that some day I would be bombing this land from a plane that hadn't been dreamed of yet.

It was through the effort of my oldest sister that I was able to go to a High School and College in the United States. It was during my second year of College that I enlisted in the Air Force. Each step was a challenge and an adventure; Preflight, Primary and Basic training in the San Fernando Valley of California, Advanced training in Texas, B-17 in New Mexico. The greatest challenge of all was when I was assigned as a copilot on the then monster of the skies, the B-29 Superfortress.

We were then assigned to the 20th air force as a replacement crew on Saipan, under General Curtis LeMay. Saipan, a tropical island, had seen many changes since the Marines had secured it from the Japanese, but there were rumors, which proved to be true, there were many Japanese Soldiers still being found on the northern part of the island. There was no question as to who the old timers were. They were heavily tanned and the replacements were, for the most part, obviously descendents of the white race.

We soon fell into the routine of things, chalking up missions and becoming the old hand, as the original crews put in their tour of duty and left for the States. Under General Curtis Le-May we were sparing nothing — droning our way with maximum effort strikes on targets of the Japanese Islands taking from 12 to 15 hours for the round trip.

One particular mission we were briefed that we were to have some Black Widow Night Fighters as cover for our night run over the target. We were to leave our 1FF (Identification Friend or Foe) on so the night fighters would know us as a friend. It was mostly a routine mission, except after the bombing run we were caught in a searchlight and no matter how we maneuvered we could not outmaneuver the searchlight.

The light was finally turned off without any ack-ack or fighter planes shooting at us. It was with a big sigh of relief that we turned our Superfortress toward our island refuge. We followed our regular procedure, so when we were about 20 miles off the coast of Japan we turned our running lights back on and settled down for the long trip home.

Then it happened. All at once, out of the darkness there was a plane flying in formation just outboard of number four engine. The pilot used his blinker to flash a message to us, not being very adept at Morse code I blinked back to let him know that we knew he was there. I asked the radio operator to come forward to see if he could understand his message. He was as unsuccessful as I had been to read his message. Finally the plane dropped out of formation, gunned the engine and was out of sight ahead of us in no time at all.

We talked of how nice it was to have one of the Black Widows flying formation with us and how thankful we were to have them over the target area with us.

The rest of the mission was uneventful until we were debriefed upon our return to Saipan. They always wanted to know everything that occurred on the mission that we had observed. We told of our experience with the Black Widow flying in formation with us for a while after we had left the Coast of Japan. We were stunned at the answer we heard, "Gentlemen the Black Widows did not fly the mission as planned." Since then I have often wondered what Japanese pilot missed a good chance to brag about shooting one of those American bombers out of the sky. However, even more often I have thanked God for His Mighty Protecting Hand.

Editorial Comment

This short story brings the P-61 (Black Widow) into play. Wallace has provided an interesting, provocative tale.

The Stanley Smith Story

It was April 28, 1945. We were called to a briefing and told, "you are going to Miyakonojo Airfield on Kyushu [Japan] and pothole the runways with general purpose bombs. The Kamikazes have been giving our sailors trouble on Okinawa. This will be formation bombing at 26,000 feet. Okay, now go get 'em!" was the last remark.

We were assigned T-Square 4. The day before we ran-in an engine on this plane, which we did by flying along the islands near Saipan (the Marianas chain) for a couple of hours. That evening a truck took us to the plane. I performed my ground check, and with a little help, pulled the props through.

We waited on the apron for our 11:55 p.m. takeoff, the plane in front seeming an apparition, its turbo exhaust a glowing ember. Max Wauchope, our commander, ran the engines up 2,800 rpm, I closed the cowl flaps. The plane vibrated wildly for a second, then we raced down the strip using all 8,500 feet plus some of the 200-foot drop off a cliff at the runway's end. We climbed to 5.000 feet with the engines at 2,400 rpm. We cruised at 5,000 feet for the next seven hours, using just enough power to stay "on the step." (To achieve the best miles per gallon I must know the weight of the plane and the power required to fly the plane straight and level, this is "flying on the step." The engines might be turning around 1,800 rpm.)

About 25 miles from the coast of Kyushu we climbed to 26,000 feet and found our formation. We were coming in from the north to exit in the south, so far no fighters in sight. Approaching the target, I saw 5 or 6 Japanese fighters 15,000 feet below us coming up fast. Moments later our bomb bay doors opened with a clunk and bombs away. Almost immediately the nearest gun turret erupted in a steady rattle of rage. I heard the bombardier say "the doors will not close!"

Then number three engine begins to vibrate and I called for Max to feather it. I saw fuel pouring from the wing behind engine two plus volumes of oil from it. I began transferring fuel to other tanks while watching for the temperature to rise on number two engine's oil. Now is the time to feather this one while we have a little oil left. I was shocked to see the plane to our right going down. The B-29 on the left passed under us and it too nosed down. I saw three bodies leave the plane.

The drag of the open bomb bay doors being significant. I increased power on our remaining engines to 2,400 rpm. With more than three hours demand on the engines, would they last? We had 500 miles to go to reach Iwo Jima in a long, gradual descent. We flew on, each emerged in our private thoughts. Some tried to manually close the bomb bay doors, others gathered flak vests to lighten the plane. On top of the pile went my knife and all was pitched out. Stocker, our navigator, calculated our rate of descent which turned out to be just perfect. There were sighs of relief when the wheels touched down on Iwo Jima, and probably a prayer or two. I will always be impressed by the expertise of every man of our crew.

My first sight upon stepping From the plane was a foot protruding from the tarmac. In the haste to make runways many things were overlooked. To my utter amazement. I caught sight of my knife sticking in a side blister---a chance in a million that could happen! I left it there. We were given a repaired B-29 and a blessing to return to Saipan only to face another day and another mission.

Editorial Comment

Stan's description of the takeoff is well done. That foot protruding from the tarmac and the knife embedded in the blister are revelations to grab anyone's attention

The Wayne Leroy Story

On 12/7/41 which was a Sunday, I, like most of my Boeing friends were enjoying the weekend. Monday morning after I got to work we were informed that starting immediately we would be on a 13 ½ hour work day, 7 days a week until further notice.

Boeing (Wichita) was assigned the task of designing the empennage section of the new secret XB-29. All the information that Seattle gave us was loads and flight data. We worked for 6 months before we were able to see a sketch of what the plane looked like. During the design stage many changes were made which meant redrawing to meet new specifications.

As soon as we could, the drawings were released to manufacturing and tooling departments. Needless to say manufacturing was in full force while we were still designing.

Eventually I transferred to Liaison Engineering with our offices located in the shop area. Our job was to take care of all problems that came up in manufacturing such as parts that didn't fit or couldn't be manufactured the way they were designed. Due to the type of work we were doing, we actually designed many parts right on the spot and had designed engineering incorporate on the drawings.

Boeing had lots of problems hiring workers for the shop. Most new hires were sent to company school classes to learn certain skills. Workers came in from surrounding states and soon learned how to build airplanes. Due to shortage of parts, including engines, a lot of work was performed outside on the ramps in sub freezing weather. Flight testing was accomplished using their runways. The engines created the most problems due to overheating which carried over into combat.

In December of 1943, 102 of my fellow engineers were informed that the company could not get us any more deferments and, that in 6 months we were subject to the draft. I immediately tried to get into cadets but was informed that there wasn't any need for more pilots. Prior to my leaving Boeing to enter the service a good friend of mine, General B. Harris, stationed at Boeing, called me to come to his office before I left for the service. When I went to his office he handed me a sealed envelope addressed to the induction officer at the induction center. When I arrived at Leavenworth K.S. the induction officer read the letter and immediately stamped Air Corps, B-29 training on my papers. I ended up as a CFC Gunner and flew out of Saipan for 17 missions. Our airplane was named Slick Dick.

Editorial Comment

Wayne had an enviable insight into the designing of the B-29. Further, how it was pressed into production while modifications were ongoing, again confirms its commitment to combat was premature. The fact he ended up flying 17 missions makes his war years unique and unusual.

The Edwin J. Seder Story

We had heard about B-29s and I was kind of hot to get one into the air. But I had trouble even enlisting because I was deaf in one ear, so when I went to sign up, the flight surgeon said "No way." And I said, "Well I'm not going to be a pilot or anything; I'm just going to sit there and look at the panel and gauges and adjust the throttle. It won't matter if I can't hear everything. Why don't you let me go and try to make it and if I get caught, they just won't let me get my wings."

So, he finally said, "Well, you're so eager, I hate to turn you down, so I'm going to sign the bottom of this thing saying that your hearing is normal. But I'm going to get in trouble if something happens and they find out your hearing is not normal." I assured him that chances were that nothing would happen. So he signed it and off I went to Denver.

Finally, graduation day came and they called me up and pinned my wings on and said O.K., you are now a flight engineer and your next assignment will be Walker, KS.

So I was put on a crew at Walker, KS and something unusual happened in that I was put on a crew with a West Point graduate as Captain. The co-pilot was just a kid, 19 or 20 years old, when he joined the crew. He was very disappointed to be assigned to a bomber crew because he wanted to be a pursuit pilot. On our base in Kansas, it happened that there was a trainer plane, maybe a Stearman biplane, and Bruce Craig, the co-pilot said "Ayed "…he was from Texas; "Ayed, let's go try that Steerman and wring it out!" So we got into this thing and he did rolls and spins and loops. I must admit that I got disoriented after that and didn't know where the horizon was. Pilots are trained to keep track of that and Bruce had no trouble with it. That was a lot of fun. He was the one who, when asked what he wanted to do after the war, said "I want to be like Ed Seder....28 years old!"

The Captain was very strict; we couldn't call the enlisted men on our crew by their first names and the enlisted men had to call us officers by our titles and last names. On the other crews they were mostly much more casual. This was on the ground and in the air and he was very strict about how we boarded the plane and everything else. So I kind of figured I'd get washed out because of my one bad ear before long, but we went ahead.

I finally went to my captain and said I had something I had to talk over with him and I told him the story. The next day he said he had decided I should stay on the crew and that as far as he was concerned my hearing was adequate for the job I was assigned to do.

So then we were all shipped off to Saipan and we started flying our missions. They were very serious about this and said that if the loss rates continued, our chances of coming home were very, very slim. So, there were a few guys, maybe two or three in our group who were so scared that they were washed out. While we were on Saipan, waiting for our assignment, we decided to build an Officers' Club; there wasn't one there and we scrounged around and got some old boards. Our Executive officer was an architect so he designed a building....and we got it done.

One night I was down there playing bridge with our flight surgeon, Doc McLaughlin and a few other guys. So I said, "Hey Doc, I bet I could get sent home tomorrow if I chose." He said, "What do you mean?" and I said what if I told you I'm deaf in one ear?" He said, "Oh, I knew that. Sullivan came to me back in Kansas and told me he had a flight engineer who was deaf in one ear, and he asked me what he should do. I told him if had someone who was stupid enough that he wanted to fly, you should hang on to him."

I think there were about a dozen ground crew assigned to our plane. An armor officer that inspected the bombs and bomb bay, an electronics man for the radar and radios. The engines had to be checked, and a lot of other things, so there was a whole crew for each plane. That crew stayed with that plane all the time we were there. Our plane insignia, on the tail vertical stabilizer, was "Z square 7" and the Nose Art was "Hells Belle." Some of the guys, in their spare time, liked to decorate the nose of the plane with pin- up art. Most of it was pretty good.

The master sergeant on our crew, the chief gunner, was a pilot. His name was Lisle Neher. He had been a pilot as a civilian. As a young fellow he had learned to fly and taught others to fly. So when the war started he enlisted in the Air Corps and was sent to flight school. He was a very self-confident guy. He'd go around saying, "You know, I'm already a pilot and I've been an instructor." Well, he got some instructor mad, I guess, and they washed him out. So then they sent him to gunner school and he was assigned to our crew as chief gunner.

In order to get to the front of the plane from his station, while we were flying, he had to crawl through this padded tunnel, actually through the bomb-bay area, up to the forward compartment. Once in a while, if the pilot or copilot was tired, he'd sit in one of the pilots' seats and take over. Lisle had no fear; the rest of us all confessed to being scared. Lisle wasn't. On maybe two occasions, when another crew had a gunner sick, and Lisle was available, he'd go on that mission as a volunteer gunner! He actually got nicked in the arm on one of those flights, and I think that made him eligible for a Purple Heart, the only one in our crew.

After he got out of the Air Corps, he started taking instrument training and soon became a pilot for United Airlines, and was for many years. We are still in touch with him and his wife. He was so self-confident, but not obnoxious about it. He had a very strong belief in himself.

Our tail gunner was the nicest guy, John Birchett. He became an MD, so he was successful, too.

Our captain, Richard Sullivan, was an all-right guy. He was career Army, a West Pointer. He got into some kind of trouble after the war, and sorta dropped out of sight.

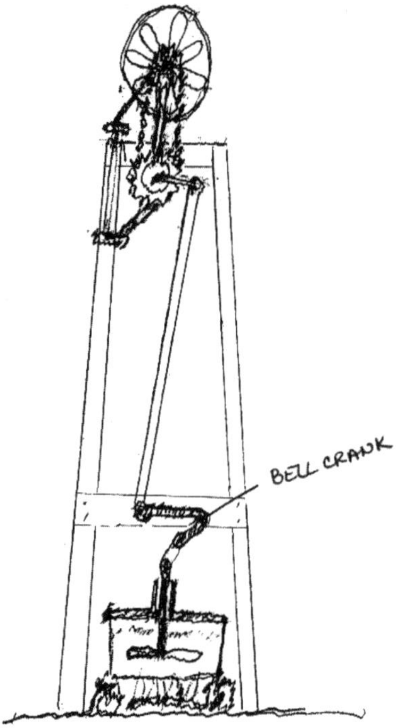

Editorial Comment

Ed is one of those people you like to call friend. He is reliable, dependable and the kind of man you want around you

The Tom Sanders Story

I have wanted to write the following experience for 50 years just never got around to it.

I was navigator on A/C Raymond Sealy's crew, arriving on Saipan, February 1945, and assigned to the 882nd Squadron of 500th Bomb Group.

We received our baptism of fire on our very first mission, a night bombing raid on Nagoya on March 24, 1945. All subsequent missions were anti-climactic.

We were a new crew without a regular co-pilot. Our Group Commander, Col. John Dougherty flew with us perhaps to "check us out."

When we arrived over Nagoya on March 24, 1945 and made the bomb run at 6,000 ft, flak was rattling off the fuseloge like hail.

The bomb release mechanism malfunctioned and the 31-500 bomb bombs didn't toggle. Wheeler, the bombardier, came roaring and cursing past my station to open the bomb bay door in search of the trouble – to no avail.

Col. Dougherty came brushing past me to the bomb bay to see if he could locate the trouble.

The second time around we did get rid of the bombs – just as a sudden jolt hit the plane.

Daugherty and Sealy were busy trying to keep control as we headed home.

Meanwhile, Mason, the radar navigator announced that his arm was bleeding from a flak hit.

When daylight came as we limped home, I looked out my window and saw a hole in the wing looking big enough to drive an automobile through. We later learned there were 100 + flak holes in the plane.

We arrived at Saipan over an hour late – with the Group wondering if they had lost their Commander.

Col. Dougherty landed the plane with the shattered left wing at a very steep elevation. When we hit the runway, we were straight and level.

On this critical mission, Col. Dougherty received the Silver Star, Sealy the DFC, and Mason the Purple Heart.

The rest of us were grateful to survive and live to fly 30 more missions – all milk runs compared to this initial introduction to combat.

Editorial Comment

Tom's baptism to fire came uncomfortably close to disaster. Having Col. Dougherty aboard was a fortunate assignment. Glad you made it, my friend.

The Jack C. Heffner Story
Tokyo Raiders
Cut in Half Over Tokyo

Marianas-- Hacked nearly in half by its own propeller, the Holy Joe, a Marianas-based B-29, nearly ditched in the middle of Tokyo Bay but managed to limp home and set a new record for the longest mission flown by Superforts before it literally fell apart after landing.

Nearly 100 Jap fighters hit the B-29 formation over an industrial suburb of Tokyo. "We were on the bomb run at the time," said Lt. James M. Pearson of Manchester, Tenn, pilot of the big plane. "Seven fighters came at us in a head-on coordinated attack one after the other. Three 20-mm. shells hit the right inboard engine. One of them hit the oil tank, dumping all the oil for that engine, which immediately began running away. Overheated, it burst into flames. We dove steeply at more than 400 miles an hour straight at Tokyo Bay, dropping from over 25,000 feet to less than 12,000 in an effort to put out the fire and spin off the prop.

"The fire went out but the prop was still spinning and wouldn't feather. The engine caught fire again. We dove another 4000 feet and that did it. The prop whirled off all right, spinning at terrific speed. It slashed back into the fuselage, ripping a hole 10 feet long and two feet wide. We'd saved ourselves from a very awkward ditch job right in Tokyo's front yard, but we were still in a rough spot."

Practically holding their breath so as not to jar or shake Holy Joe, the crew nursed the B-29 all the way back to the Marianas at reduced speed, sliding into the home field. Carefully, Lt. Pearson set her down like a crate of eggs. She shook, wobbled and finally cracked in half just as they slowed to a stop. Three crew members who were in the rear of the fuselage had to descend by sliding down a rope. But aside from a shaking up and a few scratches, no one was injured.

After landing, they glanced at their watches and found the mission had lasted 17 hours and 45 minutes. To their knowledge the longest mission flown by the Superforts since the B-29 attacks on Japan began.

S/Sgt. Jack L. Heffner received the Purple Heart and the entire crew received the Distinguished Flying Cross and a rest leave in Hawaii after this mission. S/Sgt. Heffner flew 25 more missions after this one. Heffner says 1st/Lt. Pearson was as "cool and steady as a rock."

Combat Diary Notes of S/Sgt. Jack L. Heffner
February 19, 1945 - Follow

Mission #10. Destination - aircraft plant in Tokyo.
Pilot - Lt. Pearson - Ship #1
My position - Radar operator
Mission Debriefing

Take off- 0647 Landed - 2335
Total time - 17 hours, 45 minutes!
Bombing - some radar, some visual, on primary target and also docks of Tokyo.
Altitude 26,000 feet.
Flak moderate and heavy, accurate. Thompson in #2 got one in the right wing large enough to put two barrels through. Got back OK, no one hurt.
Fighter opposition - moderate, heavy on our element, and very aggressive.
Strength - about 150 B-29's, including Tinian. I counted 87 in sight at one time.
Losses - Three over target, one ditched. Two of the three from our group, one from our squadron. Both in our four plane element. Bombing results unobserved. Our bombardier, Skinner, got an Irving, ring gunner Doan, a probable.

Longest and toughest mission for me as yet. We were lead ship of the extreme right element, low element, with Lt. Samuelson on our right (Evans, Radar) and Lt. Rouse (Johnston, Radar) as tail end Charlie, Calhoun on left wing. Picked up a few attacks after I.P., being the first formation in. Right after bombs away, an Irving came in from the front and high, the ring gunner shooting at him. He went on back and crashed into Sammy on top, almost halfway back. We think it was a deliberate ramming. The plane broke in two and burst into flames immediately, the Irving going into smaller pieces with it. Six parachutes were seen to open from the 29, one was burning and collapsed. This happened directly over Tokyo at 26,000 feet. Evans was one of my closest buddies. He, Burkie, and I traveling together ever since Scott Field. He may have been one of the parachutists. He gave me his leatherjacket to send home in case something happened. I knew every man on the crew very well, and it sure is hurting.

Rouse then pulled into Sammy's position on our right wing, and soon after was seen spiraling down to Earth. No one knows what happened to him. Johnston was also one of my closest buddies since Scott Field. Taught me lots of songs. During all this, we were getting plenty of attacks and expecting anything. No. 3 engine was bad and it started throwing huge chunks of frozen oil. The prop then ran away and the engine started burning. Unable to feather it, we soon dropped back from the formation, losing altitude fast. Course took us out of the Mainland and Maj. Fitzgerald went into a dive to follow us down.

We all expected a ditching or a crash off the mainland, but the ship leveled off at 3000 feet and the fire was put out. However, not knowing how long we'd last, everyone prepared to ditch and started throwing all loose stuff into the sea. We proceeded in ditching position for some time, Fitzgerald alongside of us (Cookson, Radar) and No. 3 whining at a high pitch. Later, the prop flew off and tore a huge gash in the fuselage, in the fore bomb bay section, tearing a bomb bay door off. We were down to 150 mph indicated, and limped all the way back, expecting to ditch at any time, or the nose to drop off. We steered clear of high islands by our Radar and our ETA seemed far beyond our gas limitations. After nearly 18 hours of flying, we came in sight of our base around midnight, a few hours overdue, Fitzgerald still aiding us. Can't commend him enough. We were leery of our landing gears and the nature of our landing, made a beautiful approach and soft landing. We were just a short ways up the runway, still clipping it off, when something happened, due to lack of hydraulic pressure for brakes, I think.

We ran off the strip, smashed into a truck, hit a cleat truck, turning if over, tore through an embankment and smashed into a parked B-29 (Z9) on its hard stand. I was standing up in the Radar room, got thrown up into the CFC (Central Fire Control) compartment, not missing anything and nothing missing me. I got out with a banged up nose.

Two other gunners in back with me didn't get hurt either, nor the remainder of the crew in the front. Driver of the truck was seriously injured, cleat truck man killed instantly. I'll never know how the boys in the front got out, the nose was ripped off completely to the wings and twisted around, the fuselage battered on all directions, cowlings, landing gears and everything imaginable lying all over.

The tail was at least 20-25 ft. in the air, the tunnel twisted, making it impossible to get through. We had to wait for a rope to climb down. Z9 was knocked off its stand and into the embankment. It was also cut in two, the tail lying all over and the fuselage flattened. By the time we got out, they were washing the blood away with a hose and a huge crowd had gathered. Our crew was intact, the pilot slightly injured. We got out of the scene immediately and were taken to the dispensary for slight treatment, received a double shot, wonderful stimulant, ate a meal and a very tired and jittery crew called it a day. Three planes out of the four in our formation, or rather element, will never fly again, but one of the crews will be back another day, less exciting, I hope.

Longest mission recorded (17 hours, 45 minutes), 1500 miles with 2 engines out on same side.

February 20, 1945

Got our pictured taken in front of both of our sections of the plane now being salvaged. Lt. Pearson said we were put in for a rest. Took Lt. Samuelson's crew's belongings out of their quonset today. Four and a half crews gone out of twenty.

February 22, 1945

Got issued clothing that was lost on the last mission. Pearson said there's a good chance of going to rest in Hawaii. Lewis, my old co-pilot got his own crew today (Capt. Brown's).

McNamer's Crew
Take off - 0750
Over Target- 1345
Altitude - 30,0000
Flak - heaviest yet
Fighter opposition very heavy, between 50 and 100 fighters. Came in through our formation and threw lots of 20's. Unestimated number shot down. Target very clear.
Forty- minute running fight.
Strength - about 70 B-29's
Losses - I B-29 (881st lead ship with Col. King and Major Goldsworthy)
Returned to Base - 2230 (Overdue, no gas left, crash landing)
Total time - 14 hours - 45 minutes

Comments - right before hitting target we got a hit that lowered our landing gears, everybody thought we were going to bail out. About 50 fighters took turns on us as we dropped behind the formation. The last they saw of us (our formation), we were still over target with gears down. Major Goldsworthy's plane was then hit, and most of the fighters took after him. It went down with two engines blazing and was later reported as crashing in Tokyo and burning, no one getting out. We lost our squad leader and our Group Commander (Two cols. on ship- Bruggie and King). S/Sgt. Welles was Radar operator. We tried to salvo our bombs and couldn't. The landing gears came back up and the doors stayed open.

Fighters clung to us and sent 20's thru our tail, making huge holes and knocking out the tail guns. Another tore a huge hole in the side of the fuselage, back of the Radar compartment, and shot up a lot of control cables. One also nipped off part of the rudder. We finally got our bombs off, the gunners still blazing at fighters as we were far behind the formation. Mac, pouring on all the coal we had, pulled away from the fighters and we headed home. Due to many things, we were very low on the petrol and ditching in the Pacific was predicted. We prepared for it by throwing out everything that was loose, then sat back to sweat. By some miracle we landed a bearing on Saipan, radar being out, Engineer saying, "Not enough gas." We finally reached the runway, using the B-24 strip as the pilot expected a crash landing, due to our landing gears gone whacky. We did! Right in on the nose, the nose gears coming up through, and the doors still stuck.

Pictures were taken, and no one was badly hurt. Number 7 was dragged off the runway and as yet (1944), it's status is unknown. Practically everything gone on it, and the props look like pretzels. To the fast accumulating B-29 graveyard,

I guess. The 881st has now lost 4 out of 10. Mac was congratulated by our CO on his crash landing. He's tops for a pilot and we'll ride with him anywhere. (Maybe)

PS Those double shots hit the spot exceedingly well for some reason tonight.

Comment - Col. King and Maj. Goldsworthy survived and spent the duration of the war as prisoners of war in Tokyo.

"A lot of things happen in the cockpit that are unknown to the rest of the crew in the back compartment. We had quite a discussion about staying at 12,000 feet until the engines quit then make a dead stick landing in the water if that was the case. As you know now we kept flying even after the engineer said we were flying on vapor and landed with only the gear problem. "Mac" made a normal landing and lowered the nose wheel and it folded back under the belly.

Also about that mission, I remember an airplane (Japanese fighter) that looked like it was going to ram us but it exploded in front of our left engines and ½ went over the wing and ½ under it.

Editorial Comment

Here is another excellent presentation. Please note most of the writings up to the start of Jack's diary are quotes from the pilot (A/C) Captain (Lt.) Pearson. Jack then describes the mission in "notes" from his diary. The two perspectives make an interesting contrast.

His mission of February 22, '45, with A/C Hugh McNamer has a special connotation since it describes the loss of Col. (Major) Goldsworthy and Cols. King and Bruggie. "Mac" has a short burst on this sortie too. Nice comparison again. Thanks to son Heffner for these stories.

The Walter Williams Story

One of the rare privileges of my long life was the opportunity given me to serve in the 875th Bomb Squadron of the 498th Bomb Group, under the Command of Lt. Col. John Harris Griffith. This privilege included interaction with dedicated and extremely motivated men who flew 16 hour flights to and from the main Islands of Japan, totally over the Pacific with no place to ditch except the ocean (before Iwo Jima was secured) and the completely committed maintenance support personnel. I have felt they (we) never got the recognition they (we) earned. We seem to have attached our nation to the glamour of D-Day and the remarkable invasion force. Certainly the 8th Air Force unit earned deserved plaudits (my college roommate flew a B-24)

I have 2 graduate degrees and taught management and managed 4 separate activities/organizations but never learned to manage (command) with the skill of Lt. Col. Griffith. That he was killed, has deprived America of a great leader. He was totally mission focused – totally which, unlike many lesser men, permitted him to make decisions out of the box because he understood human needs and knew that, fulfilled, their concentration in the air worked better. I could write pages about Lt. Col. Griffith who became my roll model throughout my life. Unfortunately I never noticed his human relations skill. Enough.

Two items might be of value. The first, in one of the early air raids one of our officers got hit in the butt and earned his purple heart by the seat of his pants. I think it was reported but my memory is fragile.

The occasion I remember above all was what transpired when the aircraft was reported shot down with no parachutes seen. That aircraft contained one of the Selby twins. The Selby boys were identical twins. I was the Squadron Sergeant Major at that time and never could tell them apart except that one had a blue stone in his class ring, the other had a red stone.

I was directed to call the remaining twin and follow Air Corps policy, offer him the opportunity to either continue combat flying or return to the U.S.

He chose the U.S and added "not for the reason I suspect you think." My brother is alive. I know it. We are identical. One's thought becomes the other's. We dated the same type girls. We were one. (I didn't put in quotes because I can't remember exactly how he said it.) He then went on to say he would not be the cause (he was a radar-gunner) of bombing an area that might contain a POW camp with his brother in it. End of story? Not quite.

When I rotated home in October 1945, I came through Sacramento. We were supposed to get a sleeper to my separation center in N.J. None were available so they put us in our old day coach with woven reed seats (very uncomfortable). To make the coast to coast trip endurable they stopped at every main city for several hours to let us eat in a restaurant and get drunk. We'd sleep it off between stops, then repeat. We ultimately stopped in Omaha which, I recalled was the Selby home.

We went to the restaurant in the Blackstone Hotel (?) had a few scotches and a great steak. I decided to call the remaining Selby lad and invite him to join us. Which Selby was the one presumed dead I now cannot remember – Let's say it was Norman. I called the Selby residence expecting to have Ed answer. Following the "Hello" I said "Ed this is Walt Williams." The voice at the other end said "This isn't Ed, I'm Norm." I was speechless. When I recovered I told him where we were and he said they'd be right down. Soon the two twins appeared and, in my mind I was witnessing a miracle.

I believe the two Selbys are alive and in the automobile business in California.

I've not interested in any personal high profiling but am most thankful to you for telling the story. Give credit to the brave flight crews and the mechanics who kept the big birds in the air.

Editorial Comment

Walter's story has a certain intrigue about it. I'm confident many of you will find the physic connection of the Selby twins unique.

The John Tillery Story

I was drafted in the army and three days later transferred to the Air Corps. I had friends who tried to go to the Air Corps but could not, and I was drafted in the army and sent to the Air Corps, one of the many things I wondered about.

During basic training I learned to keep my mouth shut and do whatever you were told.

I learned another valuable lesson at Clovis, we had just received our wings. None of us could sew but we wanted to get them on. One man in our outfit accused another man of stealing his shirt. He noticed it by the stitch it was sewn on with. At a formation when all men were present, the Captain called the man out and in front of all of us. The Captain told him not to feel too badly because every one of us would steal, if the price was right. His price was a shirt with wings on it. This lesson stuck with me forever.

While at Clovis, my wife and son came down we rented a 16 ft. camping trailer across the road from the runway. The planes came over the trailer and shook everything. One landed in our backyard. I got to know the farmer that owned the property. I worked for him on my days off. I repaired the fence the trucks tore down to get to the plane. I drove his tractor for 60¢ an hour. Pretty good money at that time because I was a PFC. Would be a PFC until I finished all my training. We were told we would not get a raise or time off until we finished all the schools. We were also told we would be the first crew to fly and do the maintenance on the plane. This was changed when we finished the training. It took too long to train crews to do both. We were all split up and sent mostly to different bases in Kansas. The group I was sent to was ready to go overseas.

I left to go to Saipan from California. Spent 30 days on ship. I sat two weeks at Pearl Harbor waiting. No way to get off. Arrived on Saipan, and the first night Tokyo Rose played a song for us on the radio; Down in the Valley. They knew we were there.

First we slept in pup tents with a stranger. Before the plane arrived we did everything. Ate rations. Our officers did the same. After the plane arrived things changed. Officers became gentlemen. We built and did things for them. We moved into 6 man tents with 10 men in each. We built barracks for the officers and flight crews. A short time before, my groups of electricians were in that group. At first most of us were mad and hurt, but as time went on we decided we were the lucky ones. Our pay was less but the future looked better for us. We could not think of any reason we were treated so different.

We fixed an old Jap truck. They had stripped all the wiring out. We used it to go to and from the line to work. When we went to lunch we were stopped at the field by the kitchen. We had to walk to the mess hall as we picked up trash. Most days we had to hurry because we had to get our spare shoes inspected or work on K.P.

When the war ended we had to get out of bed and carry our guns outside to let the officers smell them to see if we had shot them. We knew the smellers were the ones that shot their guns, but they were officers.

I pitched softball for the 883rd group and we beat most every body. When we got our book from the 500th group we found out the officers were the best team. Their pictures were in the book. We have many sore spots. If I was on a flight crew I would have to remember the men that repaired the plane and timed the engines so they could fly, even they were only enlisted men.

One time I was on the beach and saw the tip of a canvas shoe in the sand. Their shoes had a separate pocket for the big toe. I thought I would keep it. Pulled it up and it still had a foot and leg in it, so I returned it in a hurry.

We shot down one plane over our area and it crashed and burned some men. I shot at it because I had carried the rifle all the time.

I went in the army as a butcher and in 18 months, could walk up to a B-29 and fix anything electrical. Big change but the army was smart. When I came out I got my first job by showing the schools I had finished. So I gained.

Flew back on an old plane. Had trouble all the way. Two men got off before we got to Pearl Harbor to wait on a ship. Scared to fly on.

Editorial Comment

The second paragraph of John's story parallels some of my preflight training experiences. He had some bitter moments, but after discharge the training he received proved to be of great benefit to his future.

A Poem by Stan McClain (Lee)
Nipponese Round

As the thick grey dawn enveloped the land
We visioned the humor which would soon be at hand.
Our briefings completed, the co-pilot said,
"Check your 'chutes men, rough weather ahead."
Details in order without further adew
We prayed for the "Nightmare" to carry us through.
Of tenseness or fear there was never a sign
We were Nipponese-bound in that B-29.

As the wheels left the runway cold sweat veiled my brow
For our sixty ton weight was no joke to us now.
We climbed to twelve thousand and leveled in flight
And my brain painted pictures of the target in sight.
Our equipment strapped on, we seemed anchored in place
What with flak suits, helmets and knives on our waist.
The heavens poured rain and the sun wouldn't shine
We were Nipponese-bound in that B-29.

We saw the Great Wall of China cross the turbid Yangtze
And off in the distance the East China Sea.
We hovered a moment over ancient Shanghai
And tested our guns as the hours dragged by.
"Tell all hands," spoke the skipper to the flight-engineer
"For supper, we'll have plenty of steak and cold beer."
Away to the right loomed the target's design,
We were Nipponese-bound in the B-29.

A curtain of flak burst sharp on our tail
"Right rudder quick, Major," was the rear gunner's wail.
As a Zeke made a pass our fifties replied
"Good hunting, Tojo." "How useless you've died!"
"Steady, steady on course," was the Bombardier's will
Our breath came in gasps as we dived for the kill.
A satisfied feeling will always be mine
When we salvoed our bombs from that B-29.

The Matthew Darrian Story

There were others on Saipan who had an impact on the war over the Empire of Japan – namely the ground crew! It would have been impossible for the B-29 crews to complete their missions without them. I feel it is necessary to reveal one of many heroic efforts that took place, while our crews were flying over Japan.

On or about midnight, November 12, 1944 – a B-29 was being topped off and being refueled – with the flood-lights on! My husband and some buddies were returning from their duties – to their Bivouac area – over on a distant hardstand (under the flood lights), Matt saw the B-29 being refueled – without regard to his own safety – he ran across several hardstands to warn the crew of an air-raid alert, and to turn off the flood-lights! He reached the tip of the wing, and heard a man say "tomorrow we'll…" – and then the explosion of the plane and surrounding area.

Matt could not remember what happened until he found himself in the dispensary tent, being treated, by a squadron clerk for his wounds, and told to wait for the doctors to return. Because he had experienced a concussion and was confused and dazed – he somehow found his way back to his tent and collapsed on his cot and was never treated by the doctors. He tried to carry on with his duties, until Isely Field, was again thoroughly strafed (fired on by Japanese fighters), and he was unable to control his actions and evacuated to Hawaii.

Unfortunately, Matt's efforts was one of many that took place on Saipan, that was never recorded.

Editorial Comment

This is another example of a ground crewman's heroic deed. Mrs. Darian was good enough to send it to me and I feel privileged to make it a part of this book.

The Bill Andreason Poems

Ode to a Bombardier

To men who have sat in Plexiglas
And watched the clouds go whisking past
To see the fighters turn and dive
Their wings ablaze with the guns alive
And just as suddenly the sky is clear
Until the puffs of black appear
The target's near, your on the run
And now your work has just begun
The puffs are here, the puffs are there
But you are truly unaware
Your eyes and crosshairs fixed as one
With bombs away your job is done.
So man the guns and head for home
The day is done, the battle won.
At the club we stand with glasses raised
To empty chairs our eyes due gaze
Another day has made its run
Another mission is really done
The magic number is near at last
If only our luck can last and last

Ode to a Navigator

To those who have raced across the starless night
To rendezvous with a pencil dot, on a table top
To have sat alone while others slept
And had their bodies washed with sweat
To see the dawn in morning's glare
And see ahead the target's lair
To have muscles relax in silent prayer
As if to say thank God we are there
Then to sit and wait and wait
While you enter through hell's gate

While smoke and steel go round and round
Until the targets truly found
Then pencil up and homeward bound
To watch the clock hands go round and round
And then at the witching hour
You see ahead the airport tower.

Editorial Comment

Bill passed away suddenly August 27, 2004. His wife Alice was kind enough to submit these beautifully written poems in memory of his passing. Thank you sincerely, Alice.

Andy was a 1st Lt. Bombardier, serving with the 468 Bomb Group, 58th Bomb Wing.

He saw action and was decorated in both the China, Burma, India, and Marianas theatres.

The Hugh McNamer Story

Direct quotations from my small and erratic diary will give a good picture of the next few days on Saipan.

November 26, 1944 - Saipan-Things here are set up better than I expected. We live in Quonset huts (no mosquitoes). Boys just got back from Tokyo raid.

Nov. 27, 1944 - Saipan - Air raid last night - I slept through it. 4 or 5 Zekes came over today strafed the field - destroyed 3 B-29's on ground - ack-ack got one that I saw -reported getting 5 - this one bastard blew up not far from huts.

Nov. 28, 1944 - Saipan - Everyone building sand bag shelters today - The boys went over Tokyo again - Erwin ditched - they haven't found him yet, We didn't get to go.

Nov. 29, 1944 - Saipan - Searched for Erwin for 7 hrs. today - no luck - that's a dam big ocean - sure hope they locate them before long - was glad to get the crew in the air.

Nov. 30, 1944- Saipan - Briefed for a Tokyo mission - will probably go day after tomorrow - give us a chance to get ship in shape.

Dec. 1, 1944 - Saipan - Mission postponed 24 hrs.

Dec. 2, 1944 - Saipan - Mission postponed 24 hrs.

Dec. 3, 1944 - Saipan - Sunday - off at 0750- everything ok up to within sight of Fuji (Japanese volcanic mountain, a well known landmark) but formation too loose. Bill (copilot) flying- me eating when we sight Fuji - hurry to get into our flak suits (metal lined vests used for protection from anti-aircraft fire, etc,) - way out of formation. Early tactical theory had it that if you flew a very loose formation on the way to the target you would save gas. This was later dropped and we flew a fairly tight formation all the way.

When you went through clouds you sometimes couldn't see the other plane - but kept your position by the feel of his slipstream on your wing. Pull takeoff power for 30 min. trying to get in formation - going too fast - cut inside of Fuji to catch them - #28 (Gerwick) also out of formation - Bursts of flak just south of Fuji - #28 cuts underneath us directly for target - catch formation halfway from Fuji to target simultaneously fighters hit us - diving through formation out of sun - everybody on interphone at once - see Lumans (#2 man) bombs drop and Bill pushes toggle switch - Bob (Bombardier) busy shooting - no bombs drop. Bob hits salvo - no bombs drop- Sandy (Tail Gunner) starts yelling, "tails out! - tails out! - landing gear starts down - I yell to Bill - he flicks up switch and pulls out fuze.

See lead ship with Col King & Goldy (Major Goldsworthy - pilot of lead airplane) feather #4 - then unfeather and feather #3 - smoke or vapor streaming from both their engines - fighter activity eases up and we head out to sea. Check up and find only one bomb dropped - tail turret out - trim tab cables gone - C-1(automatic pilot) partially out - gear nacelle doors down- nobody hurt. Bob wants to see if bombs will drop in sea - I ask him, Weaver (navigator) and Heffner (radar operator) to figure out course and target on Bonins (some islands off the Japanese coast). We take up course to Bonins - check on fuel and decide we can't afford it. Bombs will drop on bombsight so we drop them in the drink - take up course for home. Seaver isn't sure of position or groundspeed. We continue on assumed course - radar apparently working but not picking up any islands -one engine stuck at 2,300 rpm - which uses a lot of gas - nacelle doors are giving drag - best known ETA (estimated time of arrival) and amount of gas are about same - good possibility of ditching.

Corlew (radio operator) gets a QDM (I forget the exact

meaning of the initials - but it indicated that we were on a correct course for Saipan) and one hour later another. Seavers star shoots (sextant observations) at first aren[1]t lining up - finally begin to fall pretty close. Begin picking up Saipan on command radio (this is a communications and navigating radio system aced by commercial and civilian aircraft) but very faint - radio compass not reliable - set 21:30 (24 hour clock - used in military -9:30 PM civilian time), if no indication of improvement in situation, will get set to ditch. Have Bill keep #3 at 1,600 rpm with feathering button - keep 6,500' alt. At 21:30 have crew throw all loose equipment in bomb bay - set 22:00 as distress message time - about 21:40 Saipan signal gets noticeably louder - radio compass improving - Seaver estimated 22:10 on basis of star fixes - Bond (flight engineer) estimates no gas at 21:50 (looks like we've got about 20 minutes that we don't know what to do with) - but gauges show more -gauges usually not reliable at low readings.

At about 21:50 see lights ahead and drop altitude rapidly - its Saipan - come over field - call tower - throw gear down - all gear appears to be down but no green light on left main or nose wheel (a green light on the instrument panel indicates that wheel is down and locked - a red light indicates the opposite). Suspected we would have trouble after they started down over the target. Called tower(control tower operator who directs traffic) and got clearance to land at lsley #2 (an adjacent airstrip used by the navy and for emergencies) estimated at most 15 minutes gas - told crew to prepare for crash landing.

Tried to land on one main gear first and ease down on the other (this is not as tricky as it sounds - the B-29, when lightly loaded (no bombs-no gas) handles about like a Piper Cub). Main gear held on landing, but nose gear gave way - messing up four props and lower turret but otherwise ok. Left equipment in ship and went to 52("Intelligence" dcbriefing - where they quiz you about what-all happened on that-there mission, and the Red Cross girl gives you coffee and cookies).

So that's what the diary says happened. In the usual landing the bombardier (Bob), whose flying position is up in the nose of the plane, sits back with the navigator (Weaver) and radar operator (Heffner) in the compartment behind the pilots. When we landed this time and the nose wheel failed the plane settled down on the underneath gun turret. This started to push up through the floor so the bombardier ran forward. Next the nose started to cave in so he had to run backward. Seemed like there was quite a bit of running back and forth there for a while.

When the plane came to a stop, since the nosewheel had collapsed, the tail was sticking high in the air. We wanted everybody out as soon as possible - in case of fire. Sandusky, the tail gunner, sprained his ankle when he jumped to the ground. This was the only casualty.

We thought that this was going to be a fairly exciting war if all the missions went like that one. We had named that airplane "Hells Belle". We got another after that. Its number was ZSquare7 and we named it "Sweet Chariot" (commin' for to carry me home).

We flew a couple more missions before the end of the year with no damage to us -although other planes were lost.

A few of those missions were fairly hairy. One incident sticks in my mind. We were over one of the main Japanese targets, I think it was the navel base at Osaka. Fighters were pretty thick. They seemed to be full of the Kamakazi spirit. One fighter plane was coming straight at us from dead ahead. You could see the red ball of fire made by his guns. And you could see the line of tracers from our guns toward him. There is no maneuvering in a bomber formation. You have to hold your place because the rest of the formation is close and any maneuvering would cause you to run into someone else. Just before this fighter plane was about to hit us he blew up. The engine passed under our wing and the fuselage with the pilot sailed over the top. Close but no cigar.

There was some shake up in the flight crews. Ray Taylor was sent to a job at Wing Hqs, and his crew was without a first pilot. I was in the hospital with a skin infection for a while and my old crew was broken up, and the men transferred to other crews as replacements. Bill Lewis, my co-pilot, got a crew of his own. After I got out of the hospital I was a sort of odd man around the squadron. I was assistant operations officer for a while. Then I was sent to Wing Hqs. as an instructor of incoming crews.

Finally, I was assigned to take over Ray Taylor's crew. This was a good bunch. We flew some missions and then were sent back to the States to a Lead Crew School. We were in California for about a month making practice (photographic) bombing runs on the coastal cities of Seattle, Portland, etc. Then we went back to Saipan and either led the squadron or were sent in ahead as what was called Pathfinders. We would circle the target sending radio signals for the others to home in on.

Ray Porter, who was the engineer on that crew, and who Pat and I visited at a reunion in Lexington, Ky., had some statistics on B-29 casualties. Ray said "The records show that some 3,300 men actually flew combat from our Wing. Of that number some 1,100 or 33% perished. When you consider the last missions were almost milk runs the casualty rate for original crews must have approached 50%. We can count ourselves as very fortunate to have survived." (slight understatement!)

In a letter to Porter's son when he was arranging a surprise 50th Wedding Anniversary party for his folks I made these comments: "The first mission with the new pilot must have made the crew wonder what kind of a joker they had drawn. We almost hit Kagman Point, a big rocky cliff slightly to the left of the take-off course. No real excuse - the pilot was a little rusty to be flying a heavily overloaded airplane that was performing just a notch below its peak."

As I recall that incident the plane was performing a little below par - in fact we knocked out a couple of the lights on the end of the runway. When we got into the air we were sort of staggering. The search lights cause reflections in the glass nose of the plane. You have to keep your eyes going back and forth from the instruments to outside. We wobbled off the end of the runway and apparently made a slight turn to the left - when we should have made a slight turn to the right.

The bombardier (Troop) started yelling at me about Kagman point. At the last minute I made a bank to the right. It seemed that the cliff was about 10 feet from our left wing tip and the water was about 10 feet from the right wingtip. However, the ship began to pick up airspeed and soon we were organized and on our way. I didn't say anything - just let the crew figure that's the way I always did it.

Porter was soft of a character. He wrote a poem about his flying adventures that I get a kick out of. The meter gets a little wobbly - but the spirit is great!

(The tune is "Casey Jones")

Come all you rounders if you want to hear,
A story about a Brave Flight Engineer,
Put him down in the Hall of Fame,
Because Ray Porter is his name.

He took off for Tokyo, his life was at stake.
He had to stretch the fuel or he'd land in the lake.

Now way over Tokyo at half past twelve,
The pilot gave a terrific yell;
"Listen Port, we've got to do more,
We've only got one engine and it's Number Four!"

Port pulled out his wrench, and he pulled out his pliers,
And climbed out on the wing that was on fire.
The engine sputtered, and it rumbled and it roared.
And then they had an engine 'sides Number Four

Then Lash gave Tokyo the thrill of the year,
When two engines conked and the flak burst near.
He pulled her over in a slow roll dive,
And killed two Japs with his 45!!

That's how Crew 112 and Port came back alive.

R.A. Porter 0-868658 October, 1945

I few six missions with the original crew and twenty six more with the second crew. We gathered some ribbons for our chests. I was awarded two DFCs and four Air Medals back to Saipan. We landed on Iwo Jima one time. We might have made it back - but it would have been close.

On one of the high altitude missions when we were flying a wing position we began to lose power in one engine and had a propeller control go haywire on another engine so that we had to feather it. About this time the formation went through a cloud layer that gave us quite a bit of wing icing. Between that and the loss of power we weren't able to hold our position in the formation. So we dropped down below the clouds and dropped our bombs on the target (Osaka Arsenal) by ourselves. Between the flak from below and our friends bombs from above we had a fairly lively time. But happily, everybody missed us.

After about June of 1945 our missions met pretty light opposition. I think the Japs had pretty well had it.

On August 9th my diary entry says the BIG NEWS is the atomic bomb. A few days later we went on another mission over Japan. We expected to be recalled as they were haggling over the terms of surrender and we were sent as convincers. We weren't recalled and dropped our bombs on the Osaka Arsenal. On August 15 the radio announced that the War Was Over!

We flew three or four PW missions after that. These were missions to drop supplies into the PW camps that the Japanese had scattered around in Korea and in the northern part of Japan. Supplies were packed into 55 gal drums and stowed in the bomb bay. When you located the camp you went over at low altitude and dropped the supplies. I think some of the prisoners had mixed feelings about this operation. When the barrels hit the ground they would bounce around in a crazy pattern - which kept the prisoners on their toes to keep from being hit.

On the way back from one of these PW missions we flew over Hiroshima and other cities in Japan. It seemed to me that the country was totally devastated. I don't see how the Japanese could have continued - A bomb or no A bomb.

One of these runs was to a camp in the northern part of Korea - not too far from Vladivostok. The Russians were supposed to be our Allies. If we were crippled over the targets on the Japanese mainland Vladivostok would have been the closest place for us to go. But we had orders to try to make it back to Iwo or to Saipan or else to ditch in the ocean. The Russians declared war on Japan just a few days before the Japanese surrender - big help.

On this particular PW run some Russian fighters came alongside and motioned us to land at Vladivostok. We paid no attention so they fired a few salvos across our nose.

We were fairly close to the steep cliff of the Korean coastline so we just tucked it in real close to the cliff and just above the water so that we had two sides covered. The B-29 has a lot of fire power and with it all aimed in one direction it would have been devastating. We sort of dared the Ruskies to come in. They thought the better of it and we went on our way.

Hugh McNamer

Editorial Comment

Because I enjoy saying it and I'm certain "Mac" enjoys hearing it, this B-29 flyer is the best pilot with whom I've ever flown. Not only that, but he possessed that indefinable quality – like fearless.

Also, he could fly that big bird like a pursuit ship. He actually flew, in tight formation, all the way to Japan in a thunderstorm. No one else did. He said in his story it was no big deal, but I can assure you it was. It was an unbelievable display of skill, courage, and determination.

The part of "Mac's" story I like best is the last paragraph where he outfoxes those damned Russians. Permit me to interrupt by advising you "Mac" had recommended me to become an airplane commander and thus I had my own crew. Therefore I missed seeing "Mac" effectively telling those intimidating "Ruskies" to "Go shove it where the sun doesn't shine." You gotta love this guy.

The Robert "Bob" Wirth Story

So, here goes with my personal "story."

I served as a Radio Operator. My position was up front, but behind the Pilots. Radio shared this space with our Navigator, Lt. Boyd Wilkins and the plane's upper forward machine gun turret. This compartment was nicely outfitted. My Collins transmitter/receiver was comfortably mounted on my desk where I also kept our Flight Log. Also, other radio gear such as the craft's "Command Set," a shorter range, voice controlled radio that the A/C used to communicate with other aircraft and the ground facilities when at closer range.

Also, we must not omit the "Trailing Wire" antenna, that could significantly increase the range of my ATC. Its ability to do this provided and additional means for ground facilities to aid in navigation, in the event other navigation devices were inoperable.

The Navigator's station on the left side of the cabin was nicely equipped with radar, LORAN, and easy access to the Astral Dome where the sextant could be mounted and used to establish our location by celestial means. The design of the "Nav-Rad" area was most efficient. There was yet one more feature – the Smoke Bomb Hatch, a very useful navigating feature that was mounted in the floor of the cabin. When flying over water and with poor visibility of the heavens, unknown direction and speed of the wind could have drastic effects on navigating. It was during such times that a Smoke Bomb was called upon. The tube through which the bomb was dropped, was approximately 4" in diameter and about four feet long. When the bomb hit the water, a dense, dark column of smoke arose from it. The pilots directed the plane over the smoke several times, recording headings and airspeeds. These data were diagnosed and entered on a new flight plan. It was then possible to find our way back to Saipan or Iwo Jima, which ever one was indicated by the conditions.

It was not very long before a new and novel use for the "Smoke Bomb Hatch" was thought up and put into use. When near and/or on the final bomb run, evasive action would not be used. Any effort to evade anti-aircraft "Flak" while in daylight would drastically reduce bombing accuracy. In a like manner, we could not evade "Flak" or searchlights when we were in darkness.

Some "Guardian Angel" in upper headquarters saw that we would be supplied with tapelike rolls of aluminum foil. This material (we called it "rope") was dropped into the smoke bomb hatch. Sometimes, a small amount might be blown back into the cabin by the slipstream, but most of it fell toward the earth. As it fell, it unwound and quite quickly came off of and separated from the roll and distracted the Japanese Radar. Soon, the Flak and/or searchlights could not define our flight path, at least enough as to allow us to follow our Norden Bomb Site. And so it went. When we became aware of searchlights and/or Flak, we used the Aluminum Tape. Our Skipper, Jack would order "more rope" and I would feed some rolls into the Hatch and then as quickly as I could, I'd ram them through the tube with a five foot long piece of 2"x2" that I appropriated for that purpose.

All went well for several missions. Even on daylight missions when there were no searchlights, we hoped the rope would jazz up their radar controlled anti-aircraft weapons. Then, one night it happened!

Our scheduled position for this mission was near the end of our many groups of involved aircraft. By the time we arrived over the target area, our enemy had our mission plans quite well understood. Our entire crew was busy, each member handling his responsibility with total care and expertise. Even I was busy shoving rope down the hatch, and then WE WERE HIT!

The entire inside of our cabin WAS ABLAZE!!!

We were more than somewhat stunned, and then all was OK again!!! What had happened? Well, largely due to my location, I was the first to know and to relieve those of my crew that were aware of the "Blaze," because they were located near our Nav-Rad compartment. (The relief that we felt was akin to that we might feel when our bombs fell and we were free to do evasive action; to speed up, to change altitude, etc, whatever our A/C Ewing felt was our best course of action.) So, what had happened??

Despite the improbability of it happening, the strong beam of light from a searchlight on the ground found its way straight up the 4" Dia. X 4'-0" long tube. Inasmuch as our plane was doing 340 MPH airspeed, I felt that what the beam from the ground had caused much high intensity reflections. The cabin was alive with very strong, reflected light from the aluminum tape until our forward movement broke the beam from the ground and brought understanding, courage and strength to us poor humans.

Coincidence?? Possibly … Though I'm able to write about it almost six decades later.

Editorial Comment

I've included Bob's story because it reveals such an unusual happening and the information it provides on the little known "rope." This concept was an innovation incorporated several months after the air war over Japan commenced.

The Horance G. Davis Jr. Story

Utah, Where are you?

Since this was a daytime raid, the aircraft were to be massed in formation for protection from fighter attack. Far off the coast of Japan, with a small atoll serving as a landmark, in radio silence, hundreds of B-29s circled while seeking to join with their squadrons. A starter for airplane commander Sid Fox was that the 200-odd planes of the 73rd Bomb Wing had tails painted with a large "Z." Other than that, to find the 881st Squadron, he only knew the rally altitude. The altitude made a difference, the major factor averting collisions as maybe a thousand craft total circled over the Pacific. From a distance, they appeared as hungry seagulls circling a fishing boat. In their midst, it was like ten balls fired at once in a pinball machine. The confusion was utter to an initiate like me.

Once organized and flying in formation, the landfall on the Osaka raid caught us unprepared. Over the target, oxygen masks were to be worn in the event that a shell penetrated the hull and caused depressurization. Crewmen were to don flak protection gear, consisting of metal helmets and vests with overlapping metal plates sewed in. For protection against flash fire, they had goggles and two pair of gloves, a flimsy pair to be worn under the other - the idea that all flesh would be protected.

But, by that time, the aircraft was over enemy territory. Pete, the muscle man prone to boasting of his sexual prowess, looked at me. He shrugged, reached over to grasp his flak vest and pulled it over his genitals.

About then is when I made my big mistake. In the distance, I saw the damnest sight ever, a sky blackened with curling, twisting shapes. The sight was devastating. Excitably, and regrettably, I pressed the intercom button.

"My God, look at the fighters."

Moments later, Pete Ashbaugh, took the intercom. "Those are not fighters," he replied.

So flak was the big hazard. The black bursts were all around but, unlike the movies, they were noiseless. Except one. The aircraft shook from a nearby explosion, and we were virtually sure we had sustained damage of one sort or another. But once back on Saipan, the crew chief examined a fractured dent on the wing near the fuselage and deflated our sense of heroism. The damage was an old one.

Oh, well, as a garden variety bombardier, I suspect the raid was a total washout. Sure, we got combat credit for bombing the arsenal at Osaka, and certainly the flak came from there. But my notes contend the cloud cover obscured the target so we proceeded to the secondary, Kuwana, which I cannot even find on a modern map. Bombing was by the inferior method of radar and the results were un-observed. To cap it off, this was a high-level (25,000 feet or more) daylight raid and, flying in formation, most bombardiers were like me -
- toggling out the bombs when the lead aircraft dumped its load. No aiming, no real skill involved unless you count throwing a switch to open the bomb-bay doors. This was common practice in Europe, where bombardiers suffered the indignity of being called "toggleliers."

In retrospect, our knowledge of strategy and tactics was severely limited - no doubt deliberately so. If captured, we could tell the enemy little. Even our knowledge of geography was deplorable. Osaka, for example was on the mainland Honshu. The next target, Matsuyama, was a port city on the island of Shikoku. But the on-board jobs were so specialized that I could care less and paid virtually no attention. The pilots got us in the air, the engineer nursed the gasoline consumption, the navigator set the course, the mickey used radar to make landfall and the initial point, the bombardier was acquainted enough with the immediate target area to zero in and release the bombs, the pilots swiftly turned away, and the same team that got us there also got us home. Simple.

Of course, there were differences mainly having to do with fuel. The B-29 had a peculiarity. For maximum fuel efficiency, the machine had to be put "on the step" -essentially, it flew with nose slightly down. This meant initially flying a couple of hundred feet higher than assigned, then dipping down before holding altitude. From that point on, the mission was largely controlled by the engineer, who set throttles by best fuel consumption not air speed. This worked fine during night missions when planes flew the 1,500 miles to target and returned individually. But when flying formation in daylight raids, the jockeying to keep in position did not permit such fuel-thrifty flying. The throttles were controlled by the pilot and economy be damned.

Thus inevitably, on daylight formation raids, the fuel supply teetered on the dangerous side. This was especially true of war-weary aircraft, like our Zebra Six, assigned to green crews like ours. Once as our aircraft made its final turn to land at Isley Field on Saipan, the gasoline drained from the tank in the high wing and the right engine died. On that occasion, the two fingers of booze customarily available at the infirmary after missions was especially welcome.

The B-29 was designed to do what heavy bombers did in Europe except better. The European mission of the B-17s and B-24s was to make precision demolition daylight raids at high altitude while flying in formation. The altitude was to thwart accurate groundfire, and the formation was to discourage fighter attacks. Night raids were largely left to the British.

The daylight raid strategy simply did not work with B-29s over Japan. The cloud cover was atrocious, and radar was too primitive to expose obscured targets. Further, high altitude bombing was frustrated by jet streams ranging from 100 to 200 miles per hour. Approaching upwind, the headwind exhausted fuel and exposed creeping aircraft to groundfire. When approaching crosswind, the sideways drift exceeded equipment design. Approaching downwind, the combined speed of almost 500 mph made bombing accuracy impossible.

So our unsuccessful daylight precision raid upon the Osaka arsenal was an embarrassing norm. Of my eight combat missions over Japan, only three were to be of that type.

The shift in strategy occurred on March 9, 1945, before I arrived in the Mariannas. It was inaugurated by the 20th Air Force commander, Gen. Curtis E. LeMay, and was truly revolutionary. The B-29s were to raid at night, individually and not in formation, at low altitude, and set Japan afire with incendiary bombs instead of high explosives.

Well, it worked. Obviously, entire cities enveloped in flames hammered at the enemy's morale. In addition, the Japanese war effort supposedly was supported by "shadow factories" in residential areas. Such buildings were comprised of something like 90 percent inflammatory material. A couple of pathfinder B-29s striking before dark could easily stitch a flaming cross across an urban area, making plain the target for the 200 aircraft already on the way. A piece of cake.

In the forward bay were 500-pound cluster bombs, 20 in number. These popular bombs-the E-46-were truly ingenious. Each cluster contained a large number one hundred or so-of smaller bombs made of magnesium thermite which burned with 2,300 degree heat. This substance would burn regardless of oxygen supply. Set one off in a bucket of water and it would burn a hole in the bucket.

But it was the delivery system which was so devilishly innovative. The tiny bombs were bound together by metal bands, just as barrel staves are held together by hoops. Within the 500-pounder was something like a rifle barrel equipped with a bullet. When fired, the bullet cut the metal bands and the 100 or so bomblets were released to go separate ways. Each had something called an "all ways fuse." As they fell, many hit together and created a cascade of molten metal. From a distance, the descending fire-spewing eggs from a 500-pounder took the shape of a lighted Christmas tree. And, of course, that's what we called them - the Christmas tree bomb.

Naturally, sharing an aircraft with explosives and inflammables was toying with fate. So each bomb of any type was equipped with a small propeller which was kept from turning by a wire insert. When the bomb was released, the wire stayed with the aircraft. As the bomb fell, the propeller made a hundred or so rotations and then fell off. Only then was the bomb finally armed.

So now the complexity of the cluster bomb is truly revealed. It is released, the propeller spins and drops off in the slipstream, a timer delays the rifle firing for 20 or so seconds until the cluster nears the target, the rifle slug cuts loose the bomblets, the bomblets strike against each other and spew flames, and the target is subjected to a cascade of fire which water will not extinguish.

The following couple of minutes were hairy because the aircraft had to be kept steady on course and altitude - a sitting target. Not until the intervalometer was silent and I announced "bomb bays closed" was the pilot free to break away from the target.

On our Matsuyama raid, we had distinguished visitors

aboard. One was the 881st squadron commander, Col. Jack Doughtery. The other was a major, a bombardier, who did not terribly impress me. He had gone through bombardier training "in grade" and actually graduated after I did. Doughtery rode in the co-pilot's seat, which left Co-Pilot Pete Ashbaugh and the major to squat on the flight deck as comfortably as they could. They were not belted down.

Before putting my head into the Norden, I could only stare at the monster looming over the gigantic bed of coals which was Matsuyama. We obviously were not the first fire-bombers to reach that afflicted city. Above the flames was an ominous black column extending upwards for thousands of feet and, indeed, dwarfing the aircraft. But it was just smoke, right? So why worry? I bore in, determined to do my duty. The bombs started clicking out of the ship before we hit. Then the aircraft went wild. The pilots frantically fought the thrashing controls. We soared up. We plunged down. Outside, nothing but blackness. Strange objects smeared the plexiglass. The spare bombardier and Pete Ashbaugh were crashing around loose-from deck to ceiling - and were there dangerous flying objects threatening vital switches and levers. Without a word, I hit the salvo switch to drop all bombs at once. To hell with the scientific bombing pattern.

"Salvo the damned bombs," cried out Col. Daugherty.

"Salvo the damned bombs," echoed the major, who was suspended in space.

"The damned bombs are salvoed," I shouted.

"The damned bombs are salvoed," repeated the major.

The bronco ride was the result of a fire storm. On the ground, the flames were consuming so much air and forcing it so violently upwards that they created hurricane-velocity winds in the target area, sucking even more combustibles into the maw. Entrapped humans, if not consumed by fire, died of asphyxiation. Twelve thousand feet up, we emerged safe and sound, none the worse except for soot and assorted singed debris which blocked the view until the 250 mph slipstream did its job.

But, odd as it may seem, I had not learned my lesson.

Our crew was to make three more fire raids. Two were notable for different reasons.

One was over Ichinomia on July 29. It began just like Matsuyama two days earlier.
We toted even the same bomb load. And I again stared at a 30,000-foot column of black smoke rooted in the bright red coals of a flaming city. I put my head in the Norden and bore in. We hit the thermal and the bucking ride was repeated. But we were veterans, and it was merely deja vu all over again. There were no panicky junketing passengers this trip. Nor were there fearsome cries about salvoing.

We emerged in the clear, and I reached for the switch to close the bomb-bay doors. My relief was rudely dissipated by radio operator William R. Hood, whose only outside view was through the bomb bay. "You've got bombs piled up in the forward bay," he said.

Hot damn! If they were piled up, certainly some of the wires had been jerked out of the propellers. After about a hundred spins, the bombs would be armed. Maybe 23 second later, the rifle would fire. A single 500-pounder would vomit a hundred fire-spewing magnesium bomblets. Our war-weary aircraft, good old Zebra Six, would go down like a comet.

As bombardier, this was my problem exclusively. It was nighttime. We were flying at 12,000 feet or higher and, without oxygen, there was danger of passing out.

But the options were zilch. I had to get into the bay quickly. I asked Pilot Sid Fox to depressurize, jerked off the heavy flak suit, and reluctantly abandoned my oxygen mask because breathing had suddenly become a second priority. I clambered back between the pilots and beyond engineer A. R. Ulander. Then, encumbered with survival gear, I stuck solid between the gun turret and Johnny Jones' navigation table, although he had hastily folded it up. Again, no option. I pounded the chest release, which instantly shed parachute and life raft attached to it. So I felt truly naked when I reached radioman Hood's position, opened the hatch, and peered through. The flames of Ichinomia illuminated four 500-pounders on the port side, three of them resting on the wampyjawed bottom one.

Simply put, at a critical moment within that thermal, the aircraft had plunged downward faster than the bombs.

There was a handhold or two somewhere in the bay, but only the flames illuminated the area, and the footing on the bay's edge was gear-laden and treacherous. I stepped out, virtually over open space, with the 250 mph slipstream whipping around the bay. I edged around to the side of the bombs and found, luckily, a flashlight tucked in my flight suit. Some propellers, I forget how many, were spinning. I stopped them by hand and, drawing on my training, gently unscrewed the fuses and tossed them out.

I felt impelled to unload those bombs on the enemy. I tried the standard technique of toggling out the bottom cluster by hand. But its steel shackle was twisted like a pretzel and would not give. Several times as I worked, radioman Hood shouted, conveying pilots' warnings about fighters and ordering me to douse the light. With Ichinomiya past, I worked in a bomb bay which was merely a dark hole with windy fingers which tugged at me. With the target area long past, I defused the remaining bombs but still could not free the obstructing cluster.

Getting rid of those 2,000 pounds of bombs was critical. Landing on Saipan with them was absolutely forbidden because damage to the runway could jeopardize the safe return of 200 other aircraft. If the bombs could not be shed, we would have to ditch in the water or bail out.

Hours later, in daylight as we flew over the Pacific, I reopened the bomb bay doors. Co-Pilot Pete Ashbaugh, he of the muscles and with fists which could penetrate walls in anger, volunteered to help. We went back without chutes or life rafts. Somehow, I mustered the strength to push the top cluster toward the middle of the ship and hold it there so it would not endanger Pete. With a hatchet, part of the plane's regular equipment, he attacked the steel lug holding the bottom bomb. Suddenly, my hands groped air. With surprising silence, all four clusters dropped down to the ocean deep. We were home free.

Before Nishinomiya, we had made another incendiary raid-one of the two most notable. The target was the chemical and textile manufacturing city of Toyama, population 128,000, on August 2. The bomb load was the usual 6,600 pounds of gas jell, 10,000 pounds of magnesium clusters. As we hit landfall, the number four engine conked out. The pilots were able to feather the propeller so it would not windmill. This was a lucky stroke, as the B-29 was prone to crash because of this precise problem.

The humorous point. Up front in the cockpit, we had a serious discussion about whether to dump the bombs just anywhere and head back to safety in Saipan. The decision was to be heroes and continue to target. We learned upon return to Saipan that, had we not bombed, we could have been subject to courts-martial.

All right, we decided on the spot to be heroes. Toyama was in flames already, the ominous column reaching for the heavens. I did not need instruction from the pilots of a crippled ship to avoid playing bucking bronco again. The bomb sight's horizontal hair I kept on target, ensuring the bombs would be released on time. But the vertical hair I virtually ignored, choosing to steer the aircraft just to the right of the thermal. That dark threat loomed a couple of hundred feet off the left wingtip. I can only ensure that the load fell in Toyama's vicinity.

We were among the 173 aircraft which struck Toyama that night. The raid burned out 99.5 percent of the city's roof area. It was deemed the most effective attack ever and certainly proof that war can be hell.

The B-29s were equipped with a "friend or foe" reactive radio signal to identify them as friends. This device, of course, would have aided the enemy so it was turned off during raids. But even with it, we were advised to steer clear of the notoriously trigger-happy crews on Navy ships.

The exceptions were submarines, deemed friendlies for good reason. They responded to "dumbos," unarmed B-29s loaded with enough fuel to circle constantly over our route to Japan. Dumbos were there to sometimes drop survival gear but, primarily, to circle downed crewmen and beam a radio signal to guide Navy subs to the rescue.

Even this was not ideal. En route to Japan on one mission, I spotted a one-man yellow life raft containing a fellow who had spread the yellow-green sea-dye. He looked awfully lonesome in an endless sea. But before bombing, we had to maintain radio silence. All I could do was ask navigator Johnny Jones to note the spot and, once we departed Japan hours later, have radioman Bill Hood alert rescuers by radio. So if the fellow was rescued at all, he had a hairy wait.

Of course, we would not have been troubling the Japanese at all if the Marianna Islands had not been wrested from the enemy. The important islands Saipan, Tinian and Guam cost 4,750 American lives. The Japanese had 46,000 killed and captured.

Of these three islands, seizing control of our volcanic-coral base of Saipan was the most bloody. The Marines, ultimately reinforced by the Army, invaded Saipan on June 15,1944. The American toll for that one operation was 6,500 dead and wounded. The Japanese dead included 28,000 military and, since Saipan had been under Japanese control since 1920, some 22,000 civilians also died. A great many, including women embracing their children, chose suicide by leaping off a cliff. With all that out of the way, and the passage of months to prepare facilities, the first B-29 to arrive in the Mariannas landed at Saipan on October 12.

But if survival is the game, Iwo Jima is the name. Even during my short combat career, I cheerfully acknowledge that the small atoll probably saved my hide twice.

No, the real value of Iwo was as a resting place for crippled and fuel-depleted B-29s. Before Iwo, incidents were heart-rending. In aircraft unable to make it back to base, crews had the choice of bailing out over water or crash-landing (called ditching) in the ocean. Ditching generally was favored because the B-29 was known as a good floater which provided time for the crewmen to stay together in larger life rafts. But as they wrestled with that dilemma, they were in radio contact with friends flying alongside who underwent the agony of being unable to help.

Being spared that ordeal because of Iwo, I am obligated to acknowledge unlimited tribute to those who paid the price of conquering the island. I can barely mention it without tearing up.

Our first emergency landing on Iwo followed the August 2 raid on Toyama when we bombed with three engines. As peculiar as it seems, an aircraft on three engines used more fuel than one with all four. So, low on fuel, we approached Iwo in search of a safe haven. I could hardly believe what I saw. There were, indeed, a great number of wounded birds.

On the radio, Iwo control was "Paradise" and allocated landing priority. The B-29 was a "Dreamboat." And the radio exchange was something out of Kafka. Transmissions were apt to contain drama such as this:

"Paradise, Paradise, this is Dreamboat Zebra-two-six. We're on two engines and request permission to land."

"Roger, Dreamboat Zebra-two-six, I have a priority with wounded and I'll get you soon."

A few minutes later: "Paradise, Paradise, this is Dreamboat Zebra-two-six. This is my fourth time around on two engines. Permission to land please."

"Roger, Dreamboat Zebra-two-six. You're on our list."
A few minutes later: "Paradise, Paradise, this is Zebra-two-six. We've cranked number three engine and have a fire."

"Roger, Dreamboat Zebra-two-six. You have a fire. Please advise when in position for final approach."

Our own landing on August 2 was not without drama. Pilot Sid Fox's final approach was too low. From my view in the nose, we were doomed to make impact on the bluff, below which was an abbreviated beach with rusted landing craft left over from the American invasion. That view remains branded on my retinas. Sid responded by thrusting throttles forward, and the idling engines went into a roar. Except there were three engines, not four. With the power thrust unbalanced, the aircraft tilted abruptly-one wing low.

We careened over the top of the bluff and toward the runway. Nearby was a high-nosed P-S 1 fighter which commonly taxied with a mechanic crouched on the wing to aid vision. The mechanic saw us in crash posture and rolled off the wing. Ahead, at the control tower, two men were on the ladder. They took a quick frightened look at the oncoming skewed, roaring silver giant; then one hastened up, the other hastened down.

From that impossible beginning, the aircraft touched down. We eleven cats in Zebra-six had used up one of our nine lives.

On our base at Saipan, aircraft were dispersed on widely separated paved "hard stands," the better to frustrate an air attack. On Iwo, there was not such room. Quite a sight were hundreds of the behemoths parked nose to tail as far as the eye could see. Getting them unstacked in sequence and back in the air must have taken considerable doing.

Our Zebra-six had a lot of miles on her and was truly war-weary. Her fuel consumption left a lot to be desired. So it is not surprising that Iwo saved our necks on another occasion-a daylight demolition raid on Yawata on August 8. The formation flying was too much for Zebra-six, and we put in at Iwo for fuel.

On Iwo, the radioman, William R. Hood had an experience he'll always remember. The right blister gunner, Coloradan James C. Thornton, described Hood as an eager-beaver aspiring to be a leader of men. Enroute to the tent in the darkness, he charged ahead of the escort. As Thornton put it:

"Suddenly we heard a loud 'Splash--gulp--help-help.' Hood couldn't swim but his frantic beating of water quickly brought help to him. I don't recall who the two were who pulled him out of his watery trap. I wasn't helpful, but I do recall vividly, he smelled terrible. Sgt. Hood had stumbled into an open, uncovered latrine. I joined in the short walk to the ocean and gave Sgt. Hood helpful tips on how to bathe in the nude, in the darkness of an Iwo Jima night."

In all, Superforts sought refuge on Iwo 2,400 times. Some memories of Paradise will be less favorable than others.

Christians are well acquainted with the persecuting Pharisee Saul of Tarsus who was transformed into the fervent evangelist Paul when encountering a heavenly light and the voice of the Lord on the road to Damascus. The event denotes enlightenment, renewal, fresh dedication.

An epiphany much like that is claimed by many. It hits the newspapers when celebrities claim a re-dedication, traceable to a family death or in the aftermath of an auto crash or after cancer therapy or after emerging from drug treatment or following a brush with the law. An amazing number of epiphanies are revealed in press conferences in front of the local hoosegow.

I had an epiphany on Saipan around the 11th of August, 1945.

As we returned from the predawn bombing of Nishinomiya on August 6, unknown to us another B-29 passed going the other way. It was the Enola Gay which had taken off from Tinian. Only hours later, she was to unload a nuclear bomb on Hiroshima, devastating four square miles and immediately killing 66,000.

Word quickly spread. Indeed, it had an impact in our barracks. We bunked with officers of a crew which regularly cruised Japan alone to photograph bomb damage, report on cloud cover and the jet stream, and strew propaganda leaflets. Their flights were unmolested, the Japanese having concluded that a single Superfort was harmless.

But not after August 6 and the Enola Gay. And certainly not

after the atom bombing on Nagasaki on August 9, leaving 39,000 dead. When that crew next overviewed the Empire, they were attacked by hordes of fighters and barely made it back intact. The crew's off-duty attitude shifted from placid to edgy.

We Superforts had already put the Japanese on the ropes. Certainly, Hiroshima and Nagasaki were the knockout blows. Peace was in the air.

But the stout lady had not yet exercised her vocal cords. Remember the arsenal at Osaka which escaped our effort in July? We were gathered together in the evening and briefed to put down that baby again. It would again be a precision high-altitude daylight job through all that flak.

So I went to bed that night knowing that an orderly would prowl through at 2 a.m., flashlight in hand, ensuring with a hand tap that I was awake, that I would collect a gallon of canned turkey and loaves of white bread for the six cockpit crewmen, plus a handful of amphetamines to keep them awake, that I would be hauled in the back of a truck to gather a weighty load of flight gear, that another truck would deposit me at the hard stand, and that I would be checking out equipment for an hour. I would be helping hand-turn the propellers to thwart vapor lock and, before dawn, be warning pilot Sid Fox when he'd better haul back on the steering column before running out of pavement.

When I awoke, the sun was shining. That was my epiphany.

God, what a beautiful morning. The light was brilliant, the air was exhilarating, the earth rose to meet my steps. Utterly delicious was the breakfast of Spam, powdered eggs, doughy bread and muddy coffee. The world was tremendously expanded. I was to live. There was a profession to choose, an education to acquire, a woman to find, children to sire, a society to reform, a fortune to be made.

Well, not right away. There was a small problem with the peace process. The Japanese had offered to surrender, sure enough. But there was a hitch, something about preserving the prerogative of the Emperor. That was not going over well with the war planners in Washington.

So sure enough, there was to be an Osaka raid. It was indeed strange. At briefing, we were told that if the war ended, we would be radioed the code word "Utah." Given the word, we were to salvo the bombs into the Pacific and return to base. So we departed and droned steadily toward battle and possible death as we awaited the magic word. The ultimate irony would be to go down in flames on the very eve of peace. As thoroughly as we hounded radioman Bill Hood, "Utah" was one word he never heard.

But it was eerie enough. Hood put on the intercom a broadcast from New York City; indeed, from Times Square. We heard joyful shouting, vigorous hollering, the tooting of horns, the blowing of whistles, the background rumble of a delighted mob. They were riotously celebrating. World War II was over.

It was? Why were we destined for the guns of Osaka?

Don't ask me to explain it, but I think it had something to do with time zones. The August 14 news report put it this way: "New York--At 7:03 p. m. Eastern War Time, 500,000 people jammed Manhattan's Times Square, watching as the word was flashed on the moving electric sign on the Times Tower: 'Official--Truman announces Japanese surrender.'"

Regardless, we indeed did a job on the Osaka arsenal on August 14, precisely the day that the end of the war was observed and during the celebration of peace in America. On that day, how many did we kill on the ground, what children were left orphans? How many B-29 crewmen failed to return to the Mariannas, shot out of the sky or drowned in the Pacific?

With our bomb bays empty, as we departed over Osaka bay, way below I saw what appeared to be a Superfort in a controlled spiral headed for the drink right off the shore of Japan. But it was being pursued by white foam, the wake of a speeding vessel, a surfaced submarine, presumably American, seeking to make a daring rescue virtually within the shadow of Japanese smokestacks. I silently lofted a prayer:

"Dear God, at this late hour, on this futile journey, help them make it."

When next I peered upward into the bomb bays of Zebra-six, I could scarcely believe my eyes. Instead of a bomb, each shackle contained two 100 gallon metal drums welded end to end. They were crammed with food and other supplies. Loosely piled atop were a jumble of parachutes, mattress covers stuffed with clothing, shoes and other soft goods. The bomb bays looked like a junkyard. And beneath the wings of Zebra-six was painted, in bold black, the letters "POW."

We were going on an errand of mercy.

It was the 29th of August, four days before the official signing of peace in Tokyo Bay. Our assignment was to drop supplies to prisoners of war. Our destination was Inchon, Korea, a 17-hour trip. Even for a B-29, that was quite a stretch. To get there, we refueled on Iwo Jima, my third and final stop on that battered real estate. As directed, we made rendezvous over Seoul with two other Superfortresses and skipped along low level to view the scenery. Accustomed as we were to being shot at, the eyeballing was a new experience.

The POW camp was easily spotted. It consisted of a cluster

of buildings in a compound surrounded by a wooden fence. The prisoners had managed to paint a gigantic "POW" on the roof of a building. Many stood within the compound waving shirts and towels or whatever.

The pilots had their instructions. They were to come in low - 300 to 500 feet. By cutting power and lowering flaps, they were to approach the dangerous stall speed. We bombardiers had our instructions also. We were to put a zero (straight down) angle in the bomb sight. As we peered through the optics, when the compound fence hit the crosshair, we were to toggle out the load. Parachutes were to gently lower the metal drums straight down.

It didn't work that way.
First, by radio, I consulted with the other bombardiers and agreed to make the initial dump. But playing it smart, the consensus was to toggle out one load at a time. No sense in putting all eggs in a single basket. Zebra-six made the approach, low and slow, maybe 150 mph. When the fence hit the crosshair, I toggled the forward bay. Immediately, tail gunner Lee Hoover hit the intercom button:

"All the parachutes ripped off."

Naturally, that meant my drums would overshoot the compound. I leaned forward to view the ground. I could not see the containers tumbling down. But I did observe a virtual sea of humanity-curious or greedy Koreans-crowded all around the compound. Apparently, they were freshly aware of the falling drums looming above. The crowd was parting like the Red Sea under Moses' hand. I've seen nothing like it before or since.

We bombardiers consulted again. Before they proceeded, I agreed to experiment with the load in my aft bay. This time, I treated the compound as I would a target on a low-level bombing raid. I put 30 degrees in the Norden and hit the toggle switch when the compound fence hit the crosshair.

Bingo! Tail gunner Lee Hoover reported the result. The 'chutes ripped off. The tumbling free-falling drums knocked gaping holes in the perimeter fence. Some barreled into buildings. We stayed around for the other B-29 drops, buzzed the compound together, then headed back to Saipan, satisfied that the POWs got a goodly share of grits and gravy.

But first, I had one other nasty job to do. The parachute releases had been secured in the Zebra-six bomb bay with long, sturdy static lines. Those lines, probably a dozen of them, now were streaming wildly in the slipstream and obstructing the bomb-bay doors. So, once again, feeling naked without a parachute, I was in the forward bay resisting the wind's compelling pressure while another crewman did the same in the aft. Hauling in the lines hand-over-hand without a tumble brought profound relief.

A couple of months later, while reading Air Force magazine, I came across a letter written by Major Benjamin F. Stakes of Greensboro, N.C. He reported he was "one of those fortunate enough to receive the 'bundles from heaven' via B-29s" at the POW camp near Inchon. He described the first pass, when "about 60 percent of the cargo was lost by chutes not opening," but "the cartons dropped on two succeeding trips were salvaged nearly 100 percent. . .every building in our little compound received its share-through the roof." He wished to thank the Superfortresses for "good American chow, tobacco, magazines, medicines and clothing so quickly after the surrender of the Japanese."

I corresponded with Major Stakes, and he wrote back from the Valley Forge General Hospital in Pennsylvania. Noting that the compound contained 168 prisoners who force-labored in a carbide mine, he continued:

"The first drums dropped within 75 yards of where we were standing, while the clothing bundles dropped in a nearby lumber yard. I scaled the fence and drove off the natives who had appeared from nowhere to rifle the lot. By quick action we were able to recover everything that dropped outside of the camp.

"On the next pass when you dropped and the drums crashed thru the fence, I was busy getting a can of fruit cocktail out of a battered drum, and also some Life magazines, a few yards from the fence. There were no natives hurt at this time, but one of our American officers received a broken leg when a drum pinned him against the fence on the inside of the camp.

"I can assure you that you need make no apologies for the manner in which the supplies reached us. Had they floated down, the wind would probably have carried them into the nearby bay and others would have been taken by the natives who are past masters at quickly doing away with anything found. The damage to the buildings was not at all regretted. In fact, if they had been burned down, most of us would have been happy. They were so vermin ridden that sleep was something you talked about but seldom enjoyed."

For several years following, on the anniversary of that drop, Major Stakes mailed me a gift. It was always a necktie.

We engaged in one other POW mission, on September 3, one day after the signing of the peace treaty. We had 10,000 pounds of supplies for Satte Camp 20 miles north of Tokyo. But the area was socked in with clouds and we returned to Saipan with the full load. But going and coming, this was our chance for a low-level look at the enemy's homeland.

We were in a machine which had brought the Japanese grievous misery, deaths beyond count, and massive destruction. But as we skimmed the earth, clumps of people in rural areas waved. It is, indeed, a strange world.

B-29s alone would not have brought a U.S. victory over the Empire of Japan. Indeed, before the nuclear attacks yielded final resolution, an invasion was contemplated for November 1945.

But the role of the 1,437 Superforts in the Mariannas was critical. They made 29,153 effective combat sorties and dropped 171 ,060 tons of bombs - 91 percent of all delivered to Japan. They destroyed 65 principal cities, 602 major war factories, 83 percent of oil refinery production, 75 percent of aircraft engine production, and 40 percent of all urban housing, rendering 20 million homeless. They killed 330,000 persons and wounded 476,000. Indeed the civilian casualties were higher than the Japanese armed forces during the almost four years of war with the United States.

This Superfort effort was not without American cost. Killed in combat were 576. But as to be expected of hostile hands and 3,000 miles of ocean on each mission, 2,406 were missing and declared dead.

One survivor was Col. Richard T. King, whose Superfort was shot down over Tokyo on December 3, 1944. He had been flight leader of my own outfit, the 500th Bomb Group. We were summoned to the amphitheater at war's end to hear his account of captivity. Cavernous in appearance, he had been put to spreading nightsoil on crops.

My outfit, the 73rd Bomb Wing on Saipan, had been the first in the Mariannas. It dropped 28 percent of the bomb tonnage and took the brunt of the human losses-with 1,033 ultimately declared killed. I emerged unscathed and, in fact, rewarded. In August, the month after my 21st birthday, I was promoted to first lieutenant and awarded the Air Medal. Happy days.

But this bubble was to burst. Demobilization was on the basis of points for overall service, overseas service, combat service, and parenthood. How many points it took to be homeward bound, I do not remember. But my 45 were not enough. In October, virtually my entire crew was flown to Guam (I was told Sid Fox had jaundice and was returned stateside) and disbursed to assorted outfits like candy on Halloween. I never again saw another member of Zebra-six's crew.

The entire process was demoralizing. Guam was no fun, offering only the usual round of outdoor movies and cheap booze. One of my fellows, who could arrange a date with a native only if family came along, did arrange my own "date" if it could be called that.

That is how I came one Sunday to be chatting with a bronze 13-year-old and an older woman. The youngster told a romantic story of parenthood-her father, an American, had escaped from the pursuing Japanese by small boat. His current plight was unrevealed. As for the youngster, she herself had an American military paramour who had returned to the States. She looked forward to joining him someday for her first view of skyscrapers and subways.
Fat chance, I thought to myself.

Horance
Davis

Editorial Comment

Horance has done an outstanding work. Having his enlightening story a part of this book has without question elevated it's status. Thanks ol' Buddy, for a job well done.

The Howard T. Gilchrist Story
"A War Tale"

Bill Chatlos and I were Aircraft Commander and pilot respectively on a B-29 crew that went to Tinian in the Marianna Islands as a replacement crew. Our 4th mission to bomb Japan was a bit unusual in that we ran out of gas. We sat down and wrote up our experience. Each mission was at least 3000 miles long, so fuel was an important consideration. We flew at the best power settings to conserve fuel, and our flight engineer, Bob Brown, kept a log on our power settings and fuel consumption. We did not trust the gasoline gauges. Too many planes had to ditch, before Iwo Jima was taken and we had a place to refuel.

4th Mission, August 1st and 2nd , 1945.
13:15 Briefing as usual. Target Nagiaka, Japan. A night mission.

16:20 Started engines after thorough preflight by entire crew. Ship O.K.

16:30 Trouble closing rear bomb bay doors. Finally closed them by using emergency accumulators.

16:50 Take off Weight slightly over 137, 000 pounds. Had to use entire runway to get off,(one mile) to a long shallow climb. Forty 500 incendiary bombs on board.

19:00 Went through a tropical front south of Iwo Jima.

20:00 Continued on past Iwo Jima. Ship running good, above flimsy airspeed, but below flimsy power settings. Automatic pilot precessing to the left. 23:20 Landfall. Continued on briefed course by radar. Lights off A few bursts of flak to right and left of course, ineffective. Four searchlights noted, but also ineffective in spite of no clouds.

00:10 Started bomb run on 66 degree heading, (axis of attack), 12,600 feet altitude as briefed. Flew plane manually because of bad processing in autopilot. Noted moderate to medium flak ahead, but continued to target without receiving any hits.

00:25 Bombs away. Large heavy concentrated fifes in target area. Smoke cloud ahead extending up to approximately 30, 000 feet.

00:26 Drawn into extremely strong thermal updraft in smoke cloud. Ship violently tossed around and banked sharply to the left to a vertical position. Both pilots on controls to right ship. Crew badly thrown around in ship. Bombardier rolled around in the nose compartment like he was in a cement mixer. His name is Nelson Bobb from Philadelphia. Five men hurt. Administered first aid to navigator, Robert Peterson. Also to left gunner Jerome Dutch from Texas. Navigator later had five stitches for a scalp wound. Interior of plane a shambles. Several thousand dollars damage to radar and other equipment.

00:30 Blown out of thermal at approximately 15000 feet. Picked up a Southern course. Discovered five bombs hung up in rear bomb bay and would not salvo, so bombardier and navigator climbed back and pried them out with a screwdriver. Rear bomb bay doors damaged and would not close. Finally closed doors with emergency system after one half hour. Continued first aid for cuts. Radar man badly shaken and bruised after going through the floor of the plane at the camera hatch. Right gunner, Symington from New York, suffered back injury.

00:45 Intercepted by Jap night fighters, two, who circled and stalked us 50 miles out to sea. They had a wing light on, I guess to see each other. They must have been out of ammunition, because they did not attack. Thank God for that.

Crew not really in shape to give battle.

00:50 Turned to 170 degree heading on a guess toward Iwo Jima. Navigator still dazed, but regaining control of duties, along with entire crew cleaning up the mess. Radar out completely. Could not pressurize cabin; too many air leaks, so dropped to 11,000 feet.

01:15 Navigator obtained Loran fix and directed us to Iwo Jima, still on 170 degree heading. Lucky guess.

04:20 Passed Iwo. Engineer reports 1,800 gallons fuel by his cruise control figures; 1,100 gallons registered on gauges. Still running below flimsy power settings, but above flimsy air speed. Approximately on time according to flimsy, so took engineers figures as nearly correct. Crew did not want to land at Iwo Jima unless absolutely necessary, because they would possibly have been interred in the hospital there and they were not that badly hurt.

07:10 Anatahan Island in the distance. Engineer reports 250 gallons in tanks according to gauges, which now appear to be correct on action of fuel transfer pumps. Awaken crew and prepare for eminent ditching. Begin sweating out the last few miles; the whole crew praying.

07:35 Engineer says 10 gallons in tanks to #1 and #4 engines; approximately 40 gallons in #2 and # 3. Each time fuel pressure to engines #1 and #4 drops, fuel transferred from engines #2 and #3 to #1 and #4.

07:45. Contact North Tiniaji Tower and explain emergency. Close in and ships in vicinity of field give us a clear lane. Landing gear does not go down on the approach until switch is flicked several times and fuse tapped in place. Finally O. K. down and locked. One half flaps let down. Plane nosed down on approach traps remaining fuel and engines start to cut out and cough. Right outboard engine continues at full power, but pulls the right wing up too high and full opposite controls will not get it down. Waited until plane over the cliff and cut right outboard engine #4. Leveled plane, full flaps extended and hit onto the end of the runway. Plane must have bounced high as a barn! Safe on ground and straightened ship down the runway.

08:00 All engines quit; out of gas on taxi lane. Tower sends ambulance for injured crewmembers and a cleat track to tow us in.

Our knees weak, our hearts thankful. Whole crew showed up 100% through out emergency.

Editorial Comment

Howard's account of this mission is exemplary. Please note the similarity (at 00:26) of his description and that of mine of March 9/10, '45, under "The Greatest Mission." Another similarity is found between my mission #9 and his at 08:00- out of fuel. That's another condition that's repeated with monotonous, ominous regularity throughout the book.

The Adolph Glatz, Jr. Story

My Dad, Adolph F. Glatz Jr., was a member of the 75th Seabees. Although my Dad won't talk much about his war experiences, I know that if it weren't for the Seabees, many of the B-29s would not have had runways from which to operate.

Seabees - their simple motto tells the story: "We build, we fight." From the island hopping of World War II and the cold of Korea, to the jungles of Vietnam and the mountains of Bosnia, the Seabees have built entire bases, bulldozed and paved thousands of miles of roadway and airstrips, and accomplished a myriad of construction projects.

In December 1941, with an eye on the developing storm clouds across both oceans, Rear Admiral Ben Moreell, Chief of the Navy's Bureau of Yards and Docks, recommended establishing Naval Construction Battalions. With the attack on Pearl Harbor and the U.S. entrance into the war, he was given the go-ahead.

The earliest Seabees were recruited from the civilian construction trades and were placed under the leadership of the Navy's Civil Engineer Corps. Because of the emphasis on experience and skill rather than on physical standards, the average age of Seabees during the early days of the war was 37.

More than 325,000 men served with the Seabees in World War II, fighting and building on six continents and more than 300 islands. In the Pacific, where most of the construction work was needed, the Seabees landed soon after the Marines and built major airstrips, bridges, roads, warehouses, hospitals, gasoline storage tanks and housing.

I know from my Dad's photos that he was stationed in the Philippines, and some of the photos are marked Bouganville. He talks about building roads, runways out of sea shells, and housing before the arrival of the troops.

The Seabees are trained in military tactics and were to engage in combat should the occasion arise, but he does not talk of this.

There was a sign posted around camp that read:

So when we reach the "Isle of Japan"
With our caps at a jaunty tilt
We'll enter the city of Tokyo
On the roads that the Seabees built.

According to the Navy's enlistment poster, they wanted men with construction experience and they wanted men between the ages of 17 and 50.

When the war broke out in Pearl Harbor, Dad went to the Army to enlist. They found out he was color blind, and refused to take him. He then tried the Marines and finally the Navy. (After failing the first time on the color blind test, he tried to guess the colored numbers in the test hoping to get lucky - to no avail). The Navy told him that they could not take him either, but that they were starting something new, construction crews, and that they would accept him - color blind and all. He enlisted on the spot, but had to wait 3 months until they had the Seabees and their battalions ready to go.

The enlistment period was for the duration of the war and salaries for these positions ranged from $54-126 per month and included housing (the jungle), food (dried beef and powdered milk), clothing (it was too hot to want much), transportation (PT boats, planes and ships) and medical and dental care (who had the time to worry about that).

According to their enlistment poster, "Here is a real OP-

PORTUNITY for two-fisted, red-blooded Americans to serve shoulder-to-shoulder with the combatant forces in the SEABEES, the newest arm of Uncle Sam's Navy."

By Sally Ann Wagoner (daughter)

Adolph Glatz, Jr.

Editorial Comment:

The recognition of Adolph is my way of acknowledging the splendid job done by the Seabees. I was truly amazed with what they could accomplish under a myriad of seemingly insurmountable obstacles. We all and I do mean all owe them a genuine thanks and a snappy salute.

The Harry Brenner Story
The B-29 Spin

My memory of this experience has been a keepsake - a relic no less. It is an indelible and still vivid memory because it was not supposed to be. Just recently I re-connected with Major Gen. Harold C. Teubner after 55 years. He lives in San Antonio, Texas, and was my operations officer in Tucson, Arizona. We started the B-29 program back in 1943! His first expression over the phone was, 'You old B_____. You spun a B-29 and lived to prove it could be done". (Not on purpose however!) His statement is a veneration to give credibility to this "out of the question," impossible maneuver. Through the passing of time I have kept this story to myself. Though the event is authentic, the B-29 was not built to spin, and I brought this phenomenon from the corner niche of my memory bank so I could hear myself tell the story.

We had several stripped-down B-29s that we used as cargo planes to ferry gasoline and bombs from our India base, Dudkundee, to Chengtu, China. This was a treacherous operation because of weather and the necessity to fly at least 25,000 feet. I made 51 round trips from India to China, flying over what is called "The Hump." It was over the Himalayan Mountains and the locale of Mt. Everest. Forty-nine of the round trips over "The Hump" were routine, but indeed two were not.

On this particular flight we developed ice on the leading edge of the wings at 25,000 to 27,000 feet, about three hours out from base in India. This ice spoiled the airfoil, as we had no deicer boots. When the B-29 fell off, even with complete power on, I pulled the throttle back as the nose headed down. I told the co-pilot to help me put it into a left spin maneuver. The B-29 was not aerodynamically built to spin. We were taught to spin a much smaller aircraft in training for purposes of recovery in case you did get into a spin in a plane like a small fighter.

A spin is when the nose is pointed downward and the plane is spinning like a top. The aircraft is falling with no flight control. So what you do is put the controls into a spin, then after you feel the backpressure, you reverse the controls and this gets the plane actually flying again. Then you pull up and level off. With a big B-29 it took plenty of altitude to complete this maneuver, approximately 22,000 feet.

The big surprise was that the wings didn't fold up. The questions are unanswerable to this day. Prior to this we had been in heavy cloud cover and when the spin was over we ended up in a valley with mountains all around us. We took a heading back to India and gradually gained altitude. The cloud cover had begun to break up and we could see our way clear to "pack it in" and head for home. When we landed at Dudkundee I went into the operations office and reported this incredible maneuver and achievement to Harold C. Teubner, major (at that time). He retired as a major general command pilot and was in the operations office at the time I reported in. We returned to the aircraft and he noted that the trailing antenna was wrapped around the fuselage and in addition there were some wrinkles ostensibly to be seen near the tail on the fuselage to indicate it had been twisted.

Monday, March 19, 2001, I called my only remaining crew member, our bombardier, Carlyle Dozier, in Conway, South Carolina, and he also confirmed the "Spin."

Editorial Comment

This amazing maneuver is unbelievable in a B-29. The fact that Harry accomplished this feat and lived to tell about it grabs any of us B-29 flyer's attention. It reminds me of my P.T. 17 trainer outside snap. Harry flew the "Hump" 51 times, that's a bunch. Thanks, Harry, for informing us of this remarkable maneuver.

The Morris Goddard Story

On a cool early morning, a farm boy from Missouri, a long way from home, now a Sergeant, rolled his bomb loading crew of 15 out at 3 a.m. He lined them up at the fence by the runway. He told those boys to watch the plane at the end of the runway and know they were watching history. Some complained, what, another B-29? Why do you think this one is special? It's cold. I'm tired and sleepy. "Watch her" he said.

The planes name was Enola Gay. The 20 year old Sergeant was sure he knew what she carried and she was going to Japan.

Two days later, after the world knew where she went and her load, one of the young men ask question, "Sarge, what would we have done if she had hit the ocean (many did)? His answer, "You would not have had time to kiss your ass goodbye."

Alva Morris Goddard died Dec. 4, 2000 at the age of 75. I hope I have remembered all the words correctly. His job on Tinian was to load bombs. Without him and his crew there was no need for those birds to take to the air.

He was very proud to serve his country. His son was in the Army for 6 years. He now has 3 grandsons in the Army with 2 more to go when they are old enough. One grandson is a recruiter and 1 a paratrooper and 1 just home from 10 months in Iraq. How proud we are of them.

I married him in 1958 after he was out of the service. He served 8 years. We were married 42 ½ years, had 2 daughters and 1 son, 5 grandsons and 2 granddaughters, 1 great-granddaughter. He and I built homes and barns and remolded houses in our community for many years. We had a lifetime of love and laughter. I'm very proud to be his wife and to share this story if you chose to include it or if you don't that is ok as well.

Mrs. Alva Morris (Ginger) Goddard
Proud widow of a WWII veteran

Editorial Comment

Thank you, Mrs. Goddard for submitting your husband's story. I'm grateful for your willingness to share with us all.

The A.D. Kemple Story

I was sworn into the Air Force on April 6, 1943, and by nightfall was at Sheppard Air Force Base to begin basic training as an aircraft mechanic. After completing this training I was shipped to Tinian Island in the Pacific to work on the B-29s of the 505th Bomb Group, 482nd Squadron. I remember that, just across the taxi way was a new type B-29. It had fuel injected engines, reverse pitch props and no gun turrets. We wondered why, but asked no questions. I noticed that the bomb bay doors were different from that of the conventional B-29s. the name of the aircraft was the "Enola Gay."

"Later in the week I was walking to work and saw a strange, yellow painted object in the restricted area. I was about 100 yards away. It looked like a huge yellow football. I learned later that it was the atomic bomb that was dropped on Japan.

Other incidents that come to mind include the crash of the 'Jook Girl,' a B-29 that overshot the runway and suffered brake failure. All her crew members were lost. "I remember flying over the Battleship Missouri when MacArthur took the surrender. We were in the 'Herd of Bald Goats' (the name painted on the nose of my B-29)."

A.D. Kemple

Two ol' Buddies:
A.D Kemple (left) with Francis "Rocky" Pozriak (right)

Editorial Comment

A.D.'s story is short but his happenstance opportunity to view the atomic bomb while on Tinian, I thought, was a distinction few of us experienced. Being chosen a part of the select group to overfly the Missouri during the signing of the armistice verifies he performed his assigned duties with above average dispatch.

The Charles R. Major and Martha Harman Story

My wife and I were engaged when we enlisted in the Army. The day after we married we were sent to opposite ends of the war. Here is my story, also Martha's story.

EXCERPTS FROM THE LIFE OF CHARLES ROBERT (BOB) MAJOR

I was born in the village of Bernalillo, NM, on March 27, 1918. My childhood was normal for the times.

I enlisted in the Army Air Force on October 13, 1941 in Santa Fe, NM. I was put on standby reserves until March 27, 1942, then, called to active duty. In the meantime, they offered a test for men without a college degree to apply for bombardier, navigator, or pilot. I passed easily. I was sent to Kelly Field in San Antonio, Texas, for pilot ground school; then on to Uvalde, Texas for flying school. I was air sick 14 days and had to wash that PT-19 plane every time. I talked to the girl who made out the papers and she changed it from "air sickness" to "lack of coordination." So I went back to Kelly Field as another washed-out cadet. I could fly again if I worked up to it.

M/Sgt. Lee took me out the first day and told me to wash a smoke and mud covered BT-13 trainer plane. He did not say how, so I improvised. I found rags, a bucket and gasoline and cleaned that plane. He came out at noon to see why I had missed lunch. The plane looked pretty good but, it was my skin with gasoline blisters that revealed my hard work.

After much studying and hard work, I worked as a mechanic and became a PFC (Private First Class). Then I was sent to Smyna, TN, where I received my diploma as a mechanic and flight engineer on B-24s, and now was a corporal, I was sent to Tarrant Field, Ft. Worth, TX. There I made Sergeant, Staff Sergeant and Crew Chief.

I now, felt I could afford to marry my sweetheart, Martha Harman. We met when she was a student nurse and I was a student at T.U.I. She would sneak out and we would meet for coffee and pie; take walks after our late classes, and not long after we were engaged to be married. But, I knew I was going in the Army and she was required to sign up for the Red Cross when she graduated; and, the Army wanted them as of "Now." So we put off our marriage at that time.

After we enlisted she was stationed in Wichita Falls, TX and I was in Ft. Worth, TX. She still had to sneak away for us to be together in Ft. Worth as she out ranked me and, those with a higher rank were not to be seen socializing with lower rank officers.

We decided to get married. We were separated the next day. Her Chief Nurse found out by reading her mail that 2nd Lt. Harman had married a lowly Staff Sergeant. Because of this, the Chief Nurse sent her to Chickasaw, OK to get ready for over seas duty. We were sent on all expense paid honeymoon...apart, she to Europe and I went to the Sunny Pacific. We could write to each other but our mail was sporadic. At least I can boast that we had no arguments for our first year and a half and, not many throughout our forty-seven and a half years of marriage. That's when the Good Lord took my darling to her heavenly home.

She was sent to the Battle of the Bulge, and I was one of 19 men selected to go to Lowery Field in Denver, CO to train as a B-29 engineer – ten weeks of the hardest studying I have ever done. After graduating, I was put on a crew at Pyote, TX. The enlisted men asked me, "How much flying in a B-29 have you had?" I truthfully said, "None." But I started only one engine, and it was on a test stand. After that they kept giving me a hard time. It angered me, so I didn't tell them I had 2,000 hours on B-24s and B-17s.

They felt really stupid when later they found out I had more hours than the entire enlisted crew put together! Mourning knew of my record but he never discussed it with the crew. There at Pyote I not only saw my first B-29, I flew that same day. Needless to say I was nervous, never having been in one before however, everything went smoothly.

One of our training missions at Pyote was non-stop to Batista, Cuba and back. We were so proud. Of the six planes, we were the only one to get back without landing someplace else.

From Pyote, we went to Kearney, Nebraska, by train, picked up our plane and went on to California. Then we went to Hawaii for three days, and they gave us a sealed letter. Ten minutes later we could open it; next stop – Kwajalein. There we all showed our stupidity. We went for a romp in the ocean and then a shower. We couldn't seem to get the salt water off. We finally realized the Navy brought in fresh water only for drinking and cooking.

Then it was off to our final stop – good old Saipan, 497th Sqdn, 871st Outfit. We were all guarding our new plane, two hours on, two hours off, for three days. Then they towed it off and assigned A-square-47, a war weary old plane called "Sweater Out." What a let down!

A few days later three crews on a mission never made it back, and we had our first taste of war. On one mission we almost had the same fate. Our engines were quitting one by one on the way back to base and we just made landing; we couldn't even taxi to park. We flew A-square-47 seven times and A-square-48 twelve times. We flew 33 successful combat missions using, I believe, a total of 11 different planes. We were never assigned a new one until our 34th mission., which was a POW mission, dropping supplies.

Everyone was tense on all missions. No one was ever hurt

on our crew, though one time we received 184 holes in the plane. God was our No.1 pilot. We bombed a total of 24 different Japanese cities. Helped pay for their sneak attack of Dec. 7, 1941.

After spending several hectic months in combat the war ended. And my ticket home follows.

The Charles Major Story/Martha Harman
The Easy Way Home
Chitose, Japan to Chicago, Illinois

Capt. Frank Mourning and our crew had just completed 33 successful bombing missions on Japan from Saipan. One POW mission was flown to make 34 of our 35 required missions. We were lying around listening to rumors one day, as the war had ended and we all had an excess number of points to get out of the service. We hoped we could fly one more POW mission so that maybe we could be home earlier. And then we got a welcomed break. Our 35th mission was flying top rank officers and B-29s from Tokyo to Washington, D.C. We were going home!

Our crew was selected to fly the Sept. 19, 1945, non-stop flight from Tokyo, Japan, to Washington, D.C. The crew consisted of Air Commander Capt. Frank Mourning; co-pilot 1st Lt. Mervin Kirchner, Flight Officer Charles R. Major as engineer, radio operator Vincent Minott, left blister gunner Colin McBurney and tail gunner Frank Mazzio.

We were notified to write our last letter for a while, pack a Class A uniform and anything else we would need for several weeks in a musette bag. We were flying from Saipan to Guam to pick up a new plane for a non-stop mission. So we said goodbye to our old home on Saipan at the 873rd Bomb Wing and our Bomb Group, the 497th, as well as our old beat-up B-29, A-47, "Sweater Out."

So, off to Guam for further orders. This, of course, caused more rumors. We also wondered why our crew, and only part of it, had been picked. Although we were a lead crew there were other lead crews worthy of this mission.

This was going to be the first flight to accomplish 6,000 miles in 26 hours without refueling, so no extra weight was allowed. We started to strip everything we didn't need for the flight. Off came the turrets, guns, bomb racks, armor plating, and anything else not absolutely necessary. Three new 500-gallon bomb-bay tanks were put in the bomb bay, giving us a total of 10,000 gallons of fuel. It also meant a new takeoff weight of 140,000.

Our air commander was Emmitt O'Donnell, the other air commander was Gen. Ciles (#1 plane), Gen. LeMay (No 2 plane), we were #3. #4 plane, flown by the great Gen. Jimmy Doolittle was designated the baggage carrier. He drew the shortest straw.

We all spent several days on Guam. It seemed to rain every day, as if trying to dampen our spirits. Then we flew to Chitose Field, near Sapporo, Japan. This field was selected for its long runway and because it could handle our heavy load. We were billeted in a hangar and given two Japanese-size blankets, a straw mat and wooden pillows to sleep on; pretty tough sleeping for a 6-foot man.

All four planes struggled to get airborne with such heavy loads. Gen. Giles took off at 0401 hours, Gen. LeMay at 0408 hours and we were airborne at 0415 hours. Gen. Doolittle took off a couple days later. We flew very low to conserve fuel with a very slow rate of climb. We were escorted for a short time by three Russian planes. This made us a bit apprehensive, but they only put on a show for us, wig-wagged their wings, and were off.

Near Nome, Alaska, we got our first taste of the Northern Lights – at 25,000 feet, they were prettier than on the ground. Later, St. Elmo's fire danced on our wings' leading edge and trailed off from the tips, racing on the propellers and off into the night. We started to wonder if we were going to make it home.

We sprung an oil leak on No. 4 engine shortly after that. Our navigator thought we would have less wind at 15,000 feet and that it would slow the oil leak. We asked Gen. O'Donnell for permission to change our flight plan. He agreed, but then wanted an explanation of why we did this. He said he trusted each person because of his knowledge, but he always wanted to learn why, a very good policy.

This probably saved our lives, as we landed in Chicago one hour and 20 minutes ahead of the other two planes. We couldn't wait to devour a good ole American hamburger and a glass of milk.

The biggest disappointment was our personal items, souveniers, important address book, etc., never reached home. The lockers had to be thrown out when the baggage planes had trouble. It was worth it as Gen. Giles gave all the members of the crews clothing and flight equipment, including parachutes. The proud accomplishment was that it was the first American flight to fly nonstop 6,645 miles. The only other long-distance flight was 7,158 miles from Egypt to Australia in 1938.

Our proud crew was:

NAME	RANK	DUTY
00 O'Donnell, Emmett	Brig.Gen	A/C
01 Beard, Paul	Major	Pilot
01 Mourning, Frank	Captain	Co-pilot
01 Kirchner, Mervin J.	1st Lt.	Co-pilot
01 Smith, Clyde H.	Captain	Navigator
01 Brown, Charles	Captain	Navigator
17 Major, Charles R.	F/O	Flight Engineer
17 Belshaw, Wilbur M.	F/O	Flight Engineer
01 Beahan, Kermit K.	Captain	Bombardier
38 Miller, Leo	S/Sgt.	Radio Operator
38 Minott, Vincent P.	S/Sgt.	Radio Operator
20 Grissom, Paul W.	M/Sgt.	Crew Chief

Capt. Beahan was in our crew; quite a down-to-earth man, not at all conceited because he had dropped the Nagasaki bomb. I feel he never regretted it because he was able to save thousands of American lives by having done so. It may have saved mine, too! All crews seemed to fear their last few missions as badly as they had feared their very first.

My wife Martha Harman Major, was a 1st Lt. Army nurse in Europe. She was in the Battle of the Bulge, working in the 189th General Hospital. We didn't get mail often enough to really be able to keep up with each other. The result was that I didn't know she was being shipped home with hepatitis at the time I left Saipan. That condition plus being overworked and under fed brought her weight down to 89 lbs. She was visiting her father in Phoenix, Arizona, when they heard on the radio that B-29s were flying 6,000 miles non-stop. Her dad made the comment, "Wouldn't it be wonderful if your husband were on that flight!" She laughed and said, "No way, only high rank would make that flight." She didn't know that I had become a flight officer and given a battlefield commission. I now could be seen with my wife.

The brass in Washington, D.C., telephoned my mother in Albuquerque and told her I was on my way home as head engineer for Gen. O'Donnell, and that she and my father could fly to Washington to welcome me back. She was so excited she hung up too fast. She failed to mention that my wife was stateside and she never got the rest of the message. So she didn't know that they could fly to meet me and they couldn't reach her back because the line was always busy. She had so many to call.

She also phoned Martha in Phoenix and told her I was on the No. 3 plane. As soon as Martha knew the plane had landed in Chicago, she took off hitchhiking her way to Albuquerque first with a truck driver testing tires to Flagstaff, Arizona, then by car with kind folks to Winslow, then one of her oldest friends was a conductor on the Santa Fe railroad who illegally let her ride in the caboose of a freight train. God was with her. She arrived in Albuquerque the day before we were supposed to arrive. In the meantime at Tinker Field, Oklahoma, we decided that if we were considered heroes, we would see if we could get a plane to fly me to Albuquerque, Mourning to Colorado Springs and Kirchner to San Luis Obispo, California. Otherwise, we'd fly to Seattle and on down, with me last on the trip. We got our own private flight. Fame is great, even if it is so short-lived.

Martha and my sister-in-law, Vera Major, were in town shopping when I arrived. Martha and I saw each other across a main intersection and met in the middle of the street! You can imagine the euphoria of emotion we felt to finally embrace each other. Who cared that we were in the middle of a busy street? We had so much to tell each other and so much love to share. The policeman who escorted us back to the sidewalk happened to be a school friend – lucky for us. We then went to see my parents.

This event was being watched by everyone and suddenly we were surrounded by reporters as we entered the driveway. We finally let one reporter do a story from the Albuquerque Tribune. When we decided later to go out for dinner, I called a friend of mine who owned a Mexican restaurant. He agreed to let us in the back door and he seated us in a secluded booth and didn't seat anyone near. What a thoughtful Hispanic man.

I was concerned for my wife and her condition. I was amazed at how much weight she had lost, but she was mine and we were together again. She looked great to me and always did.

We had a perfect, wonderful week together before we had to report back - Martha to Beatty General Hospital in Rome,

Georgia, to recover, and I together with the rest of the crews to New York to be honored by the Wings Club at the Waldorf. I was given my second Distinguished Flying Cross from Gen. Hap Arnold.

After Martha and I were discharged we went to Atlanta and bought the only car left in the used car lot. He advertised two, but the man ahead of us chose the Pontiac and we had to settle for the Mercury. We headed to El Paso. We were still in uniform as we had no other clothes yet, so people stopped and asked us questions wherever we went. Of course we were in no hurry, after all this was our real honeymoon.

We took three weeks to get to El Paso and as luck would have it we were able to rent a Service Station with living quarters, as housing was hard to find. We decided to stay there because of the William Beaumont hospital and the civilian El Paso General Hospital. They got my bride back to a healthy condition and gave us 47 ½ years of good family life. Remember the parachute I brought on my flight home? My wife and sister-in-law reworked the parachute into many nice slips, panties, etc. as money was tight and the fabric was quality.

The Charles Major Story/Martha Harman
Martha Harman, World War II Army Nurse
As told by her daughter: Sue Major Holmes

The Oct. 4, 1944, entry from Martha Harman's service file is terse: "Departed from the United States for foreign duty, per Secret Orders."

Army 2nd Lt. Harman was on her way to Omaha Beach with the 189th General Hospital, the second hospital to land in France after the June 6 D-Day invasion.

The 25-year-old nurse sailed on the USS American, a luxury liner converted to a troop ship, and landed in Liverpool, England. The units traveled by train to Southampton, then, after two false starts due to bad weather, crossed the English Channel and landed on Omaha Beach, a little more than four months after D-Day.

On Omaha Beach, the nurses and doctors waited amid the wreckage of ships and equipment left from the invasion. They waited for two hours for transport trucks in mud a foot and a half deep, "and we wondered how the hell a trick would make it," Harman recorded in a small diary she kept intermittently for the months she was in Europe, saving it, a book of poetry, and a Bible even after she threw away her gas mask.

The hospital's original plan, she recalled, was to set up in the bombed-out town of St. Lo, but she noted in her journal, "The Army underestimated the Germans," so the hospital set up in Lison instead.

Their first location was near an apple orchard that was strictly off limits because it had been mined by the Germans. The temptation proved too much for Harman, however, so she and another nurse she identified only as Frazier, who was with a hospital over the hill, drove a couple of cows ahead of them to blow up any mines, picked some apples, brought them back and cooked them down into applesauce.

Eventually, the nurses moved from bivouac areas to their own tents, four to a tent. In hers were Lts. Harman, Lair, Harkey and Mahoney. The tents in the French winter had a stove, a concrete floor and a light. "It's like paradise," Harman wrote. "Surprising how little it takes to make us happy."

For a time, she nursed German POWs, which she hated. She wrote that she was glad to go back on nights and work with Yanks. But night duty was rough, watching the patients and keeping the stoves going and slogging through the mud from one tent to another. "If you want some water you get a bucket and carry it in. If you want some coal you get a bucket and carry it in. Some fun!"

She wrote that one night the guards on the hospital were doubled – Germans had landed paratroopers, who killed a couple of the hospital's guards. Her patients gave her a long German knife that snapped open for her to carry while on duty.

"Damned Army! They give you hell about the kind of clothes you wear, but let the Germans drop a whole load of paratroopers in our back yard."

Not all her stories were grim. Years later, she entertained her children with stories about the shortages of such things as toilet paper. Nurses going to the latrine were allowed only two sheets, which they tore off a guarding soldier's bayonet as they went by. It took a while for both the young nurses and the young soldiers to get over their embarrassment.

The war took her all through France. Among the few things

she kept is a large fragile map of France, marked with where she went. It's difficult to read, but the line goes from Coutances to St. Lo, - there also is an album that includes small black-and-white photographs of this shattered little town – to Isigny and Caen, up to Carentan and Creances, down to St. Sever, Bourdev, Domfront and Briouze, back to St. Lo, and Isigny and on to Vaudabon, Caen again, Lisieux, Orsec, Conchas, Camylle, LaQueu, St. Cloud and Paris. The album has pictures of her and her friends, "the unholy four," in a "liberated" MP Jeep off to see Paris. The map traces the rest of the path to Neully, Meaux, Rheims (the album has pictures of the famous cathedral) Chalons, Busey L'etice. It is a map of France, and does not show the later Battle of the Bulge.

Her diary on St. Lo: "Not a building stands, just an old brick chimney on the very edge of town. The engineers took bulldozers and pushed a road through the village so supplies could go through. They are still digging bodies from the debris…"

"People will be too polite to ask about some of this hell, and we will be too kind to tell them," she wrote.

Another nurse, Chris, was killed in France as the unit moved, as usual, at night. The nurses and soldiers sat wooden benches in the back of three-quarter ton trucks, in a nurse-man-nurse-man seating arrangement, and snipes hit the convoy as it traveled though St. Marie. They learned when they reached their destination that Chris and a young sergeant were killed.

In February 1945, Harman exulted over having 32 hours off, and she went to join other Americans in Bagnoles. She wrote of jostling along in a Jeep through villages and farms.

"Some towns were so bombed and others weren't touched. Some stunk so terribly because the bodies had been left because of the danger in removing them. There is the smell of death that is peculiar to itself... Resentment of Americans still runs high in bombed areas and you can hardly blame them, for it was our artillery and bombs that wrecked their homes and killed their families. In Uire, hardly anything stands."

Sometime before the Battle of the Bulge, the hospital was split up and Harman worked triage as part of a four-person team, with another nurse named Betty, Dr. Berkofsky and an aide, Dandy, "moving fast" and following Gen. George Patton. Diary entries become more sporadic and she notes only, "Just first aid and a mess. Usually get 72 hrs on and 12 off."

Then: "Bulge is on and the damn fools at home don't know how close we are to losing this stupid, senseless war."

A half page later, her journal records Betty's death in a shelling: "Betty ceased to exist today. Just a blob of blood and mess in the mud. A tangled bit of her dog tags." Betty ran for the shelter of a trench, but Harman, too scared, stayed put.

"If she hadn't tried to make me go," Harman wrote, "those extra seconds might have saved her."

Betty was 23.

"A white Star of David in a foreign land. Shit."

Berkofsky offered her an out – return to Paris or stay with him and Dandy. She stayed.

Berkofsky later was wounded in the arm, but survived.

"The dumb nut wore his Red Cross armband," Harman fumed in her journal. "The bullet went straight through and

Dandy and I cleaned it." They also made him a big Purple Heart out of gauze and gentian violet.

After an entry noting that "Berkofsky's arm is good so he can stay," is the single paragraph: "Just had the daylights blown out of our squad tent. Only lost 1 patient."

The photo album has a few small pictures of VE Day in an unidentified town. Her diary records, "It's down, it's over! Thank God."

Afterward, she was sent by ambulance to Paris, weighing only 89 pounds on a 5-foot-8 frame, "yellow as a pumpkin," suffering from jaundice. She returned to the United States and promptly went AWOL to Florida to visit her sister, Margaret Harman, who was in the WAVES.

She was visiting her father in Phoenix, Arizona when she got word her husband, Flight Officer Charles Robert Major, had returned to the United States on one of four B-29s that made nonstop flights from Japan to Chicago. They had been married in 1943 and had not seen each other for a year and a half.

Not many couples can truthfully say they had no arguments for the first year and a half of marriage.

Editorial Comment

In this story we have the classic example of an officer and an enlisted man falling in love. I know all of us appreciate your candor in sharing your experiences with us.

The August Cline Story
The Flying Cocker Spaniel

I bought a sweet cocker spaniel in Salina, Kansas, during my training, and "Princess" became our crew's mascot. She loved flying with us all the time except for missions.

After flying to Denver, Colorado, from Salina for our gunner training, where I received my diploma from the Air Force Technical School, we flew to Clovis, New Mexico, to pick up our B-29. Then we flew on to India. We did 20 missions to China and 5 missions over the "hump." Princess was always there on our return to welcome us back and lift our spirits.

Flying over the hump, (the Himalayan Mountains) was not an easy task. The high altitude and the fierce winds and downdrafts plus other factors caused B-29 crashes in areas where rescues were impossible. We had to do 6 to 8 trips, hauling gas, over those dangerous mountains to count as one mission.

After being transferred to Tinian, we did 10 missions over Japan during the fire raids and on one mission a piece of flak shot through the plane and went through the life boat I was sitting on. Good thing we didn't have to bail out over the ocean. At least the family jewels were saved.

My job as tail gunner was to keep the Jap fighters from attacking from the rear. It was not just pointing a gun out the window. I had a very complicated maze of machinery to operate in order to bring my 50 caliber machine gun and my 20 millimeter cannon to bear. It was a frightening job, being it had to be done at fairly close range. My mission always ended with the welcome home licks of Princess. She made the trip back to the States after the war and I gave her to my co-pilot's wife. I had received several flight and mechanical diplomas before gunner training in Denver but I am very proud to finally receive my high school diploma at the age of 83 because of recent legislation allowing diplomas to be given to those that left school to serve in the military.

August W. Cline 468th bomb group, 56th bomb wing

Editorial Comment

August, like all flyers serving with the 58th bomb wing, encountered some untenable flying conditions. But the readers' interest is stimulated by that little cocker spaniel, Princess. Thanks August for sharing your story with those who love dogs.

The Sherwin Lichtenfield Story
Wild Missons

V square 46 was a plane that gave our crew many wild times. I flew 35 missions. We shot down many Zero's, Tony's and others. We made the first raids on Tokyo after Doolittle's raid. We did five fire raids in 9 days.

The one mission out of 35 that stands out in my memory was when at 4800 feet over Tokyo we got hit. It knocked out the rudder and lucky for us it jammed almost dead center or we would have been "dead meat" and the tail gunner didn't even get a scratch. And when we got back, Thank God, I found him kissing the ground. The worst was watching friends of mine getting blown out of their planes and seeing those with fire going past the tails.

The best was that we had the most capable, Pilot Marvin Mills and when he moved up to operations to get an Oak Leaf he got us the best co-pilot around, W. Ridenour, otherwise knows as "Qualified Dual."

Editorial Comment
Sherwin had one of those fluke breaks that occur during a combat mission. Had that rudder been jammed a few degrees either way the plane would have flown only in a circular pattern. "Dead meat" is an appropriate term for Sherwin and his fellow crewmen.

The Howard T. Anderson Story
Two Engines Lost – Two Many Times

Our frightening missions started in Pratt, Kansas. We had a close call upon landing one foggy morning in early 1944 when a B-26 was attempting to land on the same runway we were touching down on – only he was about to touch down on the opposite end – without any radio contact. No wonder that besides testing unproven B-29s, we called these training and testing missions "The Battle of Kansas."

Then, in September '44, we crash landed at Chakulia, India, when #2 caught fire and fell completely off the aircraft on final approach. Then, in November '44, on a mission to Omura, we had 2 engines short out at bomb release time and flew that beautiful bird for 8 hours back into an emergency field in China on two engines.

Then in early April '45, as our wing was moving over to Tinian, we lost 2 engines on takeoff, at Luliang, China, due to contaminated fuel and had to salvo everything in both bomb bays to remain aloft long enough to bring it around and land it.

Then, the final "thrill" was on May 19, 1945, after returning from Hamamatsu, we were forced to bail out over Iwo because of being unable to feather #2 and when it sheared off, it sort of tore up things kind of badly; that was our 27th mission. With our crew busted up with injuries our buddy, Flt. Surgeon stepped in and said "That's it guys, you can await transport back to Uncle "Sugar."

Editorial Comment

If ever a crew seemed snake bitten, it was Howard's. That engine dropping off really blew me away. Howard, I warrant you and your guys are still thanking your lucky stars.

The Sheldon (Smokey) Stover Story
Flying the "Hump"

I was sent to the 58th Bomb Wing in December 1943 at Smokey Hill A.B. in Salina, Kansas. There I was assigned to a combat crew: Pilot Capt. Wyatte J. Gay, Co-pilot Raymond D. Payne, Bombardier Morris E. Lescoart, Navigator Frank M. Bennett Jr., Engineer Charles F. Harlin, CFC Gunner Harold D. Skilton, Right Gunner Paul W. Adams, Left Gunner Sheldon J. Stover, Tail Gunner Carl W. Maines, Radio Operator Emil Lippmann, Radar Operator George A. Doll.

They did not have enough aircraft for all crews so our crew was sent to Clovis, New Mexico, for B-29 training. We arrived to find only 4 B-29A model aircraft and approximately 25 B-17E, F, G. aircraft. We stayed there about 3 months and had 109 hours B-17 time and 69.20 hours B-29 time. We were sent to Herrington, Kansas, on 30 June 1944 to pick up the latest production B-29 and fly overseas to Pairdoba, India. We were the first replacement crew in the 462 B. G. 768th Bomb Squadron. We arrived with a total of 155.30 B-29 hrs. We had missed only 2 combat missions.

The wing had suffered heavy operational losses and some combat loss. The wing had plenty of crews but were short aircraft, so we lost our aircraft to one of the older crews. Our crew was picked to fly the "Hump." We would take a load of bombs, 20, each 500 pounds and a full load of fuel, fly to China, leave our bombs and approximately half our fuel, and return to India. Head winds were unpredictable, so some crews left too much fuel in China and lost their aircraft coming home, since runways were too short, even if you could find one to land the B-29. The next crew would take 20, each 500 pounds and a full load of fuel over the "Hump," pick up the bombs and fuel left there and fly a mission over Japan and return to China and remain overnight for refuel and maintenance. Sometimes we would get bombed with anti-personnel bombs of poor quality so we became quite complacent and would not run to the rice paddies, until one night they dropped 3 each, 500 pound bombs off the end of the runway. We immediately got the message.

The "Ferry Command" had brought about 30 each C-109 gas tankers to India to fly fuel over the "Hump," but the "Air Transport Command" did not have the crews in place to fly them, so all spare B-29 crews were sent to fly them during the months of September and October until their crews arrived. We used those aircraft to take some of the operational losses. The chosen name for the converted B-24 was the C-One-O-Boom because they had a fuel leak problem and would 'blow up' for no reason at all. You did not smoke aboard or near that aircraft.

During my trips over the "Hump" we were always looking for lost aircraft (when you could see). The C-46 was the most prevelant since it was flying at its max both weight and ceiling. They were hauling 55 gallon drums of fuels as well as other cargo. They would hit a down draft and never recover, since they could barely clear the mountains. We called it the C-46 stepping stone. We also looked for C-47, C-109, B-29 as well as other aircraft. The area was so remote that if you bailed or crashed, your chances for survival was less than 40%. Some of the area was Japanese occupied and some areas had native "head hunters." In either case it was not good for longevity. We all carried jungle survival kits, attached to our parachutes, which had food, water, and a frying pan. We also wore a money belt which contained lots of local money as well as silk maps of the area. We had crews who bailed out that took 2 months to get back to base and some that never returned at all...

To this day, the "Hump" is considered the worst flying weather and terrain in the world. The 58th Bomb Wing lost at least 72 B-29s and an unknown number of C-109s, at least 12 I know of. November 1, 1944 we returned to our home base "Paradoba," India, where we began flying missions over the "Hump" to China on to Japan, back to China then on to India. On April 27, 1944 we made the trip without the loss of a single person or aircraft, though one aircraft clipped some power poles on our take-off from China. Then our crews had enough B-29 time. This was not a problem.

Most crews always had some members missing when they flew a mission due to malaria or dingy fever so I would not always fly with my regular crew. I flew combat till the end of the war and one POW supply drop after the war. We released our supplies but one chute did not open and the pallet went through the roof of the POW barracks. All the prisoners were outside waving at us so no one was hurt. I flew 35 missions, was awarded the D.F.C. and one cluster, the Air Medal with four clusters and the Asiatic-Pacific ribbon with seven battle stars.

Chief Master Sergeant Sheldon (Smokey) Stover
USAF Retired

The Bernard J. Reisen Story
An Event Long Remembered

Our B-29 crew was part of a bombing mission over Tachiarai Air Field located in the northern part of the Island of Kyushu of the Japanese Empire. The mission, a day raid, was to knock out the air bases used by Kamikaze aircraft to attack the U.S. Fleet during the invasion of Okinawa. The date was 18 April, 1945.

The aircraft we were assigned for this strike was Squadron number T Sq 7, whose ground crew chief was M/Sgt. Walter Leslie of Deriton, Texas.

The weather that day was CAVU over the target area and while our bombing was excellent the sky was full of Japanese fighters, eager to make us pay for the blow we had just dealt. Just as we were leaving the target area a Japanese fighter bore in on us from eleven o'clock and let go with a 20 mm burst. One shell exploded in the forward part of the airplane at the navigator's station.

At this point our navigator, Lt. Bernard J. Reisen of Chicago, Ill. screamed and called out my name. Both the radio operator and I pulled him from a slumped position onto the deck over the forward access hatch. Both of his legs were filled with shell fragments and he was bleeding profusely. After applying tourniquets and sulfa powder we were able to get him in a comfortable position using flight jackets as support. Both the radio operator and myself, as well as the rest of the crew, were pretty well occupied at our stations until the fighter attack came to an end. During this period Lt. Reisen lost quite a bit of blood and our Airplane Commander, Lt. Philip R. Fisher of Miami, Florida, set a course for Iwo Jima rather than try to make it back to Saipan.

Lt. Reisen impressed us with his determination to navigate in his prone Position with his navigation computer held high with both hands. Upon arriving at Iwo Jima he was taken out on a litter through the engineer's escape hatch by medics. We returned to Saipan with a badly shot up airplane and were greeted by a skeleton crew at the hard stand, as operations had concluded we had gone down.

For his valiant and dedicated effort Lt. Reisen received the Silver Star and Purple Heart. He later rejoined the squadron to fly again and he returned to the United States after the war. In closing I am proud to salute him.

Editorial Comment

As I have done this book, the number 7 keeps appearing with monotonous regularity. Planes assigned that "lucky" number seemed to attract a date with destiny-not a good date. Lt. Reison's actions speak for themselves. He was dedicated to his responsibilities.

The Bill Stewart Stories

The strike against the Tokyo Arsenal on the night of 13 April was at low altitude, about 4,000 feet. We put our bombs on target without incident, but on the way out, our tail gunner reported that a Japanese fighter was tailing us on the right side. Jackson told him to hold his fire and keep watching. Soon Jenkins called again to say that the fighter was crossing over behind us, and as I looked out my window, 1 saw what looked like a bushel of red-hot rivets sailing past as he fired on us. Fortunately, he missed, but he must have been awfully nervous, and he immediately broke off. Six feet higher and 25 feet to his left would have cleaned us out.

On one of the daylight incendiary missions against Osaka or Kobe, we were bombing from about 14.000 feet, and huge clouds of smoke were rising from the target areas to well above our altitude. As we left the target, we saw a Japanese fighter take out a B-29 behind us, and almost immediately a P-51 took out the Japanese. Both he and the B-29 crew bailed out; the Japanese pilot's parachute was blue. They all seemed to be drifting inland when last seen, and we thought they were sure to be captured. But one day after the war, flying with a Major Miranda in a B-17, we started swapping war stories, and I told him about this one. Guess what? He had been one of that B-29 crew, and they had all landed in the Inland Sea, and a U.S. submarine surfaced and picked them up and got out of there!

One more: On 26 June we were over Osaka again, and once more the Japanese fighters were busy. Just after bomb release, the left wing plane in our element had one engine knocked out, then another, and the fighters started coming in for the kill. We dropped back to cover him (it was Dick Sullivan), and together we made an inviting target for the fighters at our reduced airspeed. But, together we had twice the firepower, and the Japs were wary. We were about out of ammunition, but the gunners kept the turrets moving, and we finally made it out of there.

We escorted Sullivan all the way to Iwo Jima, losing altitude all the way, and we were so low on fuel that we both landed there. While sitting there on a taxiway waiting to be refueled, right outside we saw a group of GI's hard at work dragging something out of the smoking ground beneath our plane. It turned out to be a live Japanese torpedo. We weren't sorry to leave there. Sullivan's radar operator, Bob De Neve, had taken a 20 millimeter hit in his shoulder and was in a bad way. I often wondered if he survived, but years later at Wright-Patterson, I ran into Bob Rae, their engineer (a Lt.Col. then), and he told me that De Neve had not only survived his wounds, but they had patched him up pretty well.

Editorial Comment

Bill has done a superb, concise job in relating these incidents. His examples of how to present the salient facts provides an interesting format for anyone considering writing a book. You did well, Bill.

A Japanese Woman's Story
Terror of the Innocent

I recall my grandmother telling me about her escape from the fire raids in Tokyo. She was only 12 years old. She said there was a great celebration by the people around her that had just heard a news report on the radio that the Japanese fighters had shot down ten B-29s that day. But she knew great danger still lurked as 3,000 women and children were being evacuated to the countryside. All daily activities and businesses were disrupted for months.

She remembered the day bombs struck precisely on one of the subway stations right in the affluent business and shopping district, killing hundreds of civilians. Soon after, several bombs destroyed the Ginza and Geisha quarters to complete rubble. The Japanese women wanted the war to end no matter who would win the war. They knew more frightening days of destruction lay ahead, and then the horror of the fire began.

Early in '45 she said it was like living past the gates of hell. She was required to stay in the city to help the injured and assist medical personnel in their care. Then the inferno started. The Americans dropped fire bombs from hundreds of B-29s attacking Tokyo like a swarm of bees. An unbelievable 25,000 plus buildings were destroyed in that first raid.

Later hundreds of thousands of buildings and civilians were incinerated instantly by the rage of wind and fire creating sudden bursts of fire storms, leaping and trapping all who were running seeking refuge from the inferno. The napalm rained upon them from each explosion, igniting everything in sight as the people raced to the rivers and canals. The heat was so intense, steel structures and bridges would collapse, there was literally no place to hide. Even open land was swept with high fierce winds of fire. My grandmother was found in a drain leading to a deep trench. Mud covered her singed body, she said it acted as a soothing ointment that saved her burned flesh from further damage.

It took her months to recover from that and her scorched lungs miraculously healed after pneumonia almost took her life several times. She was relieved when the atom bomb ended the war as she believed millions more on both sides of the war would have perished.

This is an anonymous letter from a granddaughter living in San Francisco, Ca.

Editorial Comments

This story is so very much appreciated. It is relevant in these days of revisionists, peace nicks, and liberals. It's an enlightening inspiration to have a person of Japanese decent recognize the benefits the use of the atomic bomb provided both sides. It is particularly significant when you realize the personal suffering she endured. Thank you, Granddaughter, whomever you are.

The William R. Montone Story

Having read ------- (08/12/02) account of the Hiroshima-Nagasaki sympathizers and their 8/11 Susquehanna demonstrations, something is apparent. Or should I say obvious? It is that the ------- does not consider it newsworthy that there are two lone, conspicuous, peaceful counter-demonstrators. These were my wife and I.

I wore a large-lettered, large-pictured, T-shirt. It showed a B-29 "Saipan 1944-1945." Your article gave it resounding silence.

I served for almost two years on Saipan as ground crew support for the B-29 raids on the Japanese mainland. Tinian was just across the bay, and both islands were in the 20th Air Force. Now, in light of these Hiroshima-Nagasaki sympathizers and apologists, I feel a moral obligation to express offense on behalf of many, many of my buddies who went on bombing missions and who, today, are in repose in the bottom of the Pacific Ocean or are permanently maimed.

Also, there is great offense to the thousands and thousands of U.S. Marines who fought the bloodiest and most meaningful ground battle in the Pacific, namely Iwo Jima. Life, blood and limb were suffered and sacrificed by these Marines in order to enhance and facilitate the B-29 bombing raids on the Japanese mainland. For those who don't know the geography, Iwo Jima is mid-point between Saipan/ Tinian and Japan. Iwo Jima, again at great physical cost to the Marines, afforded a life-saving landing haven for planes disabled by enemy anti-aircraft – something not available when the bombing first started.

We ground crew people experienced frequent, heavy bombing and strafing from the enemy. More lives lost, more severe injuries. And no radar to give us warning. As the bombings progressed, and the Japanese defenses weakened, we broadcast each day before a raid what cities were going to be bombed. We urged evacuation. Is that not compassion, particularly on the civilian population?

These bombings, climaxed by the A-bomb, spared thousands, perhaps millions of American and Japanese lives, in that the surrender aborted plans for ground invasion.

I realize that letters to the editor ask for brevity. But how else to state our position without the foregoing details? These sympathizers condemn the dropping of the A-bomb as inhumane. But do their thoughts turn at all to scores of thousands of American youth bloodied, maimed and dead for today's youth. Many today would not have known life at all – or American freedom to drop candles on the Susquehanna River. Have these peace-nicks ever thought of the mothers of these boys? Do they remember Pearl Harbor?

I will admit one thing we veterans have in common with the Susquehanna River demonstrators. It is their quest for PEACE. We dropped the A-bomb for the same objective, PEACE.

We did not drop flowers and candles on the waters. Rather, we deposited life, limb and blood.

Two of my experiences on Saipan follow.

One evening, about one hundred of us were attending Mass in a tent. Without warning, Japanese bombers and fighter planes were over-head, raining bombs and bullets all around us and on the remainder of the Island. There was still about fifteen minutes to go before Mass would end. The priest continued the Service without batting an eye. Not one soldier moved; not one soldier was hurt.

Once again, we were at Mass, and at the moment when the priest elevated the Host and said, "This is My Body," the voice of President Harry Truman announced over the loud speaker the end of the war.

Editorial Comment
Bill and I have a similar view on this subject. Therefore, I feel it appropriate to enter my comments as follows:

Much has been discussed and written about our use of the Atomic Bomb. True, the B-29s were reducing the cities to dust. However, it's use saved several million lives on both sides. All the "bleeding heart activists" and others of that mind set are flat incapable of dealing with the reality of war. Particularly at this juncture. It was a monumental decision with imposing implications. The unimpeachable fact is its use ended the war and saved countless lives, eliminated pain and suffering, displacement, destruction and a litany of other factors. Their stance won't compute. I am amazed far beyond my ability to comprehend how the revisionists ever arrived at their position. I presume it developed only because they closed their eyes and minds to the obvious, overwhelming evidence. Further, the horrible animalist torture inflicted on our men is shamelessly ignored. I have elected not to incorporate much in the form of the inhuman atrocities committed against our people in this book. To those readers who wish to avail themselves of these official accounts please be advised the 73rd Bomb Wing Association at bombwing73@aol.com possesses such documents. However, rules change and they may not be available to the public. —— Thanks Bill for your story.

The Joe W. Tharpe Story

We flew some pretty hectic missions but probably the most interesting for me was the extra radio man with another crew as Super Dumbo, the night of the first low altitude incendiary raid, and also the first time B-29's landed on Iwo Jima. This is an exact copy from a little pocket diary I kept of all my missions.

March 11, 1945 – Air Sea Rescue (Super Dumbo)

This was a drastic change in tactics. Our B-29's went over Tokyo at low altitude at night and dropped incendiary bombs on the industrial area. It was a very big fire and the Japs were caught napping. Who would have thought that B-29's would be used in low altitude attacks?

They didn't expect us at night either, because they are very short of night fighters. Our crew was not scheduled for this one but I was sent along as extra radio operator on the air sea rescue (Super Dumbo) with Capt. Feather's crew.

Our mission was to follow the raiders up to a point near the coast, contact a life guard American Submarine, and fly cover for it while directing anyone in trouble to it for ditching and rescue and then follow along behind in case others were in trouble.

With two radios we could monitor two frequencies for distress signals and direct them to other American ships standing by on lifeguard duty.

The battle for Iwo Jima is still pretty hot but our forces had captured an airbase.

When we got back down to Iwo we knew of seven planes that were having trouble so we circled at 800 feet and sent a homing signal. All seven were able to land there.

I was sitting in the tunnel with my head in the astro dome and we could see the action very clearly.

Our forces were using flame throwers on Jap pill boxes and then covering them with bulldozers.

There were some Japanese fighters in the crater of Mt. Suvrabachi lobing mortars at our forces and what appeared to be a bulldozer halfway up the side of the mountain.

There was a guy on what looked like what was left of the control tower, a platform on tall legs. He had a mike and was giving the B-29's landing instructions. He told them not to go past the end of the runway cause "that ain't ours yet."

Fighters were being called into strafe past the runway.

B-29 no. 6 cracked up with it's tail hanging out on the runway about ¼ of the way from the far end, and B-29 no. 7 had his bomb bay doors stuck in the open position. The controller said to pilot no. 7, "See that B-29 with it's tail across the runway, do you still think you can make it?" His reply was "Hell yes, here I come." He greased it in smooth as silk and somehow spun it around and turned off on a ramp.

Note :

A few years ago I located my old buddy from radio school Vic Chalker who was in the 497th bomb group, now living in N. Ft. Meyers, FL. I see him every winter now. I told him this story and he said, "Heck, that was us."

After leaving Iwo, we were about halfway back to Saipan when we heard a call from a B-29 from Tinian saying he was almost out of gas and was going to ditch. Our chart showed a destroyer on standby in the vicinity and we could see it on one side and the B-29 on the other side going away.

Col. Snow who was head of Air Sea Rescue in the theatre called him to turn him around and the 522nd command set, malfunctioned.

I scampered back through the tunnel to the waist section where the set was under the floor, yanked the cover off and, on a wild guess tweeked the audio squelching relay and lucked out. Col. Snow got them turned around and they ditched near the destroyer which put out a small boat and picked them all up. About 10 minutes later the B-29 broke in half and went down nose first and tail first.

I was holding a navy camera man in the open waist door shooting the whole scene.

He had flown several hours trying to get shots of rescues for a film the navy was making on Air Sea Rescue.

Editorial Comment

Joe did a great job in relating these incidents. The reply the pilot flying No. 7 made to the controller, "Hell yes, here I come," is classic American.

The William Mason Story

We were a new crew without copilot who had been shot down while filling in with another crew prior to our first official mission. For this reason and since we were new, Colonel Dougherty elected to fly as copilot with us.

Everything was pretty routine until the bombs failed to drop on our first pass over the city of Nagoya, which was about the size of Chicago. These night raids were timed so that all of the planes alone particular group were over the target at the same time in order to scatter the searchlights and antiaircraft fire among many targets rather than a few.

I am sure that if we had been on our own, we would then have followed standard instructions and proceeded to the secondary target. However, the Colonel said, "Let's go round again.' This brought us over the city at a time when we were in-between groups. Within seconds every searchlight was on us and the plane was as bright as day. Apparently the Japanese shells were, for the most part, set to explode at a higher altitude than we were flying. The one that passed through our left wing and took out engine #1 was either a dud or was intended to explode at a higher level. In any case it did pass through the outer part of the wing leaving a hole, which was later measured to be about 40 square feet. It did take out engine #1 but it did not rupture the fuel tanks and therefore we stayed in the air. Later on the round crew said that if the shell had passed some 18 inches closer in, it would have been the end for all us.

My recollection is that there were many more small shrapnel holes in the plane than Tom Sanders is reporting. The ground crew told me according to my memory that there were about 120 small holes just in the radar room where I was sitting.

Anyway, the bombs did drop on the second pass and God

was with us in that we got out from over that city.

Nothing much happened out over the water until daylight when we discovered the magnitude of the hole in the left wing and then all of a sudden I noticed a trickle of blood down my left arm.

During the flight over Nagoya I was of course wearing a flack jacket and had flack blankets wrapped around me but my sleeves were rolled up and arms were bare.

When I discovered the little trickle of blood I went on intercom and said to Captain Sealy (who was also my perennial bridge partner), “Hey Ray, I’m wounded.”

At this point, Colonel Dougherty jumped on the intercom and insisted that the other crewmembers give me a transfusion of all kinds of medical attention while I was trying to assure the Colonel that the wound was only a scratch.

As Tom has reported, we were by far the last plane to get back to Saipan. Of course at this juncture Iwo Jima was not available for an emergency landing so we had to struggle all the way to Saipan. We had taken extra time for the second run, over Nagoya and had to conserve every drop of fuel in order to get back. Once we sighted the island, the Colonel himself called in declaring an emergency. We did land without great incident, but the people on the ground all reported that they were absolutely amazed that a plane with such a hole in the wing could have made it all the way back.

On the ground there was a reception committee of two ambulances, a doctor, a minister, a priest, a rabbi and many interested flight and ground crew members.

I jumped out of the plane along with all the rest of the crew. The doctor who was standing there asked, “Where’s the wounded?” At this point Colonel Dougherty pointed to me as said, “It’s him.” “It doesn’t look like much, but it might be serious and there might be shrapnel in his arm, 1 want this man properly treated.” About this time, the doctor remembered that he was in the Army and was being addressed by a full colonel. So all of a sudden I was tossed on a stretcher and put in the ambulance and rushed off to the hospital. When we arrived at the hospital, the doctor hopped out and said, “Come on in, I know what you need.” I went inside to an examining room where there were two nurses, one blonde and one brunette. He instructed one of them to, “Go get one of those special medicines we keep under lock and key.’ The nurse came back with a bottle of bourbon. So we all had a drink and then he said, “Which one do you want to put the band aid on your arm?” I voted for two band-aids, was given the rest of the bottle of booze and was sent “home” in a jeep.

My big wound was, of course, the joke of the entire squadron for several days. One afternoon I was walking down the road when I happened to pass the flight surgeon and he said “Hey Bill, you have to come in and fill out those papers for your Purple Heart.” My response was, “Oh come on Doc, I’m sick of all this kidding.” He promptly said, ‘Lieutenant the Colonel wants you to have a Purple Heart and you come in and fill out those papers.’ Well, of course, I did, and in due course, received my Purple Heart. Captain Sealy was awarded a Distinguished Flying Cross, and the Colonel a Silver Star for that mission.

Over the years. I have never felt that my medal was completely undeserved even though if the Colonel had not been with us that evening, I am absolutely positive that neither Ray Sealy nor I would have given the slightest thought to my deserving a Purple Heart for a minor scratch. The truth is that they were trying to kill us. That is the story of our trip to Nagoya, Japan on March 24, 1945.

—Thanks Bill for your story.

The Charles Whitehead Story

With a dead pilot, a badly wounded copilot, and the instrument panels blown away, the B-29 crew prayed for a miracle that would get them to Iwo Jima.

July's "Valor" told of the survival of a B-29, commanded by Lt. William F. Orr, that was severely damaged during the June 1, 1945, incendiary raid on Osaka, Japan. On the same mission, a B-29, K-37, of the 330th Bomb Group based at North Field, Guam, endured an equally terrifying experience.

While K-37's crew waited on the hardstand for a 2:47 am take off, the aircraft commander, Capt. Arthur Behrens, took Chaplain Paul Shade aside and told him, "Paul, I'm not coming back from this one." His prophetic words did not include the crew.

K-37 arrived over the initial point at about 11:00 am. Before bombs away, the aircraft was hit by what probably was a barrage of heavy flak. The flight engineer, MSgt. Charles Whitehead remembers a number of almost simultaneous explosions. There was 'a blinding flash inside the airplane, a tremendous roar, and a violent concussion." The left side of the nose was blown away, killing Captain Behrens instantly, shattering the left arm of copilot 2nd Lt. Bob Woliver and blinding his left eye. Sergeant Whitehead's shoulder was perforated by bits of metal.

Destruction on the flight deck was cataclysmic. The aircraft commander's instrument panel was destroyed, and the copilot's panel was left with only a magnetic compass, the needle and ball. The left control column was snapped off a foot above the floor, the flight engineer's panel and the radio knocked out, and the hydraulic system ruptured. Shattered glass, hydraulic fluid, and blood covered the floor of the flight deck. Sergeant Whitehead looked through a large hole in the top or the fuselage to see barrels of the four .50-caliber guns in the upper front turret twisted "like pieces of spaghetti."

K-37 immediately went into a spiraling dive from 20,000 feet. The dazed copilot, Lieutenant Woliver, recovered his faculties enough to pull out with his good right arm at an estimated 10,000 feet. There was undetermined damage to the flight controls, leaving the B-29 in a nose-down attitude. Keeping the nose up required heavy back pressure on the control column. The B-29 was now over water, headed toward China. Bomb bay doors could not be opened to jettison the bomb load.

Not knowing K-37's location, navigator 2nd Lt. Robert Fast computed a heading for Iwo Jima as best he could. During the four-hour flight, Lieutenant Woliver never left his seat, though periodically he became so weak from loss of blood that he could not control the aircraft. During these periods, either Sergeant Whitehead or bombardier 2d Lt. John Logerot took over the control column. With no instruments working, power settings, speed, altitude, and fuel consumption could only be guessed at. The course Lieutenant Woliver was flying would have missed Iwo Jima by 100 miles, but it did avoid the front that Bill Orr's crew had to penetrate.

As they headed for a probably fatal ditching somewhere in the Pacific, Lady Luck smiled on K-37. A P-61 Black Widow night fighter based at Iwo was on a radar calibration flight. The P-61 radar operator, Lt. Eric Shulenberger, picked up an emergency signal from the B-29's identification, friend or foe system. When the Black Widow came up on K-37 from the right side, all appeared to be well—four turning and no sign of damage. Then pilot Maj. Arthur Shepard swung the P-61 to the other side of the B-29 where they could see half of K-37's nose shot away. With hand signals, the P-61 crew got Woliver on a heading for Iwo

Jima.

Lieutenant Woliver knew he could not land the airplane in his weakened condition, with partial sight, no instruments, and no brakes. He ordered the crew to bail cut over the island. Woliver himself was too weak to get out of his seat and leave through the nose wheel well. Lieutenant Logerot, suffering from flash burns, stayed with the damaged plane, got Woliver out the wheel well, and was the last to leave K-37. He was awarded the Silver Star for his heroism. The tower at Iwo ordered the P-61 to shoot down K-37, which continued to fly erratically near the island. It took nearly all its ammunition to send the B-29 bearing Captain Behrens's body into the sea.

Lieutenant Woliver, who had stayed at his post despite grave wounds and saved the lives of his crew, was awarded the Distinguished Service Cross. He retired as a lieutenant colonel and died in 1988.

The ordeal of Woliver and the crew of K-37 is a story not only of individual valor but of shared courage by an aircrew in the face of almost certain disaster. The fulfillment of Capt. Arthur Behrens's premonition that he alone would not return from the Osaka mission is an intriguing encounter with the mysteries of human intuition.

Thanks to Don Murray for telling us about this mission and to crew members Charles Whitehead and Robert Fast for providing details.

By John L. Frisbee, Contributing Editor.
Air Force Magazine: Oct 1994

Editorial Comment

Chuck's account of this nerve-gripping saga is another great tribute to the men flying these missions. That co-pilot had to be one gutsy guy. Thanks for this fabulous story, Chuck.

Frank Reynolds Story Part A
"Don't Leave Me"

On a mission on January 27, 1945, we were under heavy fighter attacks when a 20mm cannon shell exploded against the fuselage just above my head. It knocked the plexiglass blister out. I hit the gun sight with my chest, breaking it off, as I was blown outside the plane. The right gunner could not see me and told the crew I was gone. I was pinned against the outside of the fuselage by the slipstream. The only thing that saved me was the seat belt. It was just above my knees, holding my legs inside from the knees down. The rest of me was outside.

God gave me superhuman strength and I got my hands on the rim where the blister was mounted and pulled myself back into the ship. The slipstream had stripped off my flak vest, helmet and oxygen mask, and tore the oxygen hose off the outlet. I had to have oxygen or pass out in 30 seconds and die in three minutes. Again, God came to my rescue. I unsnapped the seat belt, ran by the surprised gunner, into the radar room where there was an extra outlet and mask and got on oxygen. The outside temperature was minus 50 degrees. A gale-force wind was coming through the blown out blister, chilling us badly.

The plane took more hits; the controls were shot out, and the order came "Prepare for bail out." Everyone was getting their chutes on. Mine was blown out in the explosion so I was trying to put on the spare, but it did not fit and my fingers were so cold I could not adjust it. In sheer desperation, I grabbed the radar operator and pleaded, "Don't leave me!" He adjusted the chute for me. The pilots regained control of the plane by alternate controls and canceled the bail out. Outside of some small shrapnel in my hands and neck, I was in good shape when we landed. The flight surgeon picked the flak out and gave me a tetanus shot.

I thank God for saving my life.

I was awarded the Purple Heart for the shrapnel wounds.

When word got around about what happened, for several days people would yell at me, "Hey, Reynolds!" When they got my attention. "Don't leave me!" Followed by loud laughter.

Editorial Comment at the end of Part B.

Frank Reynolds

The Frank Reynolds Story Part B
"Living to Tell About It"

Target 357, the aircraft factory on the outskirts of Tokyo, had been our first mission's target and we had been back several times, but had inflicted very little damage. Now our Wing was told to destroy that factory. Low altitude bombing had been so successful it was decided to try it on 357 with 500-pound explosive bombs.

Easter Sunday, April 1, 1945 was the date I was promoted to Staff Sergeant and this was our crew's 17th mission. Take-offs started at 0700 P.M., at 30-second intervals. We were near the end of the stream. The plane in front of us crashed on take-off at the end of the runway and bulldozers pushed the burning debris off the cliff into the water so we could takeoff. This caused a 45-minute break between aircraft arriving at the target.

All antiaircraft guns knew our route and could concentrate on us. It was a beautiful full moon, as forecast, and I could clearly see the small island in Tokyo Bay where we began the bomb run over. There was probably only one gun down there and their first shell knocked out No. 2 engine. As we proceeded, searchlights picked us up and shell blasts rocked the plane. The interphone went out, which meant the pilot could not communicate with us. Another engine on the other side went out. The bomb bay doors came open, the bombs fell out but the doors would not close. The plane turned left, as briefed, toward the coast. We ran out of searchlights and antiaircraft fire.

For a few brief moments it looked like we were going to make it. But in the center wing section a few sparks grew into a stream and quickly into flames. I grabbed a fire extinguisher and went into the bomb bay hoping I could reach the fire, but could not. With horror I saw flames licking around a hung-up bomb and knew we were doomed.

I went back into the gunners' compartment and said, "Let's get out of here, this thing is going to blow up!" We proceeded to the rear escape hatch. The tail gunner had come forward and was crouched in the door. The last thing I did was take my .45 caliber pistol from its holster and leave it in the plane, thinking, they may kill me but not with my own gun.

We jumped through the hatch one by one. I delayed opening the chute until well below the flames, now shooting past the tail. When the ripcord was pulled the chute opened with the expected jolt. I swung around to see the burning plane; just in time to see it explode with a loud boom.

A Japanese fighter had been trailing below and behind us, and he passed below me. I fell through his propeller wash which started me swinging violently. I fought the swinging, using the shroud lines, as taught in training. I observed a chute on each side of me, and tried to see where I was going to land. Suddenly, I was brushing tree branches and came to a halt with the chute caught in the top of a tree, but I was hanging in the clear. After my vision adjusted, it looked like I wasn't very far off the ground, so unsnapping the harness, I lowered myself as much as possible and finally let loose and fell about ten feet.

I thank the good Lord for getting me out of that burning plane and safely on the ground.

It was 0400 A.M., April 2, 1945. I was on a hill and moved up to the tree trunk and sat down awaiting daylight. I was unhurt with only a couple of scratches. I had a lot of melted metal on my clothes, but no burns. It was cold, probably around freezing, but I wore a khaki uniform, covered by flight coveralls and flight jacket so I was fairly comfortable. I thought we were on the briefed withdrawal route from the target, and this must be the foothills of mountains northwest of Tokyo.

When it got good and light, I decided to go toward one of the chutes I saw while descending. I found the chute but no one was there. So, I climbed up a hill, saw a village and a path leading to it and headed that way.

As I approached the village, I saw someone on a bicycle. We both stopped. I saw it was a boy who must have been twelve to fourteen years of age, and approached him slowly and smiling not wanting to scare him. I had a couple of coins in my pocket and gave them to him. He turned his bike around and rode ahead of me a few feet. The path turned into a road. As we approached the hamlet, a village elder in a robe with writing on his long shawl was waiting for me. I saluted him and he bowed to me. He motioned me down the street. People started coming out of the houses and lining the streets, looking at me and laughing. A big teenager grabbed my arm and tried to twist it behind my back. I resisted and pushed him away, firmly but gently, and he walked along beside me. I thought, this is not too bad.

After walking about two blocks, I came to two policemen at the train station. They blindfolded me and tied my hands behind my back. School children started gathering around us and when the train came, we all got on it. Several of the kids came by and greeted me with a kick or punch. After a thirty- to forty-five-minute ride, I was led off the train and walked to a police station. The blindfold was removed. Five or six policemen were in the room. One of them in very broken English asked me a few questions. The last one was, 'Who do you think will win the war?" I replied, "America." He translated my answer and they all laughed.

About two hours passed before a truck stopped outside and military personnel came in. I instinctively knew the good times were over. The blindfold went back on. With shouts, punches, and kicks I was driven like a blind animal onto the truck bed and placed with no support for my back. I heard other voices and knew there were prisoners and guards aboard. Every time the truck took a sharp turn, I fell over — which gave the guard an excuse to jerk me back up by my hair and abuse me for falling over.

The truck finally stopped after a long ride, and we were herded into a field and tied to posts. I could hear voices and knew we had an audience. I thought, this is public execution time. I hoped they would shoot us and not behead us with swords.

A voice shouted with the equivalent of, "Attention!' The crowd grew quiet. Another voice gave a short speech and when he stopped, the guards started beating us. The crowd cheered. This was repeated four or five times. Then we just stood there for a while. We were untied and herded towards the crowd. They were lined up in two long rows and as we walked between them, they hit and kicked us. At one point my blindfold was knocked down and I saw our tormentors were high school age kids. It was a very terrorizing experience.

They put us back on the truck and after another long ride we were unloaded and taken through a gate into a courtyard. We stood there for hours waiting our turn at interrogation. I learned by listening that five of my crew were there: Lieutenant Houghton and Sergeants San Souci, Le Marca, Evans and myself. Lieutenant Houghton was injured and burned. I could smell his burned flesh. There was also a flyer from another plane.

Sergeant Peterson, the top gunner, was missing. As we were going to the rear of the plane to bail out Peterson approached me, very scared, and without his parachute on. I told him he had better get his chute on, the airplane was going to blow up. I thought he probably had time to get it on and bail out before it did explode.

San Souci, the right gunner, was added to the cell after about ten days of captivity. About four or five days later we got a shock when the guard came to the cell and said, “Reynoldo, we have your friend.” There stood Peterson, the top gunner. We had been wondering what had happened to him.

Like the rest of us, he had landed in the hills but he had decided to evade capture. (There was no escape plan from Japan.) All he had to eat was some plants and one crawfish. After fourteen days hunger drove him to approach a farm house. He saw the farmer and family were just starting to eat supper so he held his gun on them until he ate their food. Then he gave the startled farmer his gun and surrendered. The farmer got the police and then gave Pete a good beating for eating his food.

Pete had lost more weight than we had, but looked pretty good except for his foot. In his evasion he had gotten his foot wet and it had frozen and was black and swollen. It started paining him badly, so San Souci and I thought if we could get it lanced it would drain and reduce the pain. We talked the guard into lancing it by sticking his bayonet in it. We got the guard to get us a paper concrete bag from the construction outside and wrapped it around his foot to hold down the odor and drippings. We got a bag change whenever we could from a cooperative guard.

Pete’s foot was getting worse every day and he was getting weaker from the loss of blood. Near the end of April, he was taken out of the cell with some other prisoners supposedly to a POW camp and never heard of again.

The flight engineer, Lt. Houghton, was in the cell to my right. I could not see him through the cracks but knew he was injured and burned. I tried to find out what happened to those in the front of the plane. But he was in shock and could not tell me.

On about 14 June, 1945, he was delirious and yelling. The chief interrogator Kobayashi went in his cell and tried talking to him, but Houghton could not answer. Kobayashi started kicking him, knocking him unconscious. Houghton was carried out of the cell and laid on the ground outside the building. He was gone the next morning.

On May 24th and 26th the 500 B-29s fire bombed Tokyo and destroyed the rest of the city. Fire bombs rained down all around us, but none hit our wood jail. Laying on the floor with blankets covering us, the heat was almost unbearable, and the smoke choked us, but we survived.

The Lord's hand must have covered our jail. Thank you Lord! I praise your name!

About the flyers killed in June after the air raid on Fukuoka. My memory is a pilot was put in the cell next to me, a few days after I was captured 2 April 1945. He was in such shock he couldn't whisper to me through the cracks of the wood cell walls. After 2-3 days he told me his story. Nine people got out of the burning plane, and put in a jail overnight. The next day all were blindfolded and tied to a post. His blindfold was removed and he was made to watch the guards attack his crew with judo chops and kicks, then hacked and stabbed with bayonets and finally beheaded with swords. The pilot was taken with other prisoners and died in the fire when B-29 fire bombs hit the prison 24 June 1945 because the guards locked them in to be cremated alive.

On 15 August 1945, all 125 prisoners were taken to a British POW camp and joined 50 other B-29 flyers.

In July, the guards with laughter and jeers, told us, that the day U.S. Forces invaded Japan, all prisoners were to be killed. It was obvious, orders had come down from higher authority, to that effect.

We were liberated by Marines on 29 August 1945, and taken to a hospital ship.
B-29 Combat crews paid a high price to win the war.

Killed and missing in action	3,082
Wounded and evacuated	433
Prisoners burned alive	66
Prisoners beheaded	47
Savage operations & cannibalism	8

I thank God and give Him all the glory that I was one of the 175 survivors.

Later, I was interviewed by a War Crime investigator. He told me those flyers taken from Kempi Tia prison in April and May, supposedly to a POW camp, instead were taken to another prison in Tokyo. Four hundred Japanese were held there also.

During the 500 B-29 fire bombing of Tokyo on May 24th, the end cells, where the flyers were held, caught fire. All 400 Japanese were evacuated.

The flyers that tried to escape through the burning wood walls, were shot by the guards. The rest burned alive in their cells.

Authorities eventually identified 66 flyers killed in the fire.

Editorial Comment

Both of Frank's stories are compelling. They provide an insight into the horror many of our fellow airmen had to endure. These are the revelations that must be repeated and repeated so that future generations will know the truth. Remember, the revisionists are still plotting to modify history. Their purpose still remains focused on blaming America for attacking Japan. Incomprehensible, I know, but true. Please spread the word. Another item in connection with Frank's career that I admire, is his rise from enlisted man to Lt. Colonel. His career would make a great book. Thanks Frank, for your service to our country and for providing your intriguing narratives.

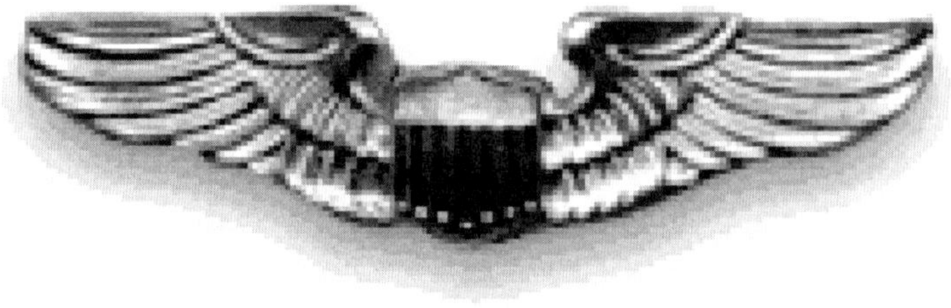

Epilogue II

I trust all in the 60 year and below age group-with particular emphasis on those in the 16 year to 40 year age group-now have an enlightened understanding of the sacrifices and commitments made by many of "the greatest generation" to protect and sustain the ideals and guarantees contained within the constitution of the United States of America.

We now pass the golden chalice, filled with priceless covenants of our enduring culture, to you. I admonish you-be alert, be aware, be vigilant-your path is precarious. It is wrought with dangers and obstacles. There are those in this world, and from within, who would do harm to America.

Thank you for reading my book. "Keep the memories alive" while preserving our republic.

"Lives of great men all remind us
we can make our lives sublime
and departing, leave behind us
footprints on the sands of time."

-Stan Lee, 58th B.W.

May God Bless the United States of America
Now and Forever.

The photographs in this book are taken from:

An Unofficial Pictorial History of the 500th Bombardment Group Stationed at Saipan, Marianas Islands
Edited and Published by Capt. Glenn E. McClure

The 20th Air Force Album
Published by the 20th Air Force Association
© 1982 by Richard M. Keenan

The 73rd Bombardment Wing History book
Published by Turner Publishing Company
© 2000, Turner Publishing Company

Line Drawing of B-29 used with permission and under
© of Squadron/Signal Publications, Inc.

Photos other than mine show photo recognition.

Editing in Part:

Judy McCollester

Helpful Hints:

Colonel John Misterly Jr.

Captain Richard Fields

Captain James L. Pattillo

Lt. Robert Copeland's Diary

Sgt. Thomas L. Check

Cathy Debreicht

Sally Ann Wagoner

<u>Our Military Legacy</u>

(Write your own story.)